Slavery and Empire in Central Asia

The Central Asian slave trade swept hundreds of thousands of Iranians, Russians, and others into slavery during the eighteenth and nineteenth centuries. Drawing on eyewitness accounts, autobiographies, and newly uncovered interviews with slaves, this book offers an unprecedented window into slaves' lives and a penetrating examination of human trafficking. Slavery strained Central Asia's relations with Russia, England, and Iran, and would serve as a major justification for the Russian conquest of this region in the 1860s–70s. Challenging the consensus that the Russian Empire abolished slavery with these conquests, Eden uses these documents to reveal that it was the slaves themselves who brought about their own emancipation by fomenting the largest slave uprising in the region's history.

Jeff Eden is a Mellon Postdoctoral Research Fellow at Cornell University. He is the author of *The Life of Muhammad Sharif* (2015) and co-editor of *Beyond Modernism: Rethinking Islam in Russia, Central Asia and Western China (19th-20th Centuries)* (2016).

Cambridge Studies in Islamic Civilization

Other titles in the series are listed at the back of the book.

Slavery and Empire in Central Asia

JEFF EDEN
Cornell University

CAMBRIDGE
UNIVERSITY PRESS

CAMBRIDGE
UNIVERSITY PRESS

University Printing House, Cambridge CB2 8BS, United Kingdom

One Liberty Plaza, 20th Floor, New York, NY 10006, USA

477 Williamstown Road, Port Melbourne, VIC 3207, Australia

314-321, 3rd Floor, Plot 3, Splendor Forum, Jasola District Centre, New Delhi - 110025, India

79 Anson Road, #06-04/06, Singapore 079906

Cambridge University Press is part of the University of Cambridge.

It furthers the University's mission by disseminating knowledge in the pursuit of education, learning and research at the highest international levels of excellence.

www.cambridge.org
Information on this title: www.cambridge.org/9781108456111
DOI: 10.1017/9781108637329

First published 2018
First paperback edition 2020

A catalogue record for this publication is available from the British Library

ISBN 978-1-108-47051-3 Hardback
ISBN 978-1-108-45611-1 Paperback

Contents

Acknowledgments

This book began as my doctoral dissertation at Harvard, under the direction of my adviser Roy Mottahedeh and committee members David J. Roxburgh and Ali Asani. Suffice to say the book and I have both benefited very much from their valuable advice and recommendations. Several other colleagues and friends read earlier drafts of this book in its entirety and offered invaluable insights: Allen J. Frank, James Millward, Alexander Morrison, William A. Wood, and the anonymous reviewers of the Cambridge Studies in Islamic Civilization series. I owe each of them my profound gratitude. Many thanks are also due to the series editors and dedicated production team at Cambridge; to Kevin Hughes for his excellent work copyediting the manuscript; and to Maria Marsh for all her help along the way.

My research trip to the archives of Kazakhstan in 2013 was supported by a grant from the Eurasia Program of the Social Science Research Council with funds provided by the State Department under the Program for Research and Training on Eastern Europe and the Independent States of the Former Soviet Union (Title VIII). (Sadly, the Eurasia Program has since been defunded and shut down.) I would like to thank the many patient and generous archivists who helped me at the Central State Archive of the Republic of Kazakhstan, the National Library of Kazakhstan, and the Kazakh Academy of Sciences.

For their time, encouragement, and enlightening conversations about the book project and/or the subject of slavery, I wish to thank Naofumi Abe, Gulnora Aminova, Christopher Atwood, Patrick Baron, David Brophy, Devin DeWeese, Michael Feener, Baber Johansen, Scott C. Levi,

Christine Nölle-Karimi, Jürgen Paul, Paolo Sartori, Ron Sela, Akifumi Shioya, Elena Smolarz, Wheeler M. Thackston, and Rian Thum.

To all my students at Cornell, Harvard College, Harvard Extension School, the University of Maryland, Baltimore County, and the University of Maryland, College Park: Being in class with you has been my greatest inspiration, as well as a joy beyond words.

This book is dedicated to my parents, Lawrence and Susan Eden. Finally, I thank Ashley, the light of my life.

A Brief Note on Transliteration

In the interests of keeping diacritics to a minimum, I have omitted them for most place-names (e.g. Bukhara, Khwarazm) as well as for commonplace titles that are widely recognized in English (e.g. Shah, Khan). I have retained diacritics for personal names as well as for transliterated samples of Persian and Turkic sources. In transliterating Persian, I have followed the *IJMES* standard. There is no commonly accepted standard for transliterating nineteenth-century Central Asian Turkic, but I have tried to be as consistent as possible on that front. In transliterating Russian, I have used the "Modified Library of Congress" system.

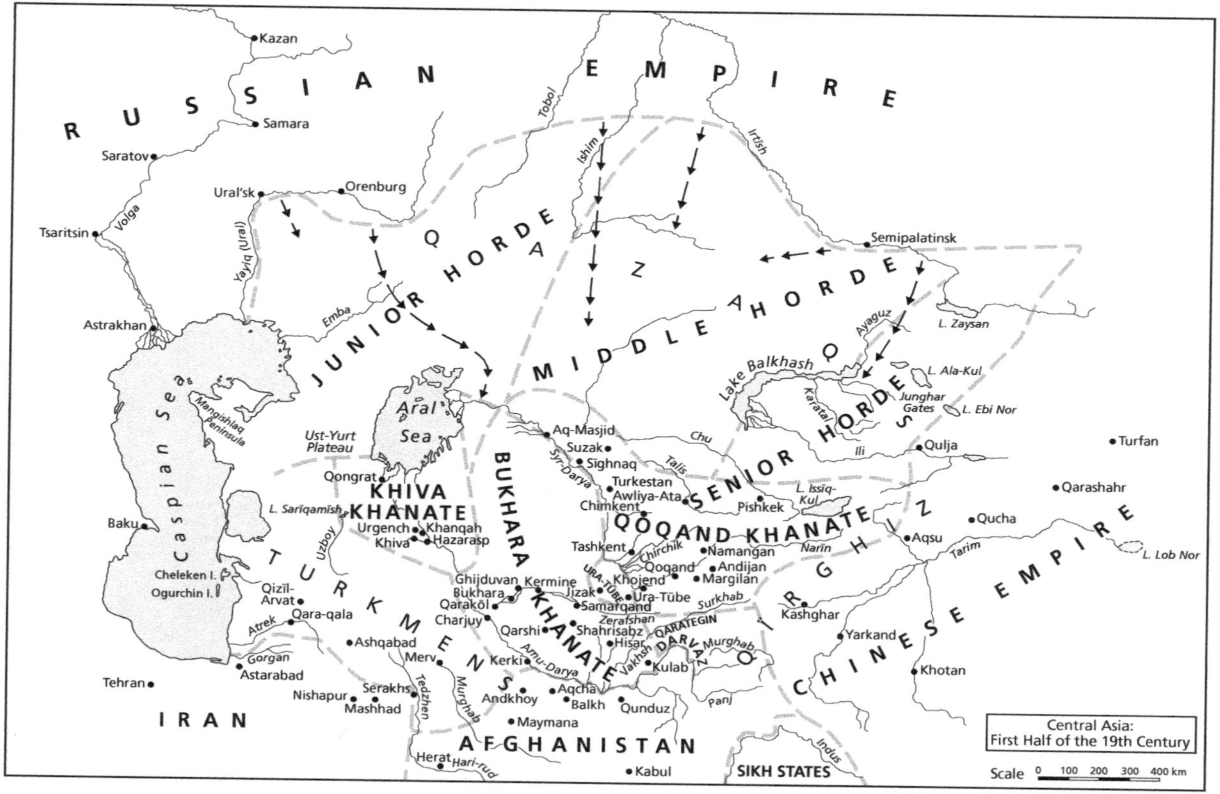

Yuri Bregel, *Historical Central Asia Maps* (Bloomington, IN: SRIFIAS Papers on Inner Asia, 2000)

Introduction

A Forgotten Slave Trade

> *The indolent, enervated Orientals may still regard with bitter resentment and rancor the efforts of Europe in the cause of humanity; but the sale and purchase of human beings is everywhere practiced with a certain reserve arising from a sense of shame, or, to speak more correctly, of fear of European eyes. This trade is now to be found unfettered and unembarrassed only in Central Asia.*
>
> Arminius Vambery, *Sketches of Central Asia*, 1868[1]

By the time of the Russian conquest of Central Asia in the 1860s and 1870s, the region's social landscape had been shaped by a millennium of slavery. Slaves served as farmworkers, herdsmen, craftsmen, soldiers, concubines, and even, in rare cases, as high-ranking officials in the region between the Caspian Sea and westernmost China. The institution of slavery in the region had never been seriously challenged by any internal or external forces down to the nineteenth century. It thrived especially in the khanates of Khwarazm and Bukhara. As the nineteenth century wore on, however, negotiations over the release of slaves began to factor heavily in these khanates' relationship to Iran, Russia, and Great Britain. By the end of the century, tens of thousands of slaves would be free.

This book examines the period from 1750 to 1873, which saw both the flourishing of Central Asia's slave trade and its collapse, and it focuses in particular on the region extending from Khurasan in the south to the Kazakh–Russian frontier in the north, and encompassing Khwarazm, Bukhara, and their environs.[2] It is not a political history of Central Asia,

[1] Arminius Vambery, *Sketches of Central Asia* (London: W.H. Allen, 1868), 205.

[2] Slavery was also prominent in other regions of Central Asia, such as Afghanistan and East Turkistan, but I have chosen not to cover those regions in the present work, in part because, as we shall see, the region extending from Khurasan north across the Caspian coast and

nor another diplomatic history of the so-called Great Game. Rather, the purpose of this book is to advance two arguments about slavery and abolition in the region. First, drawing on slaves' testimonials as well as eyewitness accounts and official sources, I challenge the historiographical consensus that Russian military force ended the slave trade and show how Russian efforts toward fostering abolition often had ulterior motives as well as wildly mixed results. Second, I argue that slaves influenced the nature of their captivity through their own initiatives and ingenuity, and I show how slaves in the khanate of Khwarazm launched an uprising, little-known even among historians of Central Asia, which served as the catalyst for abolition in the region as a whole.

While evidence of slavery and the slave trade in Central Asia is plentiful, scholarship on it is nearly nonexistent.[3] Despite its extraordinary scale,

along the Russian–Kazakh frontier can be considered a distinct and bounded (albeit roughly) ecosystem in which slaves circulated. The slave trade in East Turkistan, for example, which revolved around Tarim Basin trade networks and also involved Chinese slaves and Chinese traders, is deserving of separate study, and Laura Newby (see below) has broken ground in that effort. A recent dissertation by Benjamin Levey has offered groundbreaking insights into the fate of slaves along China's Kazakh frontier: "Jungar Refugees and the Making of Empire on Qing China's Kazakh Frontier, 1759–1773" (Ph.D. dissertation, Harvard University, 2013).

[3] The only monograph on the topic remains a slim but important Soviet-era volume in Uzbek, by Turgun Faiziev: *Buxoro feodal jamiyatida qullardan foidalanishga doir hujjatlar (XIX asr)* (Tashkent: Fan Nashriyoti, 1990). Some related works of note include Laura Newby, "Bondage on Qing China's North-Western Frontier," *Modern Asian Studies* 47:3 (2013), 968–994; Scott Levi, "Hindus Beyond the Hindu Kush: Indians in the Central Asian Slave Trade," *Journal of the Royal Asiatic Society* 12:3 (2002), 277–288; Benjamin Hopkins, "Race, Sex, and Slavery: 'Forced Labor' in Central Asia and Afghanistan in the Early 19th Century," *Modern Asian Studies* 42:2 (2008), 629–671; Alessandro Stanziani, *Bondage: Labor and Rights in Eurasia from the Sixteenth to the Early Twentieth Centuries* (New York, NY: Berghahn, 2014), 63–100; Elena Smolarz, "Speaking about Freedom and Dependency: Representations and Experiences of Russian Enslaved Captives in Central Asia in the First Half of the 19th Century," *Journal of Global Slavery* 2 (2017), 44–71; and Yuan Gao, "Captivity and Empire: Russian Captivity Narratives in Fact and Fiction" (M.A. thesis, Nazarbayev University, 2016). Valuable information on slavery along the Chinese–Central Asian frontier is provided in James Millward's *Beyond the Pass: Economy, Ethnicity, and Empire in Qing Central Asia, 1759–1864* (Stanford, CA: Stanford University Press); see, for example, 305–306n28, 238, 123. On slavery in premodern Central Asia, see Peter B. Golden, "The Terminology of Slavery and Servitude in Medieval Turkic," in Devin DeWeese, ed., *Studies on Central Asia in Honor of Yuri Bregel* (Bloomington, IN: Research Institute for Inner Asian Studies, 2001), 27–56. The paucity of published work on the subject is not entirely surprising, as the scarcity of research on slavery in Islamic Central Asia mirrors the broader scarcity of research on slavery anywhere the Muslim world. In Joseph C. Miller's comprehensive bibliography of scholarly works on slavery, published in 1999, we find a table showing the distribution of works on the subject according to their geographical focus: Among the thousands of works on slavery published between 1900 and 1991, a mere 3.3 percent focused on the Muslim world. Between 1992 and 1996, the

Central Asia's slave trade has largely been forgotten. This is no great surprise: Central Asia remains among the least-studied regions of the world. As Alexander Morrison has observed, even the Russian conquest has been the subject of surprisingly little research.[4] There is no consensus on what motivated it. This does not mean, however, that Russian imperial officials and propagandists failed to articulate a justification at the time. Ending the slave trade was at the heart of their justification.

European abolitionists, meanwhile, had high hopes for the conquest. Herbert Wood, writing soon after the Russian military took the town of Khiva in 1873, praised the Russian "civilizing mission" in the most generous terms: "Though Russia's position in the Central Asian Khanates may not yet be assured," he writes, "it is certain that without her leave no dog may bark in the bazaars of Khiva, Bokhara, and Kokand. And if a strong government which preserves social order and has put down brigandage, slavery, and man-stealing is worthy of sympathy, it is impossible not to feel that in undertaking the thankless and costly task of introducing civilisation into Turkestan, Russia is fully entitled to the good wishes and gratitude of every Christian nation."[5] It is natural, perhaps, that European observers would have expected abolition to constitute a major feature of the Russian "civilizing mission" in the East, given that Western European powers tended to cast many of their own conquests and interventions in this era as emancipating enterprises. Indeed, the nineteenth century was an age of global abolitionist intercessions, even if not all interventions were successful, and even if many were mere foils for more pressing (and more selfish) motivations. The British Empire led the way, officially abolishing the slave trade throughout its imperial holdings by 1807, and other colonial powers soon followed: Portugal signed a treaty stifling the importation of slaves into its colonial possessions in 1810; Sweden banned the trade in 1813; the Netherlands did the same the next year; and Spain and France followed soon after, the former promising to abolish the trade by 1820 and the latter by 1819. In the decades to come, the freeing of Christian captives was presented as a major incentive for the French conquest of Algiers (though, as W. G. Clarence-Smith observes, "they failed to extend their liberality"

proportion dipped slightly, to an even 3 percent (Joseph C. Miller, *Slavery and Slaving in World History: A Bibliography*, 2 vols. [Armonk, NY: M.E. Sharpe, 1999], xi–xii).

4 Morrison, "Introduction: Killing the Cotton Canard and getting rid of the Great Game: rewriting the Russian conquest of Central Asia, 1814–1895," *Central Asian Survey* 33:2 (2014), 131–142.

5 Wood, *The Shores of Lake Aral* (London: Smith, Elder, & Co., 1876), 182–183.

to non-Christian slaves),[6] while the British Empire attempted to foster abolition throughout the Ottoman world, sometimes with the assistance of Ottoman rulers and elites and sometimes in spite of their opposition.[7] The British likewise led the way in efforts to undermine the Atlantic slave trade, though the last slave ship to arrive in the American South did so as late as 1858.[8] Indeed, colonial emancipation projects often achieved their ends, if at all, only very gradually, and sometimes over the course of decades.[9] Nevertheless, in this climate of global abolition, the Russian efforts in Central Asia, which came not long after the abolition of serfdom within the Empire itself, were naturally regarded by many Western observers as yet another mission to end the misery of bondage, whatever its other motivations may have been.[10]

While historians have long cast a critical gaze on Western empires' moral pretenses for conquest, the Russian Empire has generally been sheltered from similar scrutiny. Historians within the Soviet Union shared a tendency to interpret the conquest of Central Asia purely as a means of extending Russian industry into the region, while historians in the West have generally preferred a "Great Game" narrative that explains the conquest as a simple race for regional dominance between England and Russia. Proponents of both approaches tend to avoid the question of the "civilizing mission" entirely. Meanwhile, some of the (few) recent works addressing the issue of slavery directly have tended to concur with the Russian "abolitionist" narrative: Liubov Kurtynova-D'Herlugnan has recently argued that Russian abolitionism in Eurasia culminated in the eradication of slavery in the Caucasus, suggesting that the "civilizing mission" was both sincere and effective, and M. D. Farah has argued that the Central

[6] Clarence-Smith, *Islam and the Abolition of Slavery*, 100.

[7] Ehud R. Toledano, *Slavery and Abolition in the Ottoman Middle East* (Seattle, WA: University of Washington Press, 1998); Toledano, *The Ottoman Slave Trade and Its Suppression: 1840–1890* (Princeton, NJ: Princeton University Press, 1982); Ismael M. Montana, *The Abolition of Slavery in Ottoman Tunisia* (Gainesville, FL: University Press of Florida, 2013).

[8] W. E. B. DuBois, *The Suppression of the African Slave Trade to the United States of America, 1638–1870* (New York, NY: Longmans, Green, and Co., 1904), 181–185.

[9] Clarence-Smith, *Islam and the Abolition of Slavery*, 99–218.

[10] Several recent works have offered important insights on the ulterior motives—and, oftentimes, the evident insincerity—of abolitionist efforts among Western powers: see, for example, Matthew S. Hopper, *Slaves of One Master: Globalization and Slavery in Arabia in the Age of Empire* (New Haven, CT: Yale University Press, 2015); Ehud R. Toledano, "Abolition and Anti-Slavery in the Ottoman Empire: A Case to Answer?" (forthcoming); and Behnaz A. Mirzai, *A History of Slavery and Emancipation in Iran* (Austin, TX: University of Texas Press, 2017).

Asian slave trade essentially ended with the Russian military conquest of Khiva.[11] In this book, I come to the opposite conclusions concerning the Russian "civilizing mission" in Central Asia.

Indeed, Russian abolitionism in Central Asia is a myth. The overall mechanism of abolition in Central Asia, and the means by which the region's new Russian rulers would patrol and monitor the slave trade were evidently never articulated even among the tsar's top generals and officials. If indeed there had been a grand, overarching plan for general emancipation in Central Asia (and we have no evidence such a thing existed), it was certainly implemented in a scattershot – perhaps even improvised – manner. Russian demands for abolition were applied unequally across the conquered territories, and enforcement seems to have been non-existent – a fact that, as we shall see, agitated some Russian officers who had anticipated more active antislavery efforts.

As I show in Chapter 7, the most important force behind the liberation of Central Asia's slaves was the slaves themselves – particularly the slaves of Khwarazm,[12] who seized the occasion of the Russian invasion to launch a courageous uprising against their masters. Witnessing this uprising, the Russian general in charge of the invasion hung two rebel slaves in the town square as a warning to other rebels. Evidently, this general preferred to seize an orderly town of slaveholders rather than a chaotic town of self-emancipated slaves. Russian threats notwithstanding, the slave uprising continued until the general had no choice but to support it. It was abolition *sans* abolitionism, in other words.

Notwithstanding these dramatic events, which culminated in an "official" abolition decree, the slave trade continued. Even if the Russians had attempted to patrol it, which they did not, the trade could not have been stopped without a relentless and wide-ranging enforcement strategy. This is because, as Chapter 2 shows, the slave trade was not

[11] Liubov Kurtynova-D'Herlugnan, *The Tsar's Abolitionists: Languages of Rationalization and Self-Description in the Russian Empire* (Leiden: Brill, 2010); M. D. Farah, "Autocratic Abolitionists: Tsarist Russian Anti-Slavery Campaigns," in William Mulligan, ed., *A Global History of Anti-Slavery Politics in the Nineteenth Century* (New York, NY: Palgrave, 2013), 97–117. While I do not always agree with Kurtynova-D'Herlugnan's conclusions, her work deserves recognition as a groundbreaking and important study. It is interesting to contrast this book with Irma Kreiten's valuable article: "A Colonial Experiment in Cleansing: The Russian Conquest of Western Caucasus, 1856–65," *Journal of Genocide Research* 11:2–3 (2009), 213–241.

[12] In most Russian and Western European sources, the khanate of Khwarazm is referred to as Khiva, often resulting in ambiguity as to whether an author is referring only to the capital city or to the khanate as a whole. In Central Asian sources, however, the khanate was always referred to as Khwarazm, and I will maintain that usage here.

confined to the urban centers and their bazaars; Central Asia's slave trade was decentralized and widely dispersed, with many slaves traded in villages and nomadic encampments. Indeed, the nomads of the hinterlands played a key role in the slave trade, not only as raiders but also as merchants and slave-owners. In contradiction to many previous studies, which allege that nomads did not need or use slaves, I will argue here that slave ownership in Central Asian nomadic communities was commonplace. However, while nomadic raiding was a key feature of the slave trade, helping to ensure its survival after the fall of major towns to Russian armies, it was hardly the only means by which individuals were seized for enslavement. As I argue in Chapter 1, selling captives into slavery was a normative part of warfare across the region; this practice was not limited to nomads, and the Russians themselves sometimes took part in the slave-dealing economy in Central Asia.

When it comes to the nomads, slave-raiding and slave-trading served more than just their immediate commercial interests. Turkmen and Kazakh nomads developed complex, symbiotic relationships with merchants in the towns of Khwarazm and Bukhara that revolved around the commerce in slaves. Turkmens traded slaves for grain, for example, which these desert-dwellers had no way of growing for themselves. The slaves were often put to work on plantations, growing grain – a cyclical commercial system.

Slave-raiding was also a form of resistance. In the nineteenth century, Turkmen and Kazakh nomads occupied territories encircled by sedentary powers, with the Russian Empire encroaching inexorably from the north and Qajar Iran threatening always to encroach (and occasionally invading Turkmen territories) from the south. Destabilizing sedentary borderland territories through raiding helped to keep these powers at bay. Central Asian sedentary states used this dynamic to their own advantage: Khwarazmian khans – threatened simultaneously by Iran and Russia – alternately allied with Turkmens hostile to Iran and with Kazakhs hostile to Russia, benefiting from whatever limited, proxy defensive capacity these borderland nomads provided. As Chapter 6 shows, Russia later adopted this "nomadic proxy" strategy against Iran, continually prompting "client" Turkmens to raid Iranian territory, or at least offering protection to those who did.

In the decades before the Russian conquest, the issue of the slave trade was at the heart of Russian and Iranian diplomacy with the khanates of Khwarazm and Bukhara. As we shall see in Chapter 1, diplomats from Russia, Iran, and Britain even converged simultaneously in Khiva at one point and issued a joint request – hopelessly, of course – for the emancipation of all the slaves in Khwarazm. Both Russia and Iran had expansionist ambitions in Central Asia; Both protested the enslavement of their citizens in the khanates; and both raised the issue of slavery in order to justify threats.

In other respects, however, the positions of these two empires differed dramatically. First, the total number of Russian slaves held in Central Asia was miniscule compared to the total number of Iranian slaves. Second, Russia's military resources were vastly greater than Iran's; by the mid-nineteenth century, the threat of a Russian conquest was palpable, while the threat of a major Iranian conquest anywhere in Central Asia (at least after the early 1830s) probably seemed remote. Finally, while Iranian travel literature from the nineteenth century often casts Central Asia as a historically Iranian-dominated region, and sometimes even as a rightful Iranian possession, one scarcely perceives in these "imperial" literatures the pretenses of a "civilizing mission."

British activities in Central Asia, meanwhile, were peripheral in every sense, and the British Empire will factor very little in this book. This omission may surprise some readers, given the extensive literature concerning British "players" in the Great Game. For all their great adventures, miseries, and ambitious pretenses – Captain Arthur Conolly, for example, planned in 1838 to concoct an Anti-Slavery Confederation in the region[13] – the impact of British officers and adventurers on the Central Asian slave trade was negligible. The greatest British accomplishment on this front was the alleged role of the officer Richmond Shakespear in convincing the Khwarazmian khan to release over 400 Russian slaves following General Persovskii's failed campaign against the khanate in 1839.[14] Certain other British efforts were characterized by a grandiosity that smacks of madness, such as the petition penned by the independent traveler Joseph Wolff while imprisoned in Bukhara in 1844; he addressed his dispatch "To all the monarchs of Europe":[15]

> Sires!
>
> . . . I do not supplicate for my own safety; but, Monarchs, two hundred thousand Persian slaves, many of them people of high talent, sigh in the kingdom of Bokhara. Endeavour to effect their liberation, and I shall rejoice in the grave that my blood

13 See, for example, Evgeny Sergeev, *The Great Game, 1856–1907: Russo-British Relations in Central and East Asia* (Baltimore, MD: Johns Hopkins University Press, 2013), 4.

14 Russian accounts tend overwhelmingly to deny Shakespear credit for the release of these slaves.

15 Wolff, *Narrative of a Mission to Bokhara, in the Years 1843–1845*, Vol. 2 (London: John W. Parker, 1845), 104.

has been thus the cause of the ransom of so many human beings. I am too much agitated, and too closely watched, to be able to say more.

Suffice to say, Wolff received no reply from the monarchs of Europe.

British and American travel writing on slavery is nevertheless precious, since visitors like Conolly, Wolff, Alexander Burnes, and Eugene Schuyler provide us with some of the most detailed ethnographic reportage in existence concerning slaves' experiences. The abolitionist bias of these authors is undisguised, and should always be borne in mind, but this fact by no means proves that the eyewitness evidence they provide is falsified. When it comes to the role of the British Empire in nineteenth-century Central Asia, however, this book leaves its officers and adventurers at the periphery – which is precisely where they ought to be, considering their minimal impact on Central Asian slavery.[16]

This book is not concerned only with empires, however. It is concerned with slaves' lives too, and I have tried here to illuminate something of slaves' experiences. For this effort, I have found two types of source especially useful. First, I have relied on interviews conducted by Russian border officials with slaves who escaped from the Kazakh steppe. These interviews are preserved in the archives of the Central State Archive of the Republic of Kazakhstan. Chapters 2, 5, and 6 make extensive use of these documents and shed light on their contents and implications. These interviews, while precious for the rare glimpse they provide into the nature of the slave trade, are typically quite concise, rarely running to more than a few pages, and sometimes comprising no more than a few lines. A far more detailed source – indeed, the greatest single source for the study of slavery in the region – is the Persian-language memoir of Mīrzā Maḥmūd Taqī Āshtiyānī,[17] whose extraordinary story of survival and hardship is recounted in Chapter 3.

Another key source for this book is a rare manuscript history of Central Asian slavery composed in Chaghatay Turkic in the early Soviet period. Called the *Āzādnāma*, this work offers details on the fate of Khwarazm's

[16] See Alexander Morrison's insightful recent comments on this subject: "Killing the Cotton Canard and getting rid of the Great Game: rewriting the Russian conquest of Central Asia, 1814–1895," *Central Asian Survey* 33:2 (2014), 131–142 (see especially 132–133). For those interested in the British role in Central Asia and in Anglo-Russian relations, there is no shortage of literature on the subject; Morrison's up-to-date bibliography in the above-mentioned article directs readers to the major works.

[17] Mīrzā Maḥmūd Taqī Āshtiyānī, *'Ibratnāma: Khatirati az dawran-i pas az jangha-yi herat va merv*, ed. Husayn 'Imadi Ashtiyani (Tehran: Nashr-i markaz, 1382/2003).

freed slaves that are found nowhere else.[18] Chapter 7 makes use of this manuscript in reconstructing the conquest of Khiva and its aftermath.

T. Faiziev's collection of nineteenth-century legal documents concerning the slaves of Bukhara is another crucial source for the study of Central Asian slavery. These documents, which include numerous manumission deeds, provide critical documentary proof that the slave trade continued well after the Russian conquests – and even into the late 1880s. They also demonstrate that slavery was formalized and regulated, at least to some extent, by the region's Hanafi Muslim legal system.

Russian imperial officers, diplomats, and travelers in Central Asia, like their British counterparts, were keenly interested in the issue of slavery, and their eyewitness reportage, while sometimes lurid, is likewise vital for any study of the subject. In citing Russian witnesses, I have tended to privilege reports of a "military-statistical" or diary-like nature over the more overtly "literary" products of the captivity-narrative genre, whose target readership was resolutely popular and whose details sometimes strike me as fantastical and suspect.

While I will focus here on slavery in the Muslim societies of Central Asia, it is important to observe that slavery was not introduced to the region by Muslims, and neither were captive-taking and slave-owning exclusive to Muslims. Furthermore, as I will show, Muslim Central Asia was home to a great diversity of slave systems, some of which invite comparisons beyond the Muslim world.[19] In Khwarazm, for example, where we find slaves laboring on large agricultural estates, the prevailing system of slavery shares more common features with plantation slavery in the American South than it does with urban slavery in Istanbul. Slavery among the nomadic Kazakhs, meanwhile, shares more in common with slavery among nomadic non-Muslim groups such as the Mongols than with either Khwarazm's plantation slavery or Istanbul's urban slavery. Aside from its diversity of forms, the extensiveness of slave-owning also

[18] MS IVAN Uz No. 12581. I am grateful to Paolo Sartori for providing me with a copy of this manuscript.

[19] The terminology of slavery in Central Asia is vast – *ghulām, qul, chūrī*, and *mamlūk* are just a few of the many terms for slaves that we shall encounter over the course of this book – and the word "slave" is hardly adequate in reflecting that diversity. What unites the roles defined by all of these terms is best captured in Seymour Drescher's definition of slavery: "The most crucial and frequently utilized aspect of the condition [of slavery] is a communally recognized right by some individuals to possess, buy, sell, discipline, transport, liberate, or otherwise dispose of the bodies and behavior of other individuals" (Drescher, *Abolition: A History of Slavery and Anti-Slavery* [Cambridge: Cambridge University Press, 2009], 4–5).

varied by region: Even as the trade thrived in Khwarazm and Bukhara, it remained strikingly small in scale in the neighboring Muslim khanate of Kokand.[20] Given this, it is possible to discuss Central Asian slavery as a regional phenomenon, extending beyond the borders of Muslim-majority territories.[21] A *longue durée* view of slavery in the region might inspire the view that slavery among Muslims was merely a continuation of a region-wide practice that can be traced into the distant pre-Islamic past, as well as into neighboring, contemporary, non-Muslim societies.[22]

However, we must keep in mind two facts that demonstrate that slavery among Central Asian Muslims was not regarded as a mere "pre-Islamic survival." First, Hanafi Muslim law both governed the slave system and justified it. It is clear that the Muslim jurists of nineteenth-century Bukhara and Khwarazm did not see the institution of slavery as "un-Islamic"; if they had, they would not have countenanced it by producing bills of sale for the slave trade or adjudicating disputes concerning slaves and their masters. Second, religious differences typically distinguished slaves from their Sunni Muslim owners, and the usual justification for the enslavement of non-Sunnis in Central Asia was explicitly religious. Iranian Shiʿites and Russian Orthodox Christians, among others, were licit to enslave because they were not Sunni Muslims.

Finally, a note on terminology: When I refer to Central Asian "slaves," I have in mind those people classed as *qul* and/or *ghulām* – two words that appear commonly in Turkic and Persian sources from the region. These two words are almost always rendered in English as "slave," and for good reason: both imply a condition of unfreedom in which an individual can

[20] The main reason for this is likely Kokand's relative distance from Khurasan, the region that supplied most of the slaves kept in Khwarazm and Bukhara.

[21] This approach contrasts with that taken by a number of recent works on "Muslim" slavery, most notably William Gervase Clarence-Smith's ambitious comparative synthesis, *Islam and the Abolition of Slavery* (Oxford: Oxford University Press, 2006).

[22] The last two decades have seen the steady development of research on Eurasian slavery beyond Central Asia, and I will mention just a few notable works here. On slavery in early modern China, see Pamela K. Crossley, "Slavery in Early-Modern China," in David Eltis and Stanley Engerman, eds., *The Cambridge World History of Slavery*, Vol. 3 (Cambridge: Cambridge University Press, 2011), 186–216; on South Asian slavery, see Indrani Chatterjee and Richard M. Eaton, eds., *Slavery & South Asian History* (Bloomington, IN: Indiana University Press, 2006). On slavery in Iran (still a relatively little-studied topic), see Thomas Ricks, "Slaves and Slave-Trading in Shi'i Iran, AD 1500–1900," *Journal of Asian and African Studies* 36:4 (2001), 407–418; and Mirzai, *A History of Slavery and Emancipation in Iran*. Valuable studies of slavery and the slave trade in regions to the west and southwest of Central Asia can be found in Christoph Witzenrath, ed., *Eurasian Slavery, Ransom and Abolition in World History, 1200–1860* (Aldershot: Ashgate, 2015).

typically be bought and sold licitly, and in which an individual requires a formal deed of manumission to become free.[23] By the nineteenth century, Hanafi legal norms had been used to manage issues of slavery for nearly a millennium; as one might expect, there is little evidence of confusion over something as basic as which individuals could legally be bought and sold, or which individuals required deeds of manumission to gain the same formal legal rights as those characterized as "free" in the Hanafi legal nomenclature. There were, however, a few exceptional cases in Central Asia for which I suspect that formal legal procedure was hazier: Military servitude among Kazakhs and Mongols, for example, has sometimes been described by outsiders using the language of slavery, but I have not seen any record of such military "slaves" being processed or defined as unfree people by Muslim jurists. Another ambiguous case is discussed at length in Chapter 5—namely, slaves among the Kazakhs who are alleged either to have been "adopted" as children or who have been given their own independent living-space and means as adults (typically comprising both a tent and livestock). Nevertheless, for the vast majority of the victims discussed in this book – who are generally Iranian Shiʿites taken captive in Khurasan and forced to labor on plantations or other private estates – I consider the word "slave" an appropriate description, both because it approximates the formalized free/unfree distinction made by the region's native legal system and because, as we shall see, their experiences and roles were in many respects remarkably similar to those of "slaves" in the English-speaking world.

In short, this book is an attempt to consider Central Asian slavery both from the "bottom-up" and from the "top-down." I aim to provide a window on slaves' experiences while locating their activities in the broader geopolitical framework of Central Asia in the age of imperial expansion. I hope to show how slaves' agency and resistance not only impacted their experiences, but also influenced the slave system itself, forming a pattern of autonomous activity that culminated in the Khivan slave uprising of 1873.

Slaves were certainly the most powerless, subaltern population in the region. And yet it is these slaves – as well as the trade that ensnared

[23] Mīrzā Maḥmūd, our Persian memoirist, prefers to describe himself as an *asīr*, a term generally better translated as "captive," and which can suggest a kind of temporary military imprisonment as opposed to the ten years of private ownership and forced labor that he endured. But he too required a letter of manumission to gain his freedom, and this fact – along with the other major details of his ordeal – has inclined me to translate *asīr* as "slave" in his case.

them – that bound together the "core" and the "periphery," the nomadic and the sedentary: Russian tsars and Iranian shahs were repeatedly drawn to their respective Central Asian "peripheries" on account of the trade, while for the Central Asian khanates themselves, the trade linked major towns (Bukhara, Urgench, Khiva) and remote oases via nomadic transit and caravan routes. The story of colonization, local resistance, caravan commerce, diplomatic rivalries, and imperial conquests in nineteenth-century Central Asia all converge around the problem of the slave trade.

Chapter 1 introduces historical, social, and political settings of slavery in early modern Central Asia, arguing that slavery and slave-taking were not unique to borderland nomads, but rather that they were normative features of Eurasian warfare over the course of centuries; that slavery gained particular prominence in the region with the expansion of agricultural plantations in the late Timurid period; and that, in the centuries to come, it would become a key issue in diplomacy between Iran, Russia, and Central Asia. Chapter 2 explores the geography of slavery, using evidence from slaves' testimonials to argue that slavery was a largely rural, agricultural phenomenon in the region, and that the slave trade was intimately connected with overland caravan routes. Because of the trade's decentralized nature, I argue, it was nearly impossible to police. Chapter 3 focuses on the experiences of Mīrzā Maḥmūd, who spent nearly a decade as a slave, first among the Turkmens and then in Bukhara, and has left us the richest firsthand account of slavery in the region. Chapter 4 draws on other autobiographical sources as well as eyewitness reports to describe slaves' occupations and roles, revealing that slaves could be found at all levels of Central Asian society.

Chapter 5 considers the curious fate of the many slaves who fled their masters for the Russian border, only to be pulled into serfdom as part of the Tsar's plan to settle and cultivate the borderlands. Here, I challenge the notion of Russian "abolitionism" in the region while further exploring slaves' means of resistance. Chapter 6 reveals how imperial powers employed Central Asian "native informants" in an attempt to pacify the borderlands and liquidate captive-taking among nomads. I weigh the mixed results of these efforts, further challenging longstanding assumptions about the Russian "abolitionist" program. Chapter 7 concludes the book by showing how slaves throughout Khwarazm joined together in the largest slave uprising in Central Asian history. I argue that this revolutionary, little-known episode triggered the abolition of slavery in the region as a whole.

1

The Setting

Russia, Iran, and the Slaves of the Khanates

The slave trade played a major part in Russian and Iranian diplomacy with Central Asia throughout the eighteenth and nineteenth centuries. The rulers of Khwarazm and Bukhara in particular were blamed for encouraging captive-taking, for providing markets for slaves, and for keeping tens of thousands of slaves in bondage. When it came to the actual taking and selling of captives, however, the blame cast by foreign statesmen, diplomats, and adventurers fell squarely upon nomadic Turkmens and Kazakhs. The near-exclusive focus of foreign observers – particularly Russian and British ones – on slave-trading and captivity among the Turkmens and Kazakhs has obscured a larger truth about slavery and Eurasian warfare before the twentieth century: Captive-taking was central to it, and significant armed conflicts almost invariably involved the phenomenon of mass captivity and enslavement. This chapter introduces the origins, development, and major features of the region's slave trade, as well as Russian and Qajar Iranian efforts to end the trade through diplomacy in the nineteenth century.

Ironically, the Qajars and Russians themselves engaged in both captive-taking and in the ransom economy, and even while deploring the barbarity of enslavement among the nomads, they made little effort to hide their own parallel efforts to deprive rivals, including noncombatants, of their freedom. Examples are legion, especially in "official" Persian chronicles, which often brag of captive-taking as if it was a hallmark of victory in battle.[1] At times the Turkmens would complain of Qajar captive-taking to

[1] The chroniclers had much to brag about on that front, and Turkmens – the most notorious captive-takers in the region's history – were often themselves the captives in question. In the

Russian officials, who were simultaneously hearing similar complaints about the Turkmens from the Qajars.[2]

Russian sympathies tended overwhelmingly to fall on the side of the Iranians, however, as have the sympathies of historians in the generations since. The idea of Turkmens as perennial persecutors and Iranians as their perennial victims is etched so deeply in the historiography of nineteenth-century Central Asia that it has become a kind of leitmotif. We see this, for example, in the kitschy title of Charles Marvin's earnest and classic work on Merv in the nineteenth century: *Merv, Queen of the World, and the*

Ma'āṣir-i sulṭānīya of 'Abd al-Razzāq Dunbulī, the court historian of 'Abbās Mīrzā (1789–1833), multiple assaults by the Iranian Shah's armies on Yomuts, Göklengs, and Tekes – invariably characterized as reprisals for their plundering – result in captivity for these Turkmens. In 1792, according to the chronicle, during a Qajar assault on the Yomuts and others in the vicinity of Astarabad, "great numbers of them were put to death or reduced to slavery and captivity, and on the highways were built minarets constructed with their heads" (Harford Jones Brydges, *The Dynasty of the Kajars* [London: John Bohn, 1833], 22). In 1803–1804, according to the same chronicle, Yomuts and Göklengs living along the banks of the Gurgen River, who had formerly been tax-paying subjects of the Qajars, were allegedly making trouble in the region and refused to pay taxes; the Shah's retinue attacked the Turkmens, burning their tents and taking their wives, daughters, and sons into captivity. Those left alive agreed to pay their dues (*Materiali po istorii turkmen i turkmenii, t. II. XVI–XIX vv. Iranskie, bukharskie, i khivinskie istochniki* [Moscow: 1938–1939], 217). Ten years later, in 1813, the Shah's troops intercepted a host of Tekes, claimed by the chronicler to be in the employ of Khwarazm, that had been staging attacks on the towns of Sabzavar and Juvayni. The Tekes were stripped of their loot and their prisoners; forty of them were killed, and 100 were taken captive by the Qajar army and sent to Tehran. Considering the damage insufficient, the Shah delegated Muḥammad Qulī Mīrzā, who was at that time governor of Mazandaran and Astarabad, to launch a massive assault on the Tekes. In the attack which followed, the *Ma'āṣir-i sulṭāniya* claims that some 2,000 Teke men, women, and children were taken captive, and that 50,000 camels, oxen, sheep, horses, and mares were stolen. Some Iranians who had been held among the Tekes – including pilgrims to Mashhad and merchants – were freed in the course of the attack (*Materiali po istorii turkmen i turkmenii, t. II*, 218). Similar incidents can be observed in nearly every major Persian chronicle concerning Khurasan in the eighteenth and nineteenth centuries. In 1841, for example, a Qajar force of 22,000 attacked more than 20 Turkmen *auls*, making off with 1,200 camels, 30,000 sheep, 7,000 horses, and 150 captives (*Russko-turkmenskie otnosheniia v XVIII–XIX vv.*, 339, doc. no. 245). In 1861, a Qajar unit assaulting Yomut settlements along the Atrek River stole 1,000 camels, 12,000 sheep, and 15 elderly Turkmen women; the reason, evidently, was that these Yomuts refused to become Qajar citizens and to surrender the Iranian captives held among them (ibid., 505–506, doc. no. 374).

2 Thus, in 1828, some Turkmen leaders from the Caspian coast informed the Russians that many of their people were still held in Iran even after a peace agreement had been concluded, inspiring resentment in their communities (*Russko-turkmenskie otnosheniia v XVIII–XIX vv.*, 259, doc. no. 174). It is revealing that, in this document, the Turkmens kept in Iran are referred to as being held "under arrest" (*pod arestom*) – a markedly different terminology than the language of captives (*plenniki*) and slaves (*raby, nevol'niki*) typically used to describe Iranians taken by the Turkmens.

Scourge of the Man-Stealing Turcomans,[3] and in the terrifying Turkmen brigands of *The Adventures of Hajji Baba of Ispahan*, James Justinian Morier's once-beloved picaresque novel.[4] Depictions of Iranians in nineteenth-century European literature are likewise generally negative, but they are relatively multifaceted, drawing on a wider array of stereotypes; the Turkmens, however, were either barbarous slave-raiders or slave-raiding barbarians, and nothing more, though on occasion one finds an appreciative word or two concerning their audacity.

Rare European accounts exist, nevertheless, which detail the horrific cruelty suffered by some Turkmen captives in Iran. N. G. Petrusevich, a Russian officer and scientist who was killed at the siege of Dengil Teppe, reported that in 1861, not long after the disastrous Qajar attempt to take Merv from the Teke Turkmens, these Turkmens assembled a large force and began raiding the villages around Mashhad. Qajar troops intervened and many of the Tekes were killed; up to 100 were taken captive. Petrusevich describes their terrible fate:[5]

> There followed an order by the Shah to deliver the captives to Tehran, and so, in groups of several individuals, they were shackled by the hands and feet to a single iron rod and driven on foot to Tehran, which was over 1,000 versts from Mashhad. The Shah, wishing to reassure the populace, which was displeased with the shameful showing of the substantial army [which had been defeated at Merv], ordered that all the captives be executed in front of the gates of the city. His ministers decided, for the public's great entertainment [*dlia bol'shego naslazhdeniia publiki*], to tie the captives to the city walls and begin shooting them at a distance of 300 paces. It should be clear enough that the regular infantry [*sarbazy*], never having been trained in arming and firing flintlocks, could not manage to hit the living targets which were laid out so far from them, such that the pleasure of shooting could last until evening, subjecting the unfortunate Turkmens to the torments of hell. Learning of these barbaric orders, all of the ambassadors immediately appealed for the abolition of such executions. But it was too late: the execution took place, though only when the infantry were summoned closer. Regardless, the shooting still continued until evening. Some of the bullets hit not the captives, but the ropes by which they were tied. Thus untied, they would come forward and sit before the infantrymen, in hopes that

3 Marvin, *Merv, Queen of the World, and the Scourge of the Man-Stealing Turcomans* (London: W.H. Allen, 1881).

4 Morier, *The Adventures of Hajji Baba of Ispahan* (London: MacMillan, 1902).

5 Petrusevich, "Turkmeny mezhdu starym' ruslom' Amu-Daryi (Uzboem') i severnymi okrainami Persii," *Zapiski kavkazskago otdela imperatorskago russkago geograficheskago obshchestva*, Vol. 11 (Tbilisi, 1880), 53–54; see also A. Rzhevuskii, "Ot Tiflisa do Dengil'-tepe," *Voennyi sbornik* 8 (1884), 285.

they would depart from this life more quickly if they were closer to the infantry, since they had no hope for mercy.

Another revolting "entertainment" was observed in 1875, and is worth retelling here both because it is one of the few accounts concerning the fate of Turkmen captives in Iran and because it speaks volumes about the extraordinary bitterness that could characterize the Turkmen–Qajar relationship:[6]

In 1875, the brother of the current Shah was appointed governor of Khurasan. The administration of Khurasan decided to honor his arrival at Mashhad, Khurasan's capital, by sacrificing Turkmen captives. They prepared twenty of them for this, and when the new governor arrived the captives were raised up on bayonets before him, one after another, so they could be seen by him and by the majority of the people who had gathered to welcome the Shah's brother. What must have been the mortal agony of the captives can be ascertained from the fact that the last of them, when it was his turn to be raised on bayonets, tried to offer 2,000 *tumans* (8,000 rubles at the going rate) to ransom himself. But his offer was not accepted. His hopes were dashed, and he had to go forth to be impaled. He did not make it, however: death overtook him beforehand, and he fell dead in front of the governor and the whole gathering.

Turkmens as well as Kazakhs were also taken into captivity in Khwarazm and Bukhara, and according to the chronicles produced in both of these domains, the Khwarazmians and Bukharans also very frequently seized one-another's subjects in warfare.[7] The Khivan chronicle *Firdaws al-iqbāl* contains no fewer than nineteen references to conflicts in which "innumerable," "countless," or "numerous" prisoners were taken (not including one which resulted in "an unspeakable number" of captives),[8] as well as dozens

[6] Petrusevich, "Turkmeny mezhdu starym' ruslom' Amu-Daryi (Uzboem') i severnymi okrainami Persii," 54; Rzhevuskii, "Ot Tiflisa do Dengil'-tepe," 285. Petrusevich meditated on the implications of this repulsive scene: "It stands to reason that, having neighbors characterized by such a disposition – and despite the fact that Persia is still seen as a beacon of civilization, tending to mitigate human cruelty and inspire a more rational vision of human life – the Turkmen have had nowhere else from which to receive examples of kind-heartedness, and it is for that reason that they remain primitive in their savagery" (Petrusevich, "Turkmeny mezhdu starym' ruslom' Amu-Daryi (Uzboem') i severnymi okrainami Persii," 54).

[7] Baron Meyendorff recounted meeting a group of Uzbeks in Bukhara who boasted, "if the Khan would only give us permission, we would revenge ourselves on the Khivans by conquering them, killing or taking them prisoners, as we did 10 years ago" (Georg von Baron Meyendorff, *A Journey from Orenburg to Bukhara in the Year 1820* [Calcutta, 1870], 41).

[8] Shīr Muḥammad Mīrāb Munis and Muḥammad Rizā Mīrāb Āgāhī, *Firdaws al-iqbāl: History of Khorezm*, trans. Yuri Bregel (Leiden: Brill, 1999), 118, 194, 196, 205, 210, 211, 220, 221, 297, 305, 307, 309, 331, 389, 397, 398, 448, 503, 645.

of other mentions of captives being taken in known or estimable numbers. Naturally, the elaborate bravado of the genre must be kept in mind, and some of these numbered or numberless victims may have been simply rhetorical embroidery. A typical passage informs us that in one battle between the Khivan army and a Qongrat detachment, "the ever-victorious [Khivan] army captured rich booty and innumerable prisoners. Thanks to his royal majesty's valor and courage this large army, as numerous as ants and locusts, was utterly destroyed and the late khan gained victory. No brave warrior except his majesty ever gained such a marvelous result."[9]

Whatever the exaggerations involved, the nearly constant reference to captive-taking in the region's chronicles is revealing. It reveals the normative quality of captivity as a result of warfare, as well as the prestige related to taking captives. Prisoners-of-war were listed among the other spoils of battle – such as camels, horses, and sheep – and were a hallmark of victory.[10] Combatants and noncombatants alike were captured, though the capture of young women seems to have held particular appeal in, for example, the world of the *Firdaws al-iqbāl*, where we learn that spoils – women among them – were divided between warriors and elites. Concerning the aftermath of one battle, the chronicle relates that "When the raiders gathered under the victorious banner, his majesty divided the booty amongst the troops, and everyone received a great amount of property . . . Among the prisoners were thirty seven virgin girls of perfect beauty and exceptional slenderness. His majesty entrusted the prisoners to reliable and virtuous people and went home victorious and triumphant."[11] After a particularly successful struggle in which Khivan and Yomut forces teamed up against the Kazakhs, we learn that "the ever-victorious troops captured plenty of booty and innumerable prisoners, including more than 100,000 sheep and more than 40,000 camels; and from this one may have some idea about the rest of the booty. There were 500 virgin girls among the prisoners, and from this one may estimate the number of other prisoners. The daughters and harems of Jantu Töre and Ayten Töre, sons of [the Kazakh Lesser Horde leader] Bölekey Khan, we also captured. One wife of Burkut Bay Biy and his young sons were also taken prisoner."[12]

9 *Firdaws al-iqbāl*, 211.

10 E.g. "They continued to pursue the fleeing [Turkmens] till the time of night prayers, killed many of them, took some prisoners, captured many women and children, seized ten thousand sheep as booty and went back" (*Firdaws al-iqbāl*, 197).

11 *Firdaws al-iqbāl*, 172. 12 *Firdaws al-iqbāl*, 398.

While we may assume that young women taken as captives tended to end up in the harems of elites, there is little clear information on what became of the other captives taken by Khivan, Bukharan, or Iranian armies. Arminius Vambery, in one of the only extant descriptions concerning Turkmen captives in Central Asia, claims to have seen three hundred Chawdur "prisoners of war" awaiting their fate in Bukhara. "They were separated into two divisions," he writes, "namely, such as had not yet reached their fortieth year, and were to be sold as slaves, or to be made use of as presents, and such as from their rank or age were regarded as Aksakals (grey beards) or leaders, and who were to suffer the punishment imposed by the Khan." The former were led away in groups of ten or fifteen, chained together by their iron collars. The latter, he claims, suffered a shocking, horrific punishment:[13]

Whilst several were led to the gallows or the block, I saw how, at a sign from the executioner, eight aged men placed themselves down on their backs upon the earth. They were then bound hand and foot, and the executioner gouged out their eyes in turn, kneeling to do so on the breast of each poor wretch; and after every operation he wiped his knife, dripping with blood, upon the white beard of the hoary unfortunate. Ah! cruel spectacle! As each fearful act was completed, the victim liberated from his bonds, groping around with his hands, sought to gain his feet! Some fell against each other, head against head; others sank powerless to the earth again, uttering low groans, the memory of which will make me shudder as long as I live.

Russian officers and subjects likewise took captives, and could sometimes be found raiding nomadic communities in a manner not dissimilar from that by which nomads raided sedentary districts. In the summer of 1841, the Orenburg governor-general received a complaint from representatives of a Kazakh community that Siberian Cossack bands had been attacking their village and others nearby. In one alleged assault on some twenty-five villages, the Cossacks killed forty people, including fifteen women (all of whom are named in the document), and stole 621 camels, 555 horses, 263 cattle, and 7,770 sheep. This was followed by a confrontation in which the Cossacks captured twenty-four people (including eleven women and girls and ten boys between three and ten years old), killing another eighteen.[14] As we shall see in the chapters to come, the Russian military also took part in the "ransom economy,"

[13] Vambery, *Travels in Central Asia*, 138.
[14] *Sbornik materialov dliia istorii zavoevaniia turkestanskogo kraia*, ed. A. G. Serebrennikov, Vol. 3 (Tashkent: Tip. Sht. Turkestanskogo V.O., 1908–1912), 84–85, doc. no. 48.

trading in captives as well as holding hostages in exchange for political promises and concessions.

Mass resettlement was another option for disposing of captives, and sometimes the number of people forcibly resettled at one time could total in the thousands. Entire towns could be created out of thin air in this manner, the most famous of which was Khurasan's "Khivaqābād," a Khurasanian town under Qajar jurisdiction consisting entirely of people forcibly resettled by Nādir Shah after his conquest of Khiva in 1740.[15] Turkmens were sometimes the victims of this sort of strategy as well: 1,500 families of Gökleng Turkmens were resettled by the Qajar Najaf ʿAlī Khan after battling with the Khwarazmians in 1837.[16] Resettlement could also be a defensive strategy: This same Najaf ʿAlī Khan resettled 150 households of Arabs from the vicinity of the Atrek to the walled village of Katlish in Khurasan in order to protect them from the inevitable attacks by the Turkmens.[17]

In short, captive-taking in Central Asia and its borderlands was not limited to the Turkmens and Kazakhs; it was a normative tactic of war. Nevertheless, foreign observers imposed a remarkable double-standard on this phenomenon, whereby violence done by non-nomads was dignified with a formal military language that was denied to nomadic combatants. Russian, Qajar, or Bukharan violence was described with the orderly vocabulary of campaigns, expeditions, offensives, operations, detachments, soldiers, regiments, and prisoners-of-war. Turkmen or Kazakh violence, meanwhile, was described using the contemptuous language of raiding, pillaging, plundering, looting, and slave-taking. At the heart of this division is the idea that the violence perpetrated by settled peoples – and especially by European empires – has a legitimacy that nomadic violence lacks.

These Turkmens and Kazakhs are very often called, in our Russian and English sources, "pirates" (*piraty*), "brigands" (*razboiniki*), and "predators" (*khishchniki*). Their activities were compared to those of the Barbary pirates from the North African coasts and the caravan-robbers of the Sahara. Thus, Ferrier writes that "A horse is to the Turcoman what a ship is to the pirate."[18] For Vambery, "What the Portuguese slave traders and

15 These events are described in, for example, Mīrzā Mahdi Khan Astarābādī's *Tārīkh-i nādirī* (cf. *Materiali po istorii turkmen i turkmenii, tom 2. XVI–XIX vv. Iranskie, bukharskie, i khivinskie istochniki* [Moscow, 1938], 146).

16 Muḥammad Ḥassan Khan, *Tārīkh-i muntaẓam-i nādirī* (cf. *Materialy po istorii turkmen i turkmenii, tom* 2, 235).

17 C. E. Yate, *Khurasan and Sistan* (London: Blackwood and Sons, 1900), 202–203.

18 J. P. Ferrier, *Caravan Journeys and Wanderings in Persia, Afghanistan, Turkistan, and Beloochistan* (London: J. Murray, 1857), 94. Cf. also Mikhail Khodarkovsky, *Russia's*

the Arabian ivory merchants are in Central Africa, that are the Turkomans in the north-eastern and north-western portions of Iran, indeed we may say in all Persia. Wherever nomad tribes live in the immediate neighbourhood of a civilised country, there will robbery and slavery unavoidably exist to a greater or less extent."[19] Vambery's comment is typical in associating nomadism itself with brigandage. The perceived independence and statelessness of nomads was often seen as an inherent threat to "civilization," as the nomads' seemingly unbounded migrations were thought to undermine borders and citizenship, as well as taxation, agriculture, urbanism, and all the allegiances and systems of loyalty that were regarded as hallmarks of "settled" statehood.

The nomads were also alleged to be impervious to diplomacy, or even to reason. Joseph Wolff, the eccentric, globetrotting missionary, wrote that "The Turkomauns of the desert of Mowr and Sarakhs are a people of such a perfidious disposition, and of such great rapacity, that one could not depend for a moment on their promises, or on any treaties entered into with them; for the Turkomauns, as well as the Beduins in the deserts of Arabia, do not consider consequences, but are only restrained by instant infliction of punishment."[20] Alexander Gorchakov, the Tsar's chancellor in the era of Central Asia's conquests, would echo these sentiments in his famous circular from November of 1864, in which he reasoned that "the tribes on the frontier have to be reduced to a state of more or less perfect submission" – and reduced violently, since, he wrote, "It is a peculiarity of Asiatics to respect nothing but visible and palpable force; the moral force

Steppe Frontier: The Making of a Colonial Empire, 1500–1800 (Bloomington, IN: Indiana University Press, 2004), 29; Gao, "Captivity and Empire," 3–4.

[19] Vambery, *Sketches of Central Asia*, 206. Vambery elaborates: "The poverty-stricken children of the desert are endowed by nature with an insatiable lust for adventure, and frames capable of supporting the most terrible privations and fatigues. What the scanty soil of their native wilderness denies them, they seek in the lands of their more favoured neighbours. The intercourse between them, however, is seldom of a friendly character. As the plundered and hardly used agriculturist cannot, and dare not, pursue the well-mounted nomad across the pathless deserts of sand, the latter, protected by the nature of the country, can carry on his career of plunder and rapine without fear of chastisement. In former times the cities on the borders of the Great Sahara and of the Arabian desert were in the same plight. Even at the present day the caravans in the latter country are exposed to the greatest dangers. But Persia has to suffer from these evils to a still greater extent, as the deserts which form her northern boundary are the most extensive and the most savage in the world, while their inhabitants are the most cruel and least civilised of nomads."

[20] Joseph Wolff, *Narrative of a Mission to Bokhara in the years 1843–45, to Ascertain the Fate of Colonel Stoddart and Captain Conolly*, Vol. 1 (London: John W. Parker, 1845), 272.

of reason and of the interests of civilization has as yet no hold upon them."[21]

While the nomads were typically singled out for a special degree of contempt, these same traits were sometimes attributed to Khwarazm and Bukhara as well. But even then the nomads were implicated: One of the most common critiques of these two states – and particularly of Khwarazm – is that they benefitted from the thievery of nomads, forming alliances with them or employing them as agents and mercenaries. Thus M. Ivanin, deploring Khwarazm's rulers for "inciting" the Turkmens and Kazakhs to abduct Russians and sell them into slavery, writes that "Khiva, by its actions in relation to its neighbors, could be dubbed the Algeria of Central Asia, as the foremost enterprise of its government has been to rob their neighbors and traffic in people."[22] Khwarazmian elites did indeed benefit from this traffic directly, by owning the slaves themselves and putting them to work on their estates.

Even so, Ivanin wildly exaggerates the centrality of the slave trade (not only for Khwarazm, but also for Algeria), and, in a typical fashion, simplifies the relationship between Turkmens, Kazakhs, and Khwarazmian rulers. The nomads were not just "agents" of the khan, but an essential part of the fabric of Khwarazmian society; the Turkmen and Kazakh populations of Khwarazm, though not entirely nomadic, may at times have added to as much as 40 percent of the total population of the khanate. The khan benefitted not only from their military participation, which was considerable, but also from their tax revenues and their commerce more generally. Relations between these populations and the khan were often strained; the years 1855–1867, for example, witnessed continual uprisings among Yomuts and other Turkmen groups who had formerly been considered Khwarazmian subjects.[23] Baron Meyendorff succinctly summed up a general predicament faced by the khans with respect to the Turkmen and Kazakh populace: "The Nomads, who wander about all over the country," he writes, "could easily leave it altogether, so that their Chiefs are compelled to treat them gently, and have even, sometimes, to flatter

[21] Demetrius Charles Boulger, *England and Russia in Central Asia*, vol. 1 (London: W.H. Allen and Co., 1879), 319.

[22] M. Ivanin, *Opisanie zimnogo pokhoda v khivu v 1839–1840 g.* (St. Pb, 1874), 18. Here, Ivanin echoes the sentiment articulated by General Perovskii, who, in 1835, wrote to St. Petersburg to urge a "punitive" expedition against the Khivans: "The guilt of the Dey of Algiers against the King of the French pales into insignificance in comparison with the crimes carried out by whole generations of Khivan Khans against the Emperors of Russia" (Morrison, "Twin Imperial Disasters," 284).

[23] Yuri Bregel, *Khorezmskie turkmeny v XIX veke* (Moscow, 1961), 197–228.

them. The present khan has not had enough regard for this precept, and has therefore lost many Turcomans, who, having subjected themselves to the khan of Khiva, show their fidelity by wasting and plundering the countries belonging to their former master."[24]

MAJOR FEATURES AND ORIGINS OF THE SLAVE TRADE

What did the khanates stand to gain from the slave trade, which became by the mid-nineteenth century such a flashpoint in diplomacy with Russia, Iran, and Great Britain? They gained quite a lot, as we shall see, and these gains were not limited to free labor. First, tax revenues could be gained from the trade in slaves. According to Ismāʿīl Sarhang Mīrpanja, who was imprisoned for ten years in Khiva, a tax of one *ṭilla* was extracted for every single sale of a slave.[25] N. N. Murav'ev, whose travelogue of a mission to Khiva provides some of the most detailed reportage on Khwarazmian slavery, writes that all subjects of the khan who engaged in raids into Iran would owe in taxes one-fifth of any spoils they brought back to the khanate.[26] Vambery, traveling in a caravan full of emancipated slaves, observed that the transport tax for this cargo was extracted beyond Khwarazm as well, and sometimes the levies could be considerable.[27] Slaves purchasing their own freedom from their owners were also taxed some portion of their value.[28]

The ransom economy also served as a significant financial incentive for perpetuating the slave trade. Of those captives taken in the relatively affluent district of Mazandaran and along the southern Caspian coast, Vambery estimated that one-third would be ransomed back into the care of relatives rather than being sold north to Khwarazm or Bukhara.

[24] Meyendorff, *A Journey from Orenburg to Bukhara in the Year 1820*, 50.

[25] Mīrpanja, *Khāṭirāt-i asārat: ruznāma-yi safar-i khwārazm va khiva*, ed. Safā' ad-Dīn Tabarrā'iyān (Tehran: Muʿssassa-yi Pazhuhish va Mutālaʿat-i Farhangī, 1370/1991), 119.

[26] N. N. Murav'ev, *Muraviev's Journey to Khiva through the Turcoman Country, 1819–20* (Calcutta: Foreign Department Press, 1871), 140.

[27] "Here, as everywhere," Vambery writes, while entering Jamshidi country, "our difficulties began and ended with questions respecting the customs. It had been said, all along, that with the left bank of the Murgab Afghanistan began, and that there the slave tax would cease to be exacted. It was a grievous mistake. The Khan of the Djemshidi, who treated in person with the Kervanbashi concerning the taxes, exacted more for goods, cattle, and slaves than the former claimants, and when the tariff was made known, the consternation, and with many the lamentation, knew no bounds" (Vambery, *Travels in Central Asia*, 260).

[28] James Abbott, *Narrative of a Journey from Heraut to Khiva, Moscow, and St. Petersburgh, during the Late Russian Invasion of Khiva*, Vol. 2 (London: W.H. Allen and Co., 1843), 288; Arminius Vambery, *Travels in Central Asia*, 235.

Captives taken from poorer regions of Khurasan and Sistan rarely had relatives who could pay a suitable ransom price, however, and so most were sold into slavery: "I have heard," Vambery writes, "out of the mouth of a slave dealer who had grown grey in his trade, that from these districts scarcely a tenth part are ransomed, the remaining nine-tenths being forwarded for sale in the markets of the khanats."[29] Ransom was no doubt the outcome of first resort from the perspective of the captive-takers themselves, not only for its greater financial rewards but also because it eliminated the need to transport captives across long distances. The bounty gained from ransom was also free from the fluctuating prices of the northern markets and independent of the captive's physical traits; if slave prices were down in Khiva, or if the captive in question was ill-suited to labor, relatives would still pay top dollar to liberate a loved one.

Mīrzā Maḥmūd Taqī Āshtiyānī, who was himself held for ransom among the Sarïq Turkmens, records the system by which these ransom exchanges would take place. Sometimes, the families of captives would send coins and promissory notes (called *barāt*) via caravans traveling from Iran, which merchants from the caravans would exchange for their loved ones. Otherwise, the merchants themselves might pay out-of-pocket for the captives, having received a promise of reimbursement from their loved ones back in Iran.[30] Families with the means to do so could also hire Turkmen agents to "kidnap" their enslaved relatives in their places of bondage and bring them back home.[31] Once within Khwarazm or Bukhara, however, ransom would have been a much greater challenge, as rulers of these domains – as we shall see – were disinclined to allow the repatriation of slaves into non-Sunni environs. The process of ransoming or otherwise extracting slaves from the khanates was thus always done covertly.[32]

Our sources abound with tales of former slaves who, having purchased or otherwise gained their own freedom, attempt to buy the freedom of family members who had likewise been taken into slavery. In 1804–1805, a woman named Akulina Krivobokova approached Orenburg border authorities after having lived for thirty-one years in slavery, having

[29] Vambery, *Sketches of Central Asia*, 213–214.

[30] Mīrzā Maḥmūd Taqī Āshtiyānī, *'Ibratnāma: Khatirati az dawran-i pas az jangha-yi herat va merv*, ed. Husayn 'Imadi Ashtiyani (Tehran: Nashr-i markaz, 1382/2003), 29–32; cf. Amanat and Khazeni, "The Steppe Roads of Central Asia and the Persian Captivity Narrative of Mahmud Mirza Taqi Ashtiyani," 125.

[31] Murav'ev, *Muraviev's Journey to Khiva through the Turcoman Country*, 156.

[32] "Nevol'niki v Khive," *Vestnik evropy* 80:7 (1815), 245.

apparently been owned by at least one Khivan khan (*v nevol'nichestve khivinskogo khana*). Relatives had purchased her freedom the preceding summer, but her two sons and two daughters remained in captivity. The cost of buying their freedom was more than the family could afford, and she had come to the Russian government in order to petition them to provide the necessary funds.[33] Vambery reports having met in a single caravan several people who had been in a similar position, seeking to purchase or having purchased their loved ones' freedom:[34]

There were in the karaván, as I remarked at the first station, many others besides myself who were longing to reach the southernmost frontiers of Central Asia. These were the emancipated slaves, with whom Hadjis were intermixed, and I had an opportunity of witnessing the most heart-rending incidents. Near me was an old man – a father – bowed down by years. He had ransomed, at Bokhara, his son, a man in his thirtieth year, in order to restore a protector to his family left behind – that is to say, to his daughter- in-law a husband, to his children a father. The price was fifty ducats, and its payment had reduced the poor old man to beggary. "But," said he to me, "rather the beggar's staff than my son in chains." His home was Khaf in Persia. From the same city, not far from us, was another man, still of active strength, but his hair had turned grey with sorrow, for he had been despoiled by the Turkomans, some eight years ago, of wife, sister, and six children. The unfortunate man had to wander from place to place a whole year in Khiva and Bokhara, to discover the spot in which those near members of his family were

33 TSGKaz 4.1.499 67a–69a.

34 Vambery, *Sketches of Central Asia*, 235–237. Elsewhere, Vambery records other affecting narratives concerning the vicissitudes of the ransom economy: He writes a letter to a relative on behalf of a young Iranian domestic slave "praying them for God's sake to sell sheep and house to ransom him" (*Travels in Central Asia*, 60); he meets a five-year-old who, having been captured and sold two years before along with his father, reports that his father had bought his own freedom and that he expected his father would free him too before long (ibid., 163); and he comments on the challenging position of the newly captured Iranian of wealthy background, who, on the one hand, wishes to be ransomed but, on the other, hopes to hide evidence pointing toward the vastness of the ransom that might be gotten for him: "This poor Persian was transferred, for chastisement, to [the Turkmen] Kulkhan, who had the peculiar reputation of being able most easily to ascertain from a captive whether he possessed sufficient means to enable his relatives to ransom him, or whether, being without relatives or property, he ought to be sent on to Khiva for sale. The former alternative is much the more agreeable one to the Turkomans, as they may demand any sum they please. The Persian, who is cunning even in his misfortune, always contrives to conceal his real position; he is therefore subjected to much ill-treatment until by the lamentations which he forwards to his home his captors have squeezed from his friends the highest possible ransom, and it is only when that arrives that his torment ceases" (ibid., 75–76). The ordeal described by Vambery, in which ransoms are gradually extracted by tormenting a wealthy captive, are consistent with Āshtiyānī's experiences as well (cf. Amanat and Khazeni, "The Steppe Roads of Central Asia," 126).

languishing in captivity. After long search, he found that his wife, sister, and two youngest children had succumbed under the severity of their servitude, and that, of the four children that survived, he could only ransom half. The remaining two having besides grown up, the sum demanded for them was beyond his means. Farther on sat a young man from Herat, who had ransomed his mother. Only two years ago, this woman, now in her fiftieth year, was, with her husband and eldest son, surprised by an Alaman [raid]. After seeing those near relatives both fall, in self-defense, under the lances and swords of the Turkomans, she experienced herself unceasing sufferings until sold for sixteen ducats in Bokhara. The owner, discovering a son in him who sought to ransom her, exacted a double amount, thus turning filial piety to cruelly usurious account. Nor must I omit to mention another unhappy case – that of an inhabitant of Tebbes. He was captured eight years ago, and after the lapse of two years he was ransomed by his father. They were both returning home, and were three leagues from their native city, when they were suddenly attacked by the Turkomans, taken prisoners, led back to Bokhara, and again sold as slaves. Now, they were a second time freed, and were being conveyed to their homes.

Still more important than the tax and ransom revenues, however, were the captives themselves: by all accounts, a substantial proportion of the agricultural labor both in Khwarazm and in Bukhara was performed by slaves, and slaves constituted a significant demographic in these states' militaries as well. For their part, those Turkmens and Kazakhs bringing slaves to the market would benefit from payment not only in cash, but also in goods and – most importantly – in the crucial stocks of grain that nomads of the arid zones were unable to produce themselves. This "grain-for-slaves" commerce was one aspect of the symbiotic relationship between slave-traders and the settled states.

It would be wrong to see captive-taking in purely economic terms, however, especially in light of the overarching culture of captivity discussed earlier, in which it was a standard part of the strategic vernacular of warfare. Though foreign observers did not dignify Turkmen and Kazakh raids as part of an ongoing political struggle, this is precisely what they were. For both groups, the long-term goal was often independence – either a degree of it within the confines of fealty to Khwarazm or Russia, or complete independence in regions that were increasingly encroached upon by expansionist imperial neighbors. Attacks on the villages of Khurasan provided revenue, but they also served to create a buffer zone of weakened, destabilized territory between Tehran and the Turkmen deserts. Kazakh attacks on caravans and settlements likewise came with financial benefits, but they also asserted dominance over the steppe in an era when Russian power was increasingly visible at its peripheries. Raiding was a form of resistance.

As I will show in the chapters to come, the slave trade also fulfilled many other functions for the captive-takers and slave-owners. For the slaves themselves, captivity could be as brief as a matter of days before being ransomed or as long as several decades in bonded labor. Many would die during the brutal ordeal of being transported across the deserts by their captors. Those who survived the journey would join tens of thousands of other slaves in Khwarazm, Bukhara, and the Kazakh steppe, performing all manner of work. Agricultural labor predominated, especially for Iranian slaves, but we also find slaves working as soldiers, teachers, carpenters, blacksmiths, musicians, drovers, prostitutes, miners, herders, and dancers. Most were converted to Sunni Islam. Many were married, sometimes forcibly, and most often to other slaves. Fortunate slaves were permitted to perform independent labor in their limited free time, the proceeds of which were their own to keep (if their masters did not expropriate them); by this means, a great many slaves purchased their own freedom. A very fortunate few, either during or after their period of bondage, managed to achieve prominent positions in the royal *dīvān* or in the military.

The estimated total number of slaves in Khwarazm and Bukhara varied throughout the nineteenth century from tens of thousands to hundreds of thousands. There has been consensus on one key point: The overwhelming majority of slaves were Iranians. The earliest estimates concerning the number of Iranian slaves in Khwarazm alone were generally in the range of 30,000–40,000, though on the higher end we find estimates of up to 140,000. Similarly, for Bukhara, estimates on the number of enslaved Iranians tend to range from 30,000 to 40,000; one estimate – by Joseph Wolff – put the figure as high as 200,000, a sum which seems impossible but which we should hesitate to dismiss entirely, given Wolff's claim that the estimate was offered by the Bukharan Amīr himself (albeit in passing).[35] By the mid-late nineteenth century, the claim that Iranian slaves in Khwarazm numbered as many as 50,000–60,000 became more common.

By contrast, the estimated number of Russian slaves plummeted as the century wore on. Unsurprisingly, the number of Russian slaves, despite being by all estimates a tiny fraction of the total slave population, inspired much more commentary among Russian and British travelers, officials, and observers. Estimates from the early decades of the century posited as many as 15,000 Russian slaves in Khwarazm and Bukhara

[35] Wolff, *Narrative of a Mission to Bokhara in the years 1843–45*, 226.

combined. The best-known and most widely reported estimate was relayed by Murav'ev, who, during his mission to Khiva, discovered a haunting secret letter from a representative of the Russian slave population:[36]

> As I was preparing to clean this gun, I discovered a slip of paper in one of the barrels, on which the following was written in Russian: "We venture to inform your Honor that there are over 3,000 Russian slaves in this place, who have to suffer unheard-of misery from labour, cold, hunger, &c. Have pity on our unhappy situation and reveal it to the Emperor. In gratitude we shall pray to God for your Honor's welfare." The perusal of these lines deeply affected me, and I thanked God that I should, perhaps, have the fortune to serve as an instrument of help.

These numbers align more or less with the estimate offered by Lieutenant Gladyshev, who proposed that there were 3,000 Russians, Kalmyks, and "foreigners" in the khanate, a number of whom he saw cleaning the canals when he visited Khiva in 1740–1741.[37] They also align with the estimate of an Orthodox priest named Khrisanf, who traveled in the region near the end of the eighteenth century, estimating some 4,000 Russian slaves in Khiva (as well as 6,000 in Bukhara).[38] In 1840, however, when the Khivan khan, as a concession to Russia, released what he claimed were all the remaining Russian slaves in the khanate, they totaled fewer than 500. Another twenty-one were freed on the eve of Khiva's conquest in 1873, and not many more appear to have been liberated during that event. It is possible that the early estimates were exaggerated; or that a great many of the Russian slaves had since been manumitted and returned home or assimilated totally into Central Asian communities; or – most likely – that they simply died and were not replaced, as the overall trade in Russian captives decreased over the course of the nineteenth century.

When it comes to Bukhara, meanwhile, there is general agreement, and among a greater number of eyewitnesses, that very few Russian slaves remained there by the middle of the nineteenth century. Jan Prosper Witkiewicz, a Polish exile who entered Russian service and ventured to Bukhara as a diplomat for the Tsar, met some twenty-five of them personally, and estimated their total number at no more than fifty.[39] Burnes put the number at 130,[40] and Kostenko observed simply that they were

[36] Murav'ev, *Muraviev's Journey to Khiva through the Turcoman Country, 1819–20*, 77.

[37] Gladyshev and Muravin, *Poezdka iz Orska v Khivu i obratno, sovershennaia v 1740–41 godakh poruchikom Gladyshevym i geodezistom Muravinym* (St. Pb, 1851), 18.

[38] *Puteshestviia po Vostoku v opokhu Ekateriny II*, 279.

[39] Vitkevich, *Zapiski o Bukharskom khanstve* (Moscow: Nauka, 1983), 115.

[40] Burnes, *Travels into Bokhara*, Vol. 2 (London: Carey and Hart, 1835), 115.

few.[41] Nevertheless, the freeing of Russian slaves continued to play a significant role in Russian diplomacy with both Bukhara and Khwarazm down to the age of the region's conquest.

The abundance of slaves increased during times of heavy warfare along the Iranian frontier, and the increase could reportedly be substantial. Baron Meyendorff claimed that a particularly violent struggle for Merv increased the number of Iranian slaves in Bukhara by 25,000 (bringing the total, in his estimation, to 40,000 overall).[42] Naturally, any great influx of slaves resulted in lower prices at the markets.[43] Regardless of the abundance of slaves for sale, however, prices could vary considerably. The most commonly cited market price for a slave, which may be taken as an overall average throughout the nineteenth century, is between thirty and sixty gold coins (*ṭilla, chervonits*),[44] in both Bukharan and Khwarazmian currency. Indeed, many former slaves who reported their own original sale price to Russian border officials were sold for a price in the twenty-five to forty coin range. But the price of a slave depended on a variety of factors, including age, origins, gender, and physical condition. Major Blankenagel', a physician who visited Khiva in 1792 to treat the khan for an eye malady, reported that the Kazakhs were selling Russian captives at the Khivan and Bukharan bazaars at a rate of forty to fifty coins for a man and anywhere from 50 to 100 coins for a woman.[45] Meyendorff observed precisely the opposite, claiming that "The women, as a rule, are cheaper than the men, except those still young and handsome." He writes that the price of a "well-built" man of any background averaged forty to fifty *ṭilla*s, though knowledge of a useful craft, such as blacksmithing, could raise a slave's price to 100 *ṭilla*s. Young and attractive women, meanwhile, could sometimes fetch 100–150 *ṭilla*s.[46] Murav'ev writes that Iranian men fetched a lower price than Russian men – generally twenty to thirty *ṭilla*s, as opposed to sixty to eighty *ṭilla*s for a "young and healthy" Russian – but

[41] L. F. Kostenko, *Puteshestvie v Bukharu russkoi missii v 1870 godu* (St. Pb, 1871), 107.

[42] Meyendorff, *A Journey from Orenburg to Bukhara in the Year 1820*, 61–62; cf. also M. Alikhanov-Avarskii, *Pokhod v Khivu (Kavkazkikh otriadov) 1873. Step' i oazis* (St. Pb, 1899), 280.

[43] Cf., for example, A. Maslov, "Rossiia v Srednei Azii. (Ocherk nashikh noveishikh priobretenii)," *Istoricheskii vestnik* 5 (1885), 386.

[44] I estimate that one *tilla* in nineteenth-century Bukhara was generally worth about 6.4 British pounds sterling, or 26 francs, though there was significant variation in the relative value of silver over the course of the century.

[45] Blankenagel', *Zamechaniia maiora Blankenagelia, vposledstvie poezdki ego iz Orenburga v Khivu v 1793–94 godakh* (St. Pb, 1858), 12–13.

[46] Meyendorff, *A Journey from Orenburg to Bukhara in the Year 1820*, 61–62.

that Iranian female slaves sold for much higher prices than Russian women; Kurds fetched the lowest sums.[47] Witkiewicz wrote that the ruler of Kunduz was at the time of his visit "constantly conducting raids on the peoples of the district, taking captives; and his merchants bring them to Bukhara. 20–50 *ṭilla*s – or Bukharan coins – are paid for them. A pleasant maiden fetches up to 70 *ṭilla*s; a comely (*prigozhii*) boy, up to 40. But workers usually fetch no more than 30 *ṭilla*s."[48]

Slaves were sold and traded extensively beyond the bazaars, however, and they were very often traded for objects or livestock, especially among the Turkmens and Kazakhs. Former slaves report having been traded for a wide range of goods and animals. Trading slaves for sheep was evidently quite common; they could be sold for as few as thirty-six sheep,[49] though a higher valuation is more customary. One slave who had previously been sold for forty-one *tanga*s[50] was traded for eighty sheep;[51] two others for 100 sheep each;[52] another for 150 sheep;[53] another for twenty-two sheep and a horse;[54] another for twenty sheep and three horses;[55] and another for ten "big sheep," one camel, one horse, and three large felt carpets.[56] Others report having been traded for twenty Khivan silk robes (*khalat*);[57] one camel and one horse;[58] one camel and two horses;[59] and nine horses, one fleece and fur coat, and a gun.[60] Many slaves were sold or traded multiple times, and the price for the same slave could vary dramatically from one sale to the next. The slave who had been traded for twenty Khivan silk robes had earlier been sold by Turkmens to a Khivan for nine *ṭilla*s, and he was later sold to a Kazakh for twenty-nine *ṭilla*s.[61] A slave who was traded to a Kazakh for forty mares was, twenty-one years later, traded to another for just ten mares – the difference owing no doubt to his advanced age.[62]

Among the first indignities suffered by many slaves in the region was the loss of their name. New owners were at liberty to change their slaves' names, and they very often did. Sometimes the masters proved themselves

47 Murav'ev, *Muraviev's Journey to Khiva through the Turcoman Country, 1819–20*, 57–58, 148.

48 Ia. P. Vitkevich, *Zapiski o Bukharskom khanstve* (Moscow: Nauka, 1983), 102.

49 TsGAKaz 4.1.3573, f. 132a.

50 A *tanga* is a silver coin, its value roughly twenty kopeks in this period.

51 TsGAKaz 4.1.2821, ff. 6a–b. 52 TsGAKaz 4.1.198, f. 19a; TsGAKaz 4.1.3646, f. 47a.

53 TsGAKaz 4.1.3646, f. 49a. 54 TsGAKaz 4.1.3646, f. 46a.

55 TsGAKaz 4.1.3646, ff. 75b–76b. 56 TsGAKaz 4.1.3646, ff. 74a–75a.

57 TsGAKaz 4.1.3646, ff. 77a–78a. 58 TsGAKaz 383.1.89, ff. 14a–b.

59 TsGAKaz 4.1.3646, f. 47b. 60 TsGAKaz 4.1.198, ff. 36b–37a.

61 TsGAKaz 4.1.3646, ff. 77a–78a. 62 TsGAKaz 4.1.499, ff. 104a–b.

creative in this effort, as with the Kalmyk slave who was renamed "Manas" (the legendary hero whose chief occupation was the slaying of Kalmyks).[63] More often, however, they proved themselves remarkably uncreative. In July of 1852, a Russian border official logged the arrival of eight escaped slaves, whom he identified (using the names given to them in captivity) as: "Nazar, Dawlat, Dawlat, Dawlat, Nazar, Mustafa, the women Summanaz, and Dawlat."[64]

Having been sold, transported, and often renamed in the khanates or in the steppe, accounts differ wildly concerning the sort of treatment slaves could expect in their period of bondage. The earliest Russian reports of slaves' treatment in Khwarazm are almost invariably grim. An article from 1815 reports that "[t]hese sufferers' food consists of two unleavened flatbreads per day, sometimes some gruel, and very rarely a piece of lean meat. The only vegetables and fruits allowed to them are those beginning to spoil. By way of clothing they get one shirt per year, and one robe (*khalat*) every two years. They are rarely given shoes, and the ones they are given are worn out. Their bed is of straw and reeds."[65] Khwarazmian slaves' starvation was likewise reported by Murav'ev, who writes that the "diet of the slaves and servant class is very bad, the latter have to be content with what is left from the tables of their masters, and they struggle and fight amongst themselves for the fragments ... These wretched creatures frequently go a whole day without a meal, and keep soul and body together by what they can beg or steal."[66] Conditions were reported to be similarly harsh in Bukhara and among Teke Turkmens to the south.[67]

Many travelers reported on horrific punishments that were visited upon slaves who attempted escape, or otherwise earned their owners' ill-will.

63 TsGAKaz 4.1.198 f. 54a. 64 TsGAKaz 4.1.3641 f. 56a.

65 "Nevol'niki v khive," *Vestnik evropy* 80:7 (1815), 245.

66 Murav'ev, *Muraviev's Journey to Khiva through the Turcoman Country*, 161.

67 On Bukharan slavery, Desmaisons writes that "Russian captives, although treated less barbarously than in Khiva, nevertheless live in very tough circumstances. In addition to the hard labor which they are forced to perform, they are kept in conditions demonstrating the loathsome stinginess generally characteristic of Bukharans. They are often deprived of basic necessities; they receive meager sustenance, and sometimes die of chronic malnutrition" (*Zapiski o Bukharskom khanstve*, N. A. Khalfin ed. [Moscow, 1983], 25). V. A. Tugan-Mirza-Baranovskii offers a similar appraisal of slavery among the Tekes: "The position of slaves is generally unenviable, but it is particularly so among the Tekes. To say nothing of those who languish for years shut up in some mud hut with heavy logs tied to their legs and shackles on their arms, the lives of other slaves, who enjoy more freedom relative to these ones, working the fields and grazing the herds and serving their owners, are very difficult owing to the scarcity of food given to them and to the beatings and insults constantly inflicted upon them. Turkmen or Kirghiz slaves, however, are treated much better than the Persians, [other] Shi'ites, and Russians." (*Russkie v akhal teke* [St. Pb, 1881, 71).

Some of these punishments were witnessed firsthand, some reported by slaves, and some only rumored.[68] The most terrible punishments, according to broad consensus, awaited fugitive slaves who had been recaptured. Several reports contend that such slaves were punished by impalement. "Before our arrival," one Russian observer writes, "an unfortunate one was subjected to such a fate, with the spike entering through his flank, and this Persian lived in such a situation and in terrible suffering for two days. He pleaded in vain to the people around him for a sip of water to quench the terrible thirst that was consuming him, but under penalty of death they were forbidden from carrying out the request of the convicted person, and he died, cursing the Khivans and the day they were born."[69] Another claims to have witnessed such a terrible spectacle with his own eyes: "[A]long the road" outside Khiva, "a few Persians were impaled by stakes ... With their arms tied parallel to their legs, these unfortunate people were finishing their lives in terrible pain, filling the air with loud, pathetic cries: 'Su! Su! Su!' [Water! Water! Water!]. The Khivans accompanying [our] embassy explained that the crime of these unfortunate people was that, having been captured by [Yomut] Turkmen robbers and sold into slavery in Khiva, they conspired and fled. The Khivans caught them the next day, and now, in order to teach a lesson to other Persian slaves, and for the edification of departing Russians, the cruel khan ordered all of these unfortunates staked down on the same day our embassy was accomplished, and along its route of travel."[70] One widely-reported method of impeding slaves' ability to flee involved cutting their feet or heels and stuffing horsehair in the wound.[71]

68 Meyendorff, for example, reports seeing a slave "whose master had cut off his ears, pierced his hands with nails, and, taking the skin off his back, had poured boiling oil on his arms, so as to force him to tell by what means a comrade of his had escaped" (*Journey of the Russian Mission from Orenbourg to Bokhara*, 61). Murav'ev writes of slaves being nailed to doors by an ear or having an ear cut off, being deliberately starved, having an eye gouged out, or being stabbed (*Muraviev's Journey to Khiva through the Turcoman Country*, 49, 136).

69 N. Zalesov, 'Pis'mo iz Khivy', *Voennyi sbornik* 1 (1859), 287.

70 Zakhar'in, "Posol'stvu v Khivu v 1842 godu," *Istoricheskii vestnik* 11 (1894), 445.

71 See, for example, Lucy Atkinson, *Recollections of Tartar steppes and their inhabitants* (London: John Murray, 1863), 290; Zakhar'in, "Posol'stvu v Khivu v 1842 godu," 445; MacGahan, *Campaigning on the Oxus, and the Fall of Khiva* (London: Sampson Low, 1874), 311. This manner of punishment is also inflicted on Leskov's Ivan in *The Enchanted Wanderer* during his captivity among the Kazakhs: "Some ten men threw me down on the ground and said, 'Shout, Ivan, shout louder when we start cutting. It'll be easier for you. And they sat on me, and in a trice one master craftsmen of theirs cut the skin open on my soles, put in some chopped-up horse-hair, covered it with the skin, and sewed it up with string. After that they kept my hands tied for a few days, for fear I'd harm the wounds and the bristles would come out with the pus; but once the skin healed, they let me go: 'Now,'

Notwithstanding horrors such as these, a number of visitors reported that cruel treatment was the exception rather than the rule for slaves in the khanates. The British adventurer Alexander Burnes "heard from every quarter that slaves were kindly treated," and he writes that he "never heard these [slaves], in my different communications with them, complain of the treatment which they experienced in Toorkistan . . . [T]hey are never beaten, and are clothed and fed as if they belonged to the family, and often treated with great kindness."[72] Later observers, including Arminius Vambery, Januarius Aloysius MacGahan, and N. Zalesov would follow suit in offering optimistic appraisals of slaves' treatment.[73]

Later chapters will explore slaves' treatment in terms of the opportunities available to them and the limitations imposed upon them. When it comes to general patterns of mercy or cruelty, the variation in travelers' accounts probably indicates a diverse range of experiences that were possible for slaves. To characterize slaves' treatment by emphasizing only the horrific cruelty of certain punishments – as some nineteenth-century commentators did – obscures the fact that slaves did not spend the entirety of their captivity being punished for particular offenses. On the other hand, claims of "good" treatment at the hands of slave owners obscure the fact that the slave system itself was inherently cruel and degrading even

they say, 'greetings to you, Ivan, now you're our real friend and you'll never go away and leave us'" (Leskov, *The Enchanted Wanderer and Other Stories*, trans. Pevear and Volokhonsky [New York: Alfred A. Knopf, 2013], 150).

72 Burnes, *Travels into Bokhara*, Vol. 1, 283, 342.

73 Vambery suggests, rather naively, that among Iranian slaves the greatest injury was suffered by their pride: "The Persian is," Vambery writes, "from his childhood accustomed to the most refined politeness, and to a flowery, elegant conversation; and must of course suffer mentally a great deal when first introduced to the savage manners and habits of Turkestan. His physical sufferings are by no means so great. The majority of them, destined for agricultural labour, generally gain the confidence and affection of their master by their good behavior. If a slave has during a year not incurred punishment, he is soon looked upon as a member of the new family" (*Sketches of Central Asia*, 223). He allows, however, that disobedient slaves could be punished very harshly indeed (*Sketches*, 224). MacGahan, who witnessed the conquest of Khiva, writes that the slaves he observed there were not, "so far as I could learn, treated so badly. They get enough to eat and drink; and as to their clothes, there is no difference in this respect between the master and his slave. They would not seem to have been overworked, for many of them were able to purchase their liberty by doing extra work" (*Campaigning on the Oxus, and the Fall of Khiva*, 300). Zalesov writes that the purportedly mild treatment of slaves in Khwarazm was a purely pragmatic strategy: "The Uzbeks' treatment of their slaves, except in punishment for running away, is generally quite gentle, all the more so since their owners, including the Khan himself, understand quite well that, of all the disasters which could befall the Khanate, one of the most horrible would be a general uprising of Persian slaves, of which there are here up to 10,000" ("Pis'mo iz khivy," *Voennyi sbornik* 8 [1858], 286).

for those slaves who suffered minimal punishment. Finally, given that few foreign observers spent much time in the presence of slaves, accounts generalizing about slaves' treatment may reveal more about the observers' expectations and susceptibilities than they do about slaves' ordeals.

THE ORIGINS OF IRANIAN SLAVERY IN CENTRAL ASIA

Iranian Shiʿites would constitute the majority of Central Asia's enslaved people for three centuries, and the origins of their enslavement can be traced to particular developments in the early sixteenth century. This was an age of bitter Uzbek–Safavid warfare, during which Sunni jurists in Transoxania issued multiple fatwas that made licit not only the raiding and plundering of Shiʿite communities but also the capturing of Shiʿite individuals, and by extension their enslavement. Iskandar Beg, a Turkmen historian employed at the court of the Safavid Shah ʿAbbās I, provides a striking and rare account of the origins of Shiʿite enslavement in his *Tārīkh-i ʿālamārā-yi ʿAbbāsī*. It is worth noting his emphasis on the reciprocal nature of enslavement as a tactic of war:[74]

I should comment here on a point I have mentioned before, but which can bear repetition. In earlier periods, when the Uzbeg rulers invaded Khurasan and the Ottoman sultans invaded Azerbaijan, either with the object of annexing territory or of plunder, they did not take captives from Shīʿite lands, nor did qezelbas armies commit this heinous crime in Sunni territory. However, in the reign of the Ottoman Sultan Morad, an Ottoman and Tartar army invaded Azerbaijan and Sirvan and was guilty of this practice. When the Ottomans occupied Tabriz, many children of seyyeds, who were descendants of the Prophet himself, were carried off into captivity and sold to Frankish infidels in Istanbul. The Uzbegs adopted this practice during their invasions of Khurasan under ʿAbdollah Khan and his son ʿAbd al-Mo'men Khan. For instance, at Mashhad, they took captive many descendants of the Imam Reza, and many children of the nobility, of the ʿolama, of ascetics and other honorable men, and of the military and civilians in general – several thousand altogether. These captives were sold in Turkestan and Transoxania, and even as far away as Kabul and India.

Because the heavens so decreed, the Shah was forced to overlook these crimes at the time; this world is a vale of woe, and revenge for these heinous acts could safely be left to the Lord of vengeance. At the urging of his commanders, however, the Shah allowed several thousand prisoners to be taken on this campaign and exiled from their homelands. Subsequently too, the Safavid governors of Astarabad on

[74] Iskandar Beg Munshī, *Tārīkh-i ʿālamārā-yi ʿAbbāsī*, trans. Roger Savory as *History of Shah ʿAbbas the Great*, Vol. 2 (Boulder, CO: Caravan Books, 1978), 819–820.

several occasions led punitive expeditions against rebel groups of the Ūklū and Göklen tribes, which were Muslim only in name, and many prisoners were taken on these occasions. But if impartial critics will take a searching look at the Shah's actions in this regard, they will discover that he has earned the approval of the religious authorities, because these prisoners were not taken into slavery but were treated as prisoners of war. Several thousand women and children were brought up in Shīʿite and God-fearing homes, and adopted the Shīʿite faith.

The name of the Sunni jurist who first made licit the enslavement of Shiʿites, while absent from our chronicle sources, was preserved in Turkmen oral historical tradition down to the nineteenth century: Both Iranian and European observers report having met Turkmens who identified the main jurist responsible as one Shams al-Dīn Herātī.[75] Considering that captive-taking was a standard feature of warfare among Muslim groups in the region during Herātī's lifetime (in the sixteenth century), this jurist's formal legal licensing hardly seems necessary. Nevertheless, it aligned with and legitimized the formalized discourse of sectarian struggle that was employed by both Sunni and Shiʿite statesmen and jurists.

As for the age of conflict in which these legal developments took place, a very brief overview of its major features must suffice here. As Shah Ismāʿīl (r. 1501–1524) consolidated Iran as a Shiʿite domain, Khurasan – a region divided from Transoxania during the partition of the Timurid empire – became the focus of struggles between the Shah and the Sunni Uzbeks to the north, which only increased after Ismāʿīl's death. Uzbek armies led by ʿUbaydullāh Khan made five major forays into Khurasan between 1524 and 1538, but were unable to retain control of any major towns in the region other than Balkh. Significant Uzbek campaigns in Khurasan were resumed with the conquest of Herat in 1589, led by ʿAbdullāh Khan II, and subsequently Mashhad and much of the rest of Khurasan was captured by that ruler's son, ʿAbd al-Mu'min. Uzbek raids in this period proceeded deep into Iranian territory, reaching as far south as Yazd, and relented only with the death of both ʿAbdullāh Khan and ʿAbd al-Mu'min in 1598, after which the Iranian ruler, Shah ʿAbbās, was able to retake most of Khurasan. It was likely during this century of Sunni–Shiʿite conflict that we find the initial proliferation of Shiʿite slaves in Central Asia.

The work performed by slaves in Central Asia during this period, as we shall see, appears to have been primarily agricultural, and the new influx of

[75] See Āshtiyānī, *ʿIbratnāma*, 84 (here, the name given is Shams al-Dīn Muḥammad); Vambery, *History of Bokhara from the Earliest Period Down to the Present* (London: Henry S. King, 1873), 266n1; Faiziev, *Buxoro feodal jamiyatida qullardan foidalanishga doir hujjatlar (XIX asr)*, 8.

slaves corresponds compellingly to a revolution in agriculture in the region. Maria Subtelny has shown how large plantations had developed during the late Timurid period thanks to a shrewd revenue-generating strategy by a Central Asian ruler facing the prospect of fiscal disaster. Caught up in the conflict between a largely Turkic military class covetous of its traditional landholding privileges and an Iranian bureaucratic class interested in imposing centralizing reforms, the last Timurid ruler, Sultan Ḥusayn Mīrzā (r. 1469–1506), was forced to find a new source of tax revenue that would alienate neither faction. He found it in the expansion of hydrological agriculture, which he encouraged elites to develop both for their own enrichment and the enrichment of the state treasury. At the same time, he rapidly expanded the system of pious endowments (*waqf*) such that Sufi shrine-complexes could flourish into massive agricultural estates.[76] It was through these developments that a Sufi master such as Khwāja ʿUbaydullāh Aḥrār could become one of the wealthiest landholders in the region. The Khwāja's private correspondences reveal that he also owned slaves, who worked on his estates.[77]

We have reason to believe that the new agricultural "plantations" that emerged in this period, such as those owned by Khwāja Aḥrār and others, made extensive use of slave labor. R. K. Mukminova's study of sixteenth-century *waqf* documents has revealed that most of the slaves mentioned in these pious endowments were used for agricultural labor or animal husbandry.[78] Other sources reveal large numbers of slaves working agricultural jobs on the estates of prominent Sufi leaders such as the Juybāri shaykhs.[79] Thanks to the influx of captives from conflicts further south, such landholders would hardly have needed to worry about labor scarcity in the hinterlands occupied by their expanding estates.

In the seventeenth century, most slave laborers in Central Asia would likely have been drawn from the pool of captives seized in more limited campaigns into Khurasan. The series of conquests by Uzbek rulers

[76] Subtelny, *Timurids in Transition: Turko-Persian Politics and Acculturation in Medieval Iran* (Leiden: Brill, 2007).

[77] See *The Letters of Khwāja ʿUbayd Allāh Aḥrār and his Associates*, ed. Jo-Ann Gross and Asom Urunbaev (Leiden: Brill. 2002), 19, 25, 97 (see especially 97n9. The slaves mentioned here are of Indian descent, and Scott Levi has argued that the slave demographic in Central Asia remained predominantly Indian throughout the medieval period: "Hindus Beyond the Hindu Kush: Indians in the Central Asian Slave Trade," *Journal of the Royal Asiatic Society* 12:3 [2002], 277–288.).

[78] Mukminova, *Sotsial'naia differentsiatsiia naseleniia gorodov Uzbekistana v XV–XVI vv.* (Tashkent, 1985), 122–123.

[79] Levi, "Hindus Beyond the Hindu Kush," 278.

ʿAbdullāh Khan and ʿAbd al-Mu'min that concluded the sixteenth century marked the last time for at least another two hundred years that forces from Transoxania would endeavor to permanently occupy Khurasanian towns. Smaller-scale military forays into the region, however, resumed just two decades later under Imām Qulī Khan (r. 1611–1642), and they intensified under ʿAbd al-ʿAzīz Sulṭān (r. 1645–1680) after Shah ʿAbbās' death, though ʿAbd al-ʿAzīz seems to have tempered his raiding once he became khan.[80]

During these formative centuries in the development of the Shiʿite slave economy – from which, unfortunately, sources on slavery in the region are scarce – it would probably have been Uzbek soldiers, rather than nomadic Turkmens, who engaged in most of the captive-taking. There is, moreover, no evidence that raiding of Khurasanian villages for captives was at this time the sort of near-constant phenomenon that it would later become.

The eighteenth century witnessed the increasing influence of Turkmen tribes in the affairs of Khwarazm and Bukhara, and also their migration closer to what would become the main routes of the slave trade: The Tekes migrated to northern Khurasan, while a large branch of the Yomuts, along with the Chawdurs, moved into Khwarazm. Meanwhile, the khanates were embroiled in ongoing political crises. In Khwarazm, the years 1685–1715 saw the succession of as many as thirteen khans, many of whom were installed by nomadic Uzbeks, sometimes in alliance with Kazakhs or Turkmens. The latter began at this time to factor more prominently in the khans' raiding forays into Khurasan. Slave-trading in the Bukharan khanate, meanwhile, was likely at a low ebb due to internal turmoil: Kazakhs – fleeing the steppe before the advancing Kalmyks – raided Bukharan towns and villages, leaving Samarqand and all but two districts of Bukhara itself depopulated by the time they returned to the steppe in the late 1720s. The regions of Ferghana, Hisar, and Shahrisabz were all more-or-less independent of Bukhara at this time, and the influence of the Bukharan ruler – nominally the khan, but in reality his *ataliq* – was confined to the capital and its adjacent provinces.[81]

[80] On the political history of this period and the conflicts in question, see Yuri Bregel, "Bukhara iv. Khanate of Bukhara and Khurasan," *Encyclopedia Iranica*, Vol. 4, fasc. 5, 521–524; Martin Dickson, "Shāh Tahmāsb and the Uzbeks: The Duel for Khurāsān with ʿUbayd Khān: 930-946/1524-1540" (Ph.D. dissertation, Princeton University, 1958); Iskandar Beg Munshī, *Tārīkh-e ʿĀlamārā-yi ʿAbbāsī*.

[81] Yuri Bregel, "The New Uzbek States: Bukhara Khiva and Qoqand: *c.* 1750–1886," in Di Cosmo et al., eds., *The Cambridge History of Inner Asia: The Chingghisid Age* (Cambridge: Cambridge University Press, 2009), 392–393.

In 1740, Nādir Shah of Iran launched an ambitious raid into the region, winning submission (as well as the services of a 10,000-strong cavalry force) from the Bukharan khan before marching on Khiva. The Khwarazmian ruler, Ilbars Khan, surrendered and was promptly executed, and Khiva suffered an intense assault. The city was surrendered after just a few days. In the aftermath of these attacks, the Shah reportedly liberated several thousand Iranian slaves as well as a smaller number of Russian slaves. The former were sent to Khurasan, and the latter were turned over to the Russian officers Gladyshev and Muravin, who conducted them back to Russia. The Shah, who has since often been depicted as a liberator of captives, also took some corvée laborers for himself: somewhere between 4,000 and 18,000 Khwarazmian cavalrymen were pressed into service in the Iranian military.[82] The presence of so many Iranian slaves in the khanate indicates that the slave system that would become well-known to foreign observers in the nineteenth century, by which Iranians from Khurasan were pressed into bondage on Khwarazmian and Bukharan estates, may already have been firmly in place by the mid-eighteenth century.

For the remainder of the eighteenth century, Iran would launch no major campaigns into the khanates, even as raids on Khurasanian towns, often carried out by Turkmens, continued to supply the Khwarazmian and Bukharan markets with Iranian slaves. The first few decades of the nineteenth century saw a renewed effort by Iran – now led by the dynasty of the Qajars – to secure Khurasan against these incursions, and to establish a military vanguard against the khanates and the nomads who sometimes served as the khans' allies.

In the 1820s and 1830s, Iranian troops made considerable gains in reducing the trade in Qajar slaves. In 1831–1832, acting as the Qajar ruler Fath 'Alī Khan 's governor of Khurasan, the crown prince 'Abbās Mirzā led successful campaigns against defiant chieftains in Quchan, Amirabad, Turshiz, and Turbat, and he inspired the formerly hostile Salar Turkmens of Herat to make a plea for peace. In 1832, he launched a successful attack on Sarakhs, sacking the Salar stronghold and liberating hundreds of Iranian captives. After his death in 1833, however, Qajar fortunes in Khurasan quickly and decisively turned. From their base at Merv, the Khwarazmians patronized Turkmens who patrolled and plundered the border region, taking captives when they could; their spoils also included heavy-laden caravans bound for Iran. An Iranian campaign in

[82] Bregel, "The New Uzbek States," 393.

1837 to take Herat was a disaster, due in part to the ability of the Merv-based Khwarazmian forces to interrupt Iranian supply lines at will. In 1841, Allāh Qulī Khan, ruler of Khwarazm, ordered a direct offensive against Iran which was evidently a success; among the results was the deportation of some 15,000 Jamshidi tribesmen from Badghis to Merv.

In the years to come, Khwarazm would lose its foothold in Merv, as many of the Sarïq Turkmens of the oasis threw off and continually rejected their former state of subjection to the khan. Unwilling to abandon Merv completely, however, Khwarazmian rulers would spend the next decade launching annual assaults on the Sarïqs, draining both their own resources and those of their entrenched Turkmen adversaries. Khwarazm was sometimes supported in these efforts by confederations of Turkmens, which included members of the Yomut, Chawdur, Yemreli, Qaradashli, and Taze Qongrat tribes. Meanwhile, the Khwarazmians and their Turkmen clients continued to plunder caravans bound for Iran, and in 1851 the khan's troops were among the forces that repulsed Iranian efforts to take Sarakhs.[83] In short, the constant presence of Khwarazmian troops and mercenaries in Khurasan was a major obstacle against Iranian efforts to exert control over the region, and the lack of control – as well as the continual armed conflict fomented both by the Qajars and their opponents – allowed for new victims to be channeled constantly into the Central Asian slave trade.

QAJAR MISSIONS TO END THE SLAVE TRADE

Qajar military efforts in Khurasan during the nineteenth century were inspired not only by a desire to end the plague of captive-taking, but also by the Iranian government's consistent ambition to expand its control northward.[84] This fact may come as a surprise, since, for decades, historians have presented this era of Central Asian history as a contest between England and Russia, in which local powers like Iran, Bukhara, and Khwarazm were alternately pawns, victims, or bystanders.[85] This Qajar project was played out on both military and diplomatic fronts, and gave rise to a genre of travel literature – combining intelligence-gathering,

[83] William A. Wood, "The Sariq Turkmens of Merv and the Khanate of Khiva in the Early Nineteenth Century" (Ph.D. dissertation, Indiana University, 1998), 137–226.

[84] James M. Gustafson. "Qajar Ambitions in the Great Game: Notes on the Embassy of 'Abbas Qoli Khan to the Amīr of Bokhara, 1844." *Iranian Studies* 46:4 (2013), 536, 551.

[85] Alexander Morrison, "Killing the Cotton Canard and getting rid of the Great Game: rewriting the Russian conquest of Central Asia, 1814–1895," *Central Asian Survey* 33:2 (2014), 131–142.

ethnography, geography, political commentary, and history – which thrived especially from the 1840s through the1870s.[86] Some of the most important and well-known works within this genre arose from missions that were tasked with freeing Iranian slaves from Khwarazm and Bukhara and ending the slave trade.

The two best-known missions tasked with ending the trade in Iranian slaves are those of ʻAbbās Qulī Khan and Riżā Qulī Khan Hidāyat.[87] ʻAbbās Qulī Khan undertook an embassy to the Bukharan ruler Naṣrullāh Khan between May and August of 1844, apparently for the purpose of asserting Qajar dominion over Merv, for seeking Bukharan cooperation in ending Iranian slavery in the khanate, and – at the behest of the British – for retrieving the missionary and adventurer Joseph Wolff from his temporary imprisonment. The envoy successfully stakes his rhetorical claim to Merv and retrieves the ailing Wolff, but when it came to general emancipation ʻAbbās Qulī Khan's efforts came up short. The Bukharan ruler denies responsibility for his subjects' enslaving of Iranians, claiming that the blame rests exclusively upon the *ʿulamāʾ* who continued to countenance the practice. Therefore, the only solution – according to the Naṣrullāh – is for the *ʿulamāʾ* of Iran and Bukhara to discuss the matter together and arrive at some kind of joint resolution. Even then, the ruler cautions, old habits die hard, and it would be impossible to reverse this unsavory custom right away.[88]

Riżā Qulī Khan Hidāyat traveled to Khwarazm in 1851 to meet with the ruler, Muḥammad Amīn Khan (r. 1845–55), and his bid to free Iranian slaves in Khiva would be no more successful than that of his counterpart, ʻAbbās Qulī Khan, in Bukhara. Before setting off on his trip, Riżā Qulī

[86] Arash Khazeni. "Across the Black Sands and the Red: Travel Writing, Nature, and the Reclamation of the Eurasian Steppe circa 1850," *International Journal of Middle East Studies* 42 (2010), 594–595; Abbas Amanat and Arash Khazeni, "The Steppe Roads of Central Asia and the Persian Captivity Narrative of Mirza Mahmud Taqi Ashtiyani," in Nile Green, ed., *Writing Travel in Central Asian History* (Bloomington, IN: Indiana University Press, 2013), 113–134; Gustafson. "Qajar Ambitions in the Great Game," 541.

[87] ʻAbbās Quli Khān, *Safarnāma-yi Bukhārā*, ed. Hussain Zamani (Tehran, 1373/1995); Rizā Quli Khān Hidāyat. *Sifāratnāma-yi Khwārazm (Relation de l'Ambassade au Kharezm [Khiva] de Riza Qouly Khan. Texte Persan)*, ed. Charles Schefer (Paris: Ernest Leroux, 1876). Both works have been the subject of insightful recent studies: Nölle-Karimi. "'Different in All Respects': Bukhara and Khiva as Viewed by Ḳāğār Envoys," in Yavuz Köse, ed., *Şehrâyîn: die Welt der Osmanen, die Osmanen in der Welt: Wahrnehmungen, Begegnungen und Abgrenzungen; Festschrift Hans Georg Majer* (Wiesbaden: Harrassowitz, 2012), 435–446; Khazeni. "Across the Black Sands and the Red"; Gustafson, "Qajar Ambitions in the Great Game."

[88] ʻAbbās Quli Khān, *Safarnāma-yi Bukhārā*, 36–38.

Khan had received the names of a number of men and women from Astarabad and elsewhere who were held as slaves in Khwarazm. Some individuals whose parents were among the enslaved had begged Riżā Qulī Khan for permission to accompany him on the journey.[89] The envoy recounts meeting with a great number of Iranian slaves over the course of his travels in the khanate. He hosts them at his residence, serves them tea, and learns of their backgrounds and circumstances. Some had been enslaved for more than fifty years, and some for less than three.[90] At one point he overhears a cacophony of cries and moans from two of the slaves coming to visit him: It turns out that they are cousins who had not had any news of one-another for some time before meeting by coincidence at Riżā Qulī Khan's residence and realizing that they shared the same awful fate.[91] Riżā Qulī Khan collects many slaves' names, and he thrills them with the news that he will request their freedom from the khan. Slaves of diverse backgrounds gather to follow him through the streets. Their excitement is such that Riżā Qulī Khan nearly expected the start of a slave uprising as he and his retinue move through the city.[92]

But all of the excitement is in vain. He is unable to free the slaves. The Khwarazmian ruler, Muḥammad Amīn Khan, after consulting with some of his top officials, declines the envoy's emancipation request on the grounds that it would embolden the "*qizilbāsh*" (Iranians), reinforcing among them the notion that the concession was a result of their troop-movements around Astarabad and in Khurasan. The result, the khan says, would be an onslaught of new demands on the part of the Qajars.[93] Simply releasing thousands of Iranian slaves at the Qajars' behest was out of the question.

Along with the two well-known missions discussed previously, there was at least one other Qajar embassy to free slaves in this period – one that appears to be largely forgotten. This is the mission of Muḥammad ʿAlī Khan Ghafūr, who was dispatched to Khiva in 1842.[94] His primary aim was to negotiate for the release of the lieutenant and nephew of

[89] Rizā Quli Khān Hidāyat, *Sifāratnāma-yi Khwārazm*, 52.
[90] Hidāyat, *Sifāratnāma-yi Khwārazm*, 85–86.
[91] Hidāyat, *Sifāratnāma-yi Khwārazm*, 86.
[92] Hidāyat, *Sifāratnāma-yi Khwārazm*, 86–87.
[93] Hidāyat, *Sifāratnāma-yi Khwārazm*, 111.
[94] Muḥammad ʿAlī Khan Ghafūr, *Ruznāmah-i safar-i Khwārazm* (Tehran: Daftar-i muṭālaʿāt-i siyāsī va bayn al-milalī, vizārat-i umūr-i khārija, 1373/1994). An important recent article assesses the motivations of this embassy: Christine Nölle-Karimi, "On the Edge: Eastern Khurasan in the Perception of Qajar Officials," *Eurasian Studies* 14 (2016), 135–177.

Mashhad's Qajar governor, who had been captured by Turkmens while hunting and brought to the Khwarazmian capital. Muḥammad ʿAlī Khan was also tasked with making a more ambitious request – the same one that Riżā Qulī Khan had made: that the slave trade in Khwarazm be ended, and that the Iranian slaves there be freed.

Muḥammad ʿAlī Khan arrives in Khiva at the same time as embassies from Russia and England, whose ambassadors he regards as amenable to his cause in liberating the slaves. He has good reason to assume this; indeed, Russian accounts claim that Muḥammad ʿAlī Khan had been sent to Khwarazm at Russia's behest, alleging that the shah, having petitioned the Russians to intercede with the khan for the liberation of Iranian slaves, had begun preparing for war, "and only the combined efforts of Russian and British ambassadors in Tehran convinced him to postpone military action and to send to Khiva, as an envoy, Muḥammad ʿAlī Khan, offering him [also] the services of an official of the British mission [named] Thomson."[95] As we shall see, the Iranian envoy would leverage these alliances to little effect.

At his first meeting with the khan in Khiva, Muḥammad ʿAlī Khan assures the ruler that ending the slave trade and emancipating Iranian slaves would "bring friendship and brotherhood" between Iran and Khwarazm. On the other hand, he threatens, if the khan declined, he would find that "nothing comes of enmity but the ruin of a country and the trampling of its people."[96] The envoy alludes to previous Iranian missions to free captives that had been unsuccessful, and alleges that the khan had broken promises to stop Turkmens under his sway from taking Iranian captives. In response, the khan alleges transgressions by Iranian governors and elites, but at first he appears to agree to take a firmer hand with the offending Turkmens. As an underwhelming sign of goodwill, he consents to release fifteen slaves. The Iranian envoy replies, "O glorious khan, it is not a matter of ten slaves or a hundred. The Shah of Iran wants *all* of his people [returned], and his wishes must be fulfilled."[97] The envoy then meets with the khan's *mihtar* and outlines his demands in more detail: He asks for nothing less than the liberation of all the slaves that had been taken since the time of Fath ʿAlī Khan (d. 1838).

What follows this initial meeting with the khan is a series of negotiations with both the *mihtar* and the ruler that are practically comical in their

[95] N. Zalesov, "Posol'stvo v Khivu podpolkovnika Danilevskogo v 1842 g," *Voennyi sbornik* 3 (1866), 46.

[96] Ghafūr, *Ruznāmah-i safar-i Khwārazm*, 19.

[97] Ghafūr, *Ruznāmah-i safar-i Khwārazm*, 20.

elaborate futility. First, the *mihtar* suggests that only those slaves taken since the relatively recent conclusion of peace between Khwarazm and Iran should be freed, but that Muḥammad ʿAlī Khan would be welcome to buy the rest of the slaves, just as the Khwarazmians had once ransomed their own people from the Qajars. Muḥammad ʿAlī Khan replies that this would not suffice, and stresses again that all the slaves must be freed. He asks the *mihtar* how many, then, he was willing to offer. The *mihtar* replies with a story that, if true, reveals something of the high-handed manner in which the Qajars had formerly dealt with the khanate: Some time previously, the khan had sent a Khivan ambassador to Tehran along with some Iranian slaves who had been freed as a gesture of goodwill. In exchange, the *mihtar* claims, the ambassador asked for the liberation of two or three Sarakhsi slaves that were held in Iran, but was told that this was impossible, since they had become close to the Shah's mother, and that respecting one's mother was as necessary as respecting the holy *kaʿba* in Mecca.[98] Thus, the *mihtar* explains, the last time Khwarazm had offered concessions on the issue of slavery, their goodwill had not been returned; instead, the khan had been insulted.

Nevertheless, the *mihtar* agrees to bring Muḥammad ʿAlī Khan's entreaty before the khan. Because the khan was busy with some other pressing issues, however, Muḥammad ʿAlī Khan would in the meantime have to carry out further negotiations with the *mihtar*. At their next meeting, Muḥammad ʿAlī Khan and the *mihtar* carry out their discussions in the presence of the imprisoned notable that the Iranian envoy had come to liberate – the nephew of Mashhad's governor. This time, Muḥammad ʿAlī Khan evokes the specter of Russian and British disapproval, warning the *mihtar* that "three countries [i.e. Iran, England, and Russia] that are friends of the Khan ask that the slaves of Iran be given leave to depart, and there are 30,000 slaves in Khwarazm." Of these, he asks, how many would the khan be prepared to emancipate "so that the Pādishah of Islam [i.e. the Shah of Iran] will be satisfied" with him? "The slaves," the *mihtar* replies, "are in the hands of the citizens and the populace. Each was bought for 30 *ṭilla*s, for 40 *ṭilla*s. It is not our custom to force or harass our people." He reiterates that Khwarazm had previously been forced to buy its citizens back from Iran, and that the Iranians were welcome to do the same. This offer does not appease Muḥammad ʿAlī Khan: "The Shah," he replies, "does not give money to buy back his own slaves."[99]

[98] Ghafūr, *Ruznāmah-i safar-i Khwārazm*, 22.
[99] Ghafūr, *Ruznāmah-i safar-i Khwārazm*, 23.

Muḥammad ʿAlī Khan's claim to negotiate on behalf of a troika of great empires was only partly accurate. While the Russians and British may have been sincere in their hopes of averting warfare between Iran and Khwarazm, they had little reason to be optimistic about the emancipation of tens of thousands of Iranian slaves, especially considering that a previous Russian embassy, less than two years prior, had made no headway on that front – which is no surprise, considering the disastrous results of the military expedition recently launched against the khanate. The ambassador at that time, Nikoforov, had been coached on his mission in a revealing debriefing from March 19, 1841:[100]

> In addition to the instructions which you received directly from the Asian Department, the Ministry of Foreign Affairs entrusts you with another mission, of no small importance. Though it does not concern our own relations with Khiva, successful execution of [the mission] may nevertheless have a beneficial influence on the course of our affairs in Asia generally . . . [R]ecently the Persian government appealed to us with the earnest request that we render our assistance in Khiva toward the liberation of Persian subjects there, adding that if for some reason the Russian state finds it inconvenient to take part in this matter, then in such a case the Persians will need to resolve upon their last resort, namely the achievement of their aim by force of arms.
>
> We have no doubt that the fulfillment of the Persian Court's request will meet strong resistance in Khiva, especially since Persians are the most numerous class of people being used as slaves. Nevertheless, we consider it necessary to make you aware that the liberation through your mediation of even some number of Persian captives would be extremely good for us. For that reason, do not fail to take advantage of any opportune moment to try to achieve that goal. Explain to [the khan] Allah Kuli what the consequences could be for him with respect to Persia if he continues to follow the same hostile system in his relations with her and, on the other hand, what he would gain in personal esteem if he takes as his principal neighborliness (*dobroe sosedstvo*) and justice. And while the complete release of the Persian captives cannot be hoped for, it may be possible for you to at least persuade the khan to send an envoy to Tehran with the proper authorization to work with the Persian Court on mutually-agreed terms, on the basis of which the liberation of Persians from Khiva may be enacted . . .
>
> If, however, the demands of the Khivans should be entirely unmanageable, and your advice concerning abolition be in vain, then in that case the Khivans can by no means hope for the assistance of our mission in Tehran, and will have to come to an agreement with the Persians at their own discretion.

[100] *Sbornik materialov dlia istorii zavoevaniia Turkestanskogo kraia*, ed. A. G. Serebrennikov, Vol. 3 (Tashkent, 1912), doc. no. 24, pp. 41–44.

On the basis of this quote, one might conclude that the issue of Iranian slaves was of great significance, a crucial corollary to the primary goals of Nikoforov's mission. But following this, the memorandum delivers Nikoforov a strong word of caution in raising the subject with the khan, urging him to remember that emancipation was not, in fact, one of the mission's foremost concerns, but merely a supplementary issue to be discussed after other matters had been concluded, and then only if a convenient opportunity presented itself:[101]

It goes without saying that the matter of the Persians should not harm the arrangement of our own affairs with Khiva. For that reason, do not initiate negotiations on this subject before fulfilling the other political errands with which you have been entrusted, and in any case only after being well received, because on top of an inauspicious reception this would serve only to excite greater antipathy toward you on the part of Allah Kuli. Consequently, it would be completely contrary to the purposes for which you were sent to Khiva.

As it happens, Nikoforov did not find a suitable moment to broach the subject with the khan. He later concisely summarized the matter in a letter to his comrade, Captain Khanykov: "Concerning negotiations on the Persian captives . . . The agent did not initiate [these negotiations] for the following reasons: 1) Up to now, there is nothing positive about our relationship with Khiva . . . "[102]

Danilevskii, the Russian ambassador who joined Muḥammad ʿAlī Khan in Khiva the very next year, had no more reason to expect success on the emancipation front. Still, Danilevskii was commissioned to "clarify" to the khan that permitting the enslavement of Iranians in his domain was not worthwhile.[103] As for Danilevskii's British counterpart, a man named William Taylour Thomson, hardly any information exists in English sources concerning his experiences,[104] but the mission debriefing provided

[101] *Sbornik materialov dlia istorii zavoevaniia Turkestanskogo kraia*, doc. no. 24, p. 44.

[102] "*Do sego vremeni net nichego polozhitel'nogo otnositel'no otnoshenii k Khive.*" *Sbornik materialov dlia istorii zavoevaniia Turkestanskogo kraia*, doc. no. 58, p. 111.

[103] Zalesov, "Posol'stvo v Khivu podpolkovnika Danilevskogo v 1842 g," 45.

[104] Strangely, the only publication featuring any substantial information on Thomson's mission appears to be Lady Sheil's memoir of her time in Iran, which includes extracts from Thomson's diary in an appendix. These extracts contain no useful information concerning the emancipation of slaves, however, nor any useful details concerning the content of Thomson's negotiations with the khan: Lady Sheil, *Glimpses of Life and Manners in Persia* (London: 1856), 358–370. Thomson observes, in any case, that "The number of Persian slaves imported and also bred in the country [of Khiva] is immense, and in almost every house where servants are kept, one or more, according to the means of the proprietor, are to be found" (Lady Sheil, *Glimpses of Life and Manners in*

for Danilevskii at least describes his position *vis-à-vis* the other ambassadors. Thomson, "according to the instructions given to him," was charged "exclusively with arranging matters relating to Persian slaves," and "has been given the fundamental duty to consult with the Russian agent in Khiva on this matter and act together with him." He was, moreover, "positively forbidden from intervening in our agent's negotiations on matters relating to Russia,"[105] and it appears that Danilevskii did indeed use the occasion of his visit to advance a number of Russian positions, including the liberation of Russian slaves, who were far fewer in number.[106]

After raising the dubious specter of Russian and British anger over the issue, and declining the opportunity to buy Iranian slaves at their market price, Muḥammad ʿAlī Khan finally wrings a small concession from the *mihtar*: the latter agrees to release some captives, albeit only a small number of them. "If you want ten or fifteen people," the *mihtar* tells him, "I will give them over so that you will not go away empty-handed." Muḥammad ʿAlī Khan balks at this, and demands 5,000 slaves. This back-and-forth continues for three or four hours, and Muḥammad ʿAlī Khan eventually reduces his demand from 5,000 to 2,000 slaves, but this does not satisfy the *mihtar*. The imprisoned Khurasanian notable, Muḥammad Walī Khan, who was present as an intermediary, pleads with the Iranian envoy to reduce his demand still further, to 1,000. Muḥammad ʿAlī Khan comes down to 1,000, and the *mihtar* agrees to bring the proposition before the khan.

After this, the khan summons Muḥammad ʿAlī Khan before him once again, this time for a meeting which would prove to be, in the envoy's retelling, far tenser than the first.[107] After exchanging pleasantries, the khan asks the envoy what he had been discussing with the *mihtar*. "I was explaining to him my mission," Muḥammad ʿAlī Khan replies. "The circumstances of its resolution are for you to decide." The khan extends his initial offer: He is willing to give over those slaves who had already been manumitted, but any others would have to be purchased. Just as he had in his negotiations with the *mihtar*, Muḥammad ʿAlī Khan objects that the Shah does not buy slaves. The khan then makes a still less generous proposition: "The viziers of Russia and England wrote to me that the Shah

Persia, 365). Cf. also Wood, "The Sariq Turkmens of Merv and the Khanate of Khiva in the Early Nineteenth Century," 41.

105 Zalesov, "Posol'stvo v Khivu podpolkovnika Danilevskogo v 1842 g," 45.

106 Zalesov, "Posol'stvo v Khivu podpolkovnika Danilevskogo v 1842 g," 49.

107 Ghafūr, *Ruznāmah-i safar-i Khwārazm*, 24.

wanted to come [and attack Khwarazm], but that they did not permit it... If the Shah comes, we will be here [waiting for him]. Whatever God wishes will come to pass."[108]

In Muḥammad ʿAlī Khan's telling, he meets this threat with one of his own: "God forbid the retinue of the Shah of Islam should venture hither. In such a case, neither your country nor your people would remain."[109] The khan scoffs at this: "You think you can frighten me?" "I am not trying to scare you, Your Benevolence," the envoy replies. "I came to converse with you." With negotiations thus deteriorating, the khan finds an opportunity to stall: He asks Muḥammad ʿAlī Khan to contact the Shah and ask him to convey precisely how many slaves he would like the Khan to surrender. Muḥammad ʿAlī Khan objects that it could take two or three months to go back to Tehran and return with a courier.[110]

Thus the talks drag on, and finally they conclude in a manner thoroughly unsatisfying for the Iranians: The slaves were not to be freed. Danlievskii, for his part, petitioned for the release of "even just 1,500" Iranian slaves, "but unfortunately all of [Danilevskii's] admonitions on this subject to the khan were useless." The one significant concession offered by the khan was the release of Muḥammad Wali Khan, the imprisoned nephew of the Mashhad governor. This, the Khan allegedly told the Russian envoy, "would have in the eyes of the Persian government more value than the liberation of 5,000 [other] people"[111] – a dubious assumption, of course.

The Qajars soon resumed their hostilities toward Khwarazm, and it is worth considering whether Muḥammad ʿAlī Khan's demands were merely a pretext to justify the impending conflicts. If, as the khan claimed, there were in fact Khwarazmians held in Iran that the Shah had shown no intention of freeing, it is reasonable to sympathize with the khan's reluctance to put himself in a position of such blatant weakness at the negotiating table. More importantly, however, the freeing of even 1,000 slaves from private hands would have been no simple matter: If the khan managed it by force, he would inspire the anger of the aggrieved slave-owners, and if he purchased their freedom he could do so only at great expense. The objection, moreover, that liberating slaves would be a sign of Khwarazmian weakness and could inspire further Iranian demands – an argument articulated by the khan to Riżā Qulī Khan – does not seem far-fetched.

[108] Ghafūr, *Ruznāmah-i safar-i Khwārazm*, 25.
[109] Ghafūr, *Ruznāmah-i safar-i Khwārazm*, 25.
[110] Ghafūr, *Ruznāmah-i safar-i Khwārazm*, 25.
[111] Zalesov, "Posol'stvo v Khivu podpolkovnika Danilevskogo v 1842 g," 52.

All of this would have been well-understood by Muḥammad ʿAlī Khan and his Qajar patrons. They would also have known that Khwarazm's degree of influence over those Turkmens funneling victims into the slave economy was highly variable. The khan's troops may have been unable to patrol the Turkmens of the southern deserts, and even policing the caravan routes to Khwarazm would have been only a half-measure against the slave trade; the markets of Bukhara would surely receive any slaves that the Khwarazmians did not purchase. Finally, neither the shah nor the tsar showed any inclination to offer the khan any significant compensation for his efforts. In other words, there is good reason to suspect that the failure of these negotiations was a foregone conclusion even for the ambassadors that took part in them. The main accomplishment of Muḥammad ʿAlī Khan's mission, then, along with the rescue of the Khurasanian notable, was perhaps the very fact of his emancipation demand and its legitimation by the British and Russian ambassadors.

RUSSIAN INTERVENTIONS IN THE CENTRAL ASIAN SLAVE TRADE DOWN TO THE NINETEENTH CENTURY

The slave trade in Central Asia was not limited to the Iranian frontier. Many Russian citizens and others were also caught up in the trade, and the Tsars – no less than Qajar Shahs – made a significant effort to safeguard and liberate their own subjects. This targeted effort was generally limited to the liberation of Russian subjects alone, and should not, as we shall see, be mistaken for an "abolitionist" campaign in the region.

Between the mid-sixteenth century, a period marked by Muscovy's eastward expansion, and the mid-nineteenth century, the risk that Russian diplomats in Central Asia would be killed, taken captive, or sold into slavery made such missions relatively rare. Those ambassadors who did venture to the region usually had the liberation of Russian slaves high on their state-mandated agendas, and scarcely an envoy reached Bukhara or Khiva without broaching the subject of Russians held in captivity. In the effort of liberating Russian slaves, these missions failed unanimously and miserably. A brief overview will suffice to make the point that the Russian Empire had hardly any impact on the slave trade or on the phenomenon of slavery in Central Asia down to the nineteenth century.

In the mid-sixteenth century, an English explorer and merchant named Anthony Jenkinson returned from a grueling voyage to Central Asia, leaving us a personal account of what would remain the most ambitious

Western mission to the region for decades to come. Jenkinson traveled as a member of the Muscovy Company, a mercantile venture with both English and Russian backing, and he has left us with the earliest account of slaves being sold at a Central Asian bazaar. Surveying the wares on display at a Bukharan market in 1558, Jenkinson observed that both Indian and Persian merchants were buying slaves, though of their origin he records only that they were "*of divers Countreis.*"[112] He brought twenty-five of these slaves back with him, all of them Russians.[113] He also described the awful and perilous landscape that his mission traversed on the way to Central Asia. In the region around Kazan and Astrakhan, he witnessed Tatars suffering from extreme poverty and plague, and Noghay children being sold as slaves.[114] The mission was later stalled by raiders who searched the party for non-Muslims to take as captives, as well as terrible storms, unwelcoming locals, and a hard passage through the desert. There would scarcely be a Russian mission to Central Asia for decades to come; there would not be another British mission to the region for nearly two centuries.[115]

In the early seventeenth century, the Bukharan ruler Imām Qulī Khan attempted to make contact with the newly crowned Russian tsar, the first of the Romanovs. After the tsar failed to receive the first Bukharan ambassador, the Khan sent another, requesting the establishment of permanent diplomatic relations. This time, he offered in exchange to return some number of Russian slaves that had been purchased from Crimean and Noghay traders who were residing in Bukhara. The tsar received this ambassador, and promptly sent an ambassador of his own to collect the slaves and to learn more about conditions in Bukhara. As Ron Sela observes, this ambassador, Ivan Khokhlov, would have an experience much like that of his predecessor Anthony Jenkinson. He visited both Khiva and Bukhara, and reported that circumstances in the region were extremely perilous for travelers. His party faced hostile nomads, grueling travel conditions, extortion-minded officials, and poor hospitality.

[112] Anthony Jenkinson, *Early Voyages and Travels to Russia and Persia by Anthony Jenkinson and other Englishmen*, ed. E. Delmar Morgan and C. H. Coote, Vol. 1 (London: Hakluyt Society, 1886), 88–89.

[113] Jenkinson, *Early Voyages and Travels to Russia and Persia*, 95.

[114] Jenkinson, *Early Voyages and Travels to Russia and Persia*, 57. Jenkinson arrived soon after the Russian conquest of both khānates, during a time when Kazan was racked with rebellions.

[115] Ron Sela, "Prescribing the Boundaries of Knowledge: Seventeenth-Century Russian Diplomatic Missions to Central Asia," in Nile Green, ed., *Writing Travel in Central Asian History* (Bloomington, IN: Indiana University Press, 2014), 71–73.

It would be another two decades before a Russian diplomat set foot once more in the region, though the Bukharans maintained consistent diplomatic contact in the meantime.[116]

In the 1640s, another Russian ambassador – Anisim Gribov – was dispatched to Central Asia with the mission of freeing and retrieving Russian slaves, visiting both Khwarazm and Bukhara. He managed to ransom only three slaves. Forty others came before him in order to beg his intervention, but he had no choice but to disappoint them.[117] In the years 1669–1673, an embassy led by two brothers – Boris and Semen Pazukhin – was dispatched to Bukhara and Khwarazm, as well as to Balkh, and again the task of ransoming Russian slaves was high on the list of priorities. In Bukhara, the ambassadors were received warmly and treated to lavish banquets and entertainments, but negotiations for the release of captives were scarcely more effective than in previous missions. Upon demanding the release of all Russian Christians who had been enslaved, the Bukharan khan countered that there were no Christian slaves in Bukhara: All had converted to Islam. Finally, the khan allowed for the free release of nine slaves and offered that the Pazukhins could purchase another twenty-two. Discouraged, the ambassadors nevertheless managed to make contact with some of the Russian slaves in the khanate and learn valuable information about the workings of the slave trade. They learned that the Bukharans purchased many of their Russian slaves from Khiva; that they were often sold by Kalmyks or Bashkirs; and that some slaves were sold even to India by Persians or Kalmyks. The Pazukhins' report estimated that 150 Russians were kept in the city of Bukhara, 100 in Balkh, and 50 in the khan's palace complex in Khiva; many more were assumed to be residing in the suburbs and hinterlands.[118]

The reign of Peter the Great witnessed the most disastrous Russian mission to date: the infamous Bekovich-Cherkasskii expedition of 1717, which was dispatched to Central Asia in order, among other things, to gain the Khwarazmian khan's submission and to establish possible trade routes with India. Arriving with a considerable military retinue, the Russian officer Alexander Bekovich-Cherkasskii reportedly found himself under siege some 120 kilometers from Khiva, facing a Khwarazmian army that some of the expedition's survivors estimated to be more than 20,000

116 Sela, "Prescribing the Boundaries of Knowledge," 77–79.

117 Sela, "Prescribing the Boundaries of Knowledge," 79–80. Gribov resolved to return on a second mission just a few years later, but decided not to travel any further than the Iranian frontier once he realized how dangerous conditions in Central Asia had become.

118 Sela, "Prescribing the Boundaries of Knowledge," 83.

strong. The expedition survived the attack, and Bekovich-Cherkasskii met with the khan, who welcomed him peaceably and offered to accommodate his retinue in five different encampments. Once divided, the expedition was again attacked, and the majority of Bekovich-Cherkasskii's party was reportedly killed or sold into slavery. Future Russian ambassadors to Khiva would have to contemplate the rumor that Bekovich-Cherkasskii himself had been flayed alive, his skin made into the head of a ceremonial drum.[119]

The remaining decades of the eighteenth century saw relatively few Russian diplomatic missions to Central Asia, and as a result little in the way of new information emerged for Russian observers concerning slavery in the region's southern expanses. It was known, however, that some number of Russians was continually being captured, particularly Caspian fishermen and merchants, the latter sometimes taken in caravan raids. In 1819–1820, a Russian officer and envoy named N. N. Murav'ev reported learning of 3,000 Russians in Khiva alone, though he – like his predecessors – was unable to free them.[120] In 1833, Russian foreign minister Karl Nesselrode corresponded with the chief of the Orenburg Border Commission, General G. F. Gens, concerning the possibility of launching a military mission to liberate these Russian slaves, but the minister expressed skepticism over the feasibility of such a mission. That same year, a well-connected general named V. A. Perovskii, former aide to Tsar Nicholas I, was appointed Orenburg's military governor, and soon requested that a list be drawn up of all the Russians known to be held captive in Khiva. The list was some 599 names long, and Perovskii wrote to St. Petersburg to advocate for a military expedition against the khanate.[121]

Allāh Qulī Khan, the ruler of Khwarazm, was not insensible to the growing Russian anger over the question of Russians held in the khanate. In 1836, after some 500 Khwarazmian merchants were detained in Orenburg and Astrakhan along with their goods, the khan freed eighty Russian captives, having freed another twenty-five that same year.[122] The remaining Russians, however many there were, would be fewer in

[119] N. N. Murav'ev, *Muraviev's Journey to Khiva through the Turcoman Country, 1819–20*, trans. Philipp Strahl (Calcutta: Foreign Department Press, 1871), 136.

[120] Murav'ev, *Muraviev's Journey to Khiva through the Turcoman Country*, 77. More on this below.

[121] Alexander Morrison, "Twin Imperial Disasters: The Invasions of Khiva and Afghanistan in the Russian and British official mind, 1839–1842," *Modern Asian Studies* 48:1 (2014), 283–285.

[122] V. I. Dal', "Pis'ma k druz'iam iz pokhoda v khivu," *Russkii arkhiv* 3 (1867), repr. "Khivinskii pokhod," *Gostynnyi dvor* 2 (1995), 168.

number than when Murav'ev visited the khanate: According to Zakhar'in, their numbers had been halved during a cholera epidemic in 1829.[123] Notwithstanding the Russians given over by the khan, Russian authorities found other reasons to proceed with Perovskii's plan, and in any event the number of captives freed was deemed insufficient. Intercession by British envoys likewise came to naught, not because the khan was unwilling to release Russians as a concession to the tsar, but rather because these concessions, along with the khan's repeated efforts to negotiate and come to some agreement short of violence, were regarded with suspicion or outright disdain by Perovskii and other Russian officials. Claiming that there were 3,000 Russians held in Khwarazm – a number he may have derived from Murav'ev's travelogue, then nearly twenty years old – Perovskii demanded that this same number of Russians be freed.[124] Plans for the military expedition to Khiva would proceed.

The expedition, which set out in the winter of 1839–1840, was a spectacular disaster. Blindsided by an especially harsh desert winter, Perovskii's force of 4,000 to 5,000 men and as many as 10,000 camels did not even reach Khiva. The entire expedition was forced to retreat, and hundreds of men perished in the cold. Despite his easy, default "victory," the khan hoped to stave off future Russian campaigns: As open as ever to negotiating, Allāh Qulī passed a decree forbidding his subjects from robbing or capturing Russian citizens, under penalty of death. After this, he freed all of the Russian slaves that had been in his own service, and ordered that other Khwarazmians follow suit. The Russians that were liberated in this effort were brought to the Russian ambassador so that he could verify that they had indeed been captives. Once this was done, each freedman was given a Khivan gold coin (worth about four rubles at that time) and a bag of flour. One camel was provided for every two men and women, and by mid-October some 416 freed Russians had arrived in Orenburg.[125] E. M. Kosyrev has left an affecting description of these Russians' condition:[126]

[123] I. N. Zakhar'in, *Khiva. Zimnii pokhod v Khivu Perovskago v 1839 godu,—i 'Pervoe posol'stvo v Khivu' v 1842 godu* (St Petersburg: Tip P.P. Soikina, 1898), 202.

[124] Morrison, "Twin Imperial Disasters," 285, 291.

[125] M. I. Ivanin, *Opisanie Zimnego Pokhoda v Khivu v 1839–40g* (St. Pb: Tip. Tov. "Obshchestvennaya pol'za," 1874), 157. Cf. also Dal, "Khivinskii pokhod," 169. These Russians were escorted by the British envoy Richmond Shakespeare, whose role in freeing them is generally omitted from Russian accounts.

[126] E. M. Kosyrev, "Pokhod v Khivu v 1839 godu (Iz zapisok uchastnika)," *Istoricheskii vestnik* 8 (1898), 544.

The captives were a pitiful sight. In ragged Khivan robes, with shaven heads or with shaggy hair, they barely resembled people. On their faces one could read the suffering they endured in captivity among the wild Khivan tribes. These unfortunate martyrs discussed the horrid details of the torments they bore. They were sold into slavery, beaten with whips and lashes, held in vermin-infested places without food, left at the mercy of horrible insects. Deep scars on their shoulders and backs gave testimony to the tortures these unlucky ones had borne. Several people had had their eyes gouged out and, returning their homeland, which they could no longer see, sobbed and hugged their countrymen. What was in the hearts of these unfortunates – God only knows. The women were terrible to behold: exhausted, and with mercilessly defiled honor. It was impossible to look upon them without crying. The soul seethed for vengeance on behalf of this group of brethren, for whom life had already withered, and for whom no rosy future opened up, as their best years and the best of their strength had withdrawn under slavery, violence and abuse. Many did not survive this crushing slavery, and left their bones in Khiva; many were executed for trying to escape. Some managed to flee, but their fortune was no better: they died of hunger and thirst in the endless steppe, to be covered over in sand or snow. There were also those who converted from their Christian faith and began to live in high esteem among the Muslims, but there were very few such cases – most longed violently for their homeland, keeping their faith in Christ and their love for Russia.

Russian accusations concerning the presence of Russian captives in Khwarazm – and, more generally, Khwarazmian interference in Russian efforts, mercantile or otherwise, to travel through the region – did not end upon the liberation of these 416 captives. But it would be thirty years before another major military expedition would be launched on the pretext of ending the alleged Khwarazmian threat to Russian subjects and Russian interests in the region.

While Turkmens took scores of Russians into captivity along the Caspian shores or at sea, Kazakh raiders found easy prey further north, along the steppe frontier. In 1766, an envoy and military officer named Bogdan Aslanov reported the presence of some 200 Russian slaves in Khiva and Bukhara who had originally been taken by Kazakhs near Orenburg. Hundreds more were taken during the chaos of the Pugachev Rebellion, and some estimates – unsubstantiated, but noteworthy – posited that the khanates held anywhere from 2,000 to 5,000 Russian slaves in total.[127] These included officers and local officials, serfs, Chuvash, Mordvins, Poles, and Maris. An unknown number of captives, rather than being

[127] M. A. Terent'ev, *Istoriia zavoevaniia Srednei Azii*, Vol. 1 (St. Pb, 1906), 106; I.I. Kraft, *Sudebnaia chast' v Turkestanskom krae i stepnykh oblastiakh* (Orenburg, 1898), 33–34.

sold southward, were held among the Kazakhs in the steppe. Early efforts to affect the return of these captives included a decree, passed in the winter of 1767, commanding Russians to take "Asian" captives of their own, so that these captives might be ransomed in trade for their Russian counterparts.[128] These efforts were in vain, however, and eventually the governors of Orenburg and Astrakhan resolved to set aside a yearly allocation of 3–6,000 rubles for paying off the ransom. The standard rate of ransom in the mid-eighteenth century was 150 rubles per captive, though some could fetch a higher price.[129]

These allocations, according to I. I. Kraft, were not sufficient to ransom all of the captives, and many "laid down their lives in that distant land" (*slozhili svoi golovy na dal'nei chuzhbine*). Kraft writes of the new ransom economy as marking a new era in Russian–Kazakh relations (albeit, unfortunately, without citing his sources):[130]

> [These circumstances] also spawned a new view of trade between Russians and Asians and of that most shameful trade, as history knows it, the trade in living people. The Kazakhs took Russian people not so much in battle or as revenge for some injustice, but simply for profit in the slave trade. Into that shameful trade came intermediaries and large enterprises [*krupnye predprinimateli*], competing with one-another. It is impossible to pass over in silence the fact that numbered among the large enterprises with respect to the trade in Russian people were sometimes also Russians, although, fortunately, these fanatics are considered but few . . .

The numbers of Russians taken by Kazakhs doubtless rose and fell according to the state of Russian–Kazakh diplomacy, the character and tenor of which fluctuated considerably throughout the eighteenth and nineteenth centuries. As we shall see in coming chapters, however, the capture and enslavement of Russians would be an ongoing issue in frontier diplomacy down to the mid-nineteenth century.

In this chapter, I have briefly summarized more than a century of failed diplomatic efforts on the part of Russia and Iran to negotiate for the return of their captured subjects and to end captive-taking along their contested frontiers. Iranian efforts in this respect were generally ineffective, but they

[128] Terent'ev, *Istoriia zavoevaniia Srednei Azii*, Vol. 1, 106. This, Terent'ev writes, was the natural outcome of circumstances by which Khivan traders could move about freely in Russia but Russians could not go anywhere in Khiva "without the danger of falling into perpetual slavery" ("*opastnosti popast' v vechnoe rabstvo*"; p. 106).

[129] Kraft, *Sudebnaia chast' v Turkestanskom krae i stepnykh oblastiakh*, 34–35; cf. also Terent'ev, *Istoriia zavoevaniia Srednei Azii*, Vol. 1, 106.

[130] Kraft, *Sudebnaia chast' v Turkestanskom krae i stepnykh oblastiakh*, 35.

are crucial to consider because the ongoing crisis of captive-taking in Khurasan served as a major justification for Iranian military action in the region, defined Iranian relations with the khanates for decades, and in several key instances – the campaigns of ʿAbbās Mīrzā, for example – had an immediate impact on the lives of many slaves. Russian efforts tended likewise to be ineffective, but they too are crucial to consider because the liberation of Russian slaves (and, more generally, the "pacification" of Bukhara and especially of Khwarazm) helped justify Russia's conquest of the region. In short, in the nineteenth century, the issue of slavery became the nexus of competing imperial claims over Central Asia.

2

Beyond the Bazaars

Geographies of the Slave Trade in Central Asia

By the late nineteenth century, as we have seen, the Central Asian khanates of Bukhara and Khwarazm had long been notorious among Russian and Western European observers for their part in the region's thriving slave trade. This notoriety would have severe consequences: As Alexander Morrison has recently argued, the ongoing slave trade, as a pretext for war, "played a crucial role in legitimizing and motivating the Russian advance" into the region, which culminated in the conquest of Bukhara in 1866–1868 and of Khwarazm in 1873.[1] The conquest of the latter was followed by official proclamations of emancipation and abolition in both khanates, issued by the khans at the behest of the Russian Governor-General. These events were widely assumed to have brought about the end of the slave trade in this part of Central Asia, which has been characterized – according to the standard narrative – by the phenomenon of nomadic Turkmen and Kazakh slave-raiders transporting their captives for sale to the region's major urban centers. There has been little research into how the trade actually functioned, however, and little evidence to confirm that the Russian conquests brought about its demise. In this chapter, I will argue two points: (1) that the urban centers of Khwarazm and Bukhara were, for many slaves, merely transit points in a decentralized network of trade extending well beyond the major towns and their bazaars; and (2) that the decentralized nature of the slave trade demands that we reject long-held notions about Russian and local authorities effectively

[1] Alexander Morrison, "Twin Imperial Disasters. The Invasions of Khiva and Afghanistan in the Russian and British Official Mind, 1839–1842," *Modern Asian Studies* 48/1 (2013), 282–283.

abolishing the slave trade in the 1870s. I will draw evidence for these arguments from eyewitness accounts of the trade, as well as from the firsthand experiences of Central Asian slaves themselves, preserved in unpublished interviews found in Central Asian archives.

A DECENTRALIZED SLAVE TRADE

According to a longstanding consensus among historians of Eurasian economies, the rise of maritime trade linking Western Europe with India and China in the fifteenth and sixteenth centuries had a devastating effect on the caravan trade across Central Asia, rendering it largely obsolete.[2] This overland trade had formerly brought prosperity to Central Asia's cities by promoting the urban-centered production of everything from paper to textiles. Isolation from the new oceanic trade routes was thus (the story goes) catastrophic for the regional economy as a whole, and it resulted in decentralization and rapid deurbanization. In recent decades, however, research into overland trade in the region after the sixteenth century has revealed that it was far from stagnant. Audrey Burton's landmark work on Bukharan trade networks, for example, reveals how the khanate engaged in extensive trade with nomadic, sedentary, rural, and urban peoples throughout Eurasia, thanks to overland commercial networks extending through Khwarazm, East Turkistan, Iran, China, Muscovy, Siberia, the Ottoman Empire, and India.[3] James Millward has shown in remarkable detail how Qing China engaged neighboring Central Asian regions by maintaining overland trade networks in a multitude of commodities throughout the eighteenth and nineteenth centuries.[4] Trade

[2] Recent examples include Christopher I. Beckwith, *Empires of the Silk Road: A History of Central Eurasia from the Bronze Age to the Present* (Princeton, NJ: Princeton University Press, 2009). For summaries and critiques of this approach, see especially the work of Scott C. Levi, *The Indian Diaspora in Central Asia and Its Trade, 1550–1900* (Leiden: Brill, 2002); "Early Modern Central Asia in World History," *History Compass* 10:11 (2012), 866–878; "India, Russia and the Eighteenth-Century Transformation of the Central Asian Caravan Trade," *Journal of the Economic and Social History of the Orient* 42:4 (1999), 519–526. See also Morris Rossabi, "The 'Decline' of the Central Asian Caravan Trade," in James Tracey, ed., *The Rise of Merchant Empires* (Cambridge: Cambridge University Press, 1990), 351–370; and Robert D. McChesney, *Central Asia: Foundations of Change* (Princeton, NJ: Darwin Press, 1996), 41–42.

[3] Audrey Burton, *The Bukharans: A Dynastic, Diplomatic, and Commercial History 1550–1702* (New York, NY: St. Martin's Press, 1997).

[4] Millward, *Beyond the Pass: Economy, Ethnicity, and Empire in Qing Central Asia, 1759–1864*; Millward also offers important comments challenging the Silk Road "decline" hypothesis on pp. 98–101.

by Indian merchants in Central Asia during this period has, meanwhile, been the subject of important studies by Scott C. Levi, Stephen Dale, Muzaffar Alam, Claude Markovitz, and others.[5] While the mere existence of overland trade, as Ron Sela has observed, is not sufficient to prove that Central Asia as a whole was a thriving, flourishing region during these turbulent centuries,[6] it is nevertheless worthwhile to consider the nature of the existing commerce and how some types of trade managed to flourish. The trade in slaves can be counted among those types of commerce that thrived in the eighteenth and nineteenth centuries, and it was bolstered by continual conflict in Khurasan and the Kazakh steppe as well as by demand for slaves in Bukhara, Khwarazm, and among rural nomads.

As we shall see, much of the slave trade took place outside major urban centers, with slaves being transported along caravan routes across rural Central Asia and traded in rural caravanserais and settlements. They were often traded by and among nomads, and it may be for precisely this reason that studies describing this slave trade remain so rare. Nomadic commerce, after all, has most often been considered not in relation to the wide-ranging caravan trade but rather in relation to specific urban centers, and the most common approach has followed a core/periphery model: The city is the core and the nomads populate the periphery, like spokes radiating from a hub. In the decades since Anatoly Khazanov published his influential *Nomads and the Outside World*, the relationship between Eurasian nomads and the urban "core" has frequently been described as a symbiotic one, with the former providing the cities with goods or services in exchange for food, handicrafts, and luxury items; the urban "core" constituted the final destination of the nomads' goods, as well as the source of goods and revenue they gained in trade.[7]

In Central Asia, slaves were undoubtedly a major source of trade revenue for many nomads, particularly Turkmens, and they were most

[5] Levi, *The Indian Diaspora*; Stephen Dale, *Indian Merchants and Eurasian Trade, 1600–1750* (Cambridge: Cambridge University Press, 1994); Muzaffar Alam, "Trade, State Policy and Regional Change: Aspects of Mughal-Uzbek Commercial Relations, c. 1550–1750," *Journal of the Economic and Social History of the Orient* 37:3 (1994), 202–227; Claude Markovitz, *The Global World of Indian Merchants, 1750–1947: Traders of Sind from Bukhara to Panama* (New York, NY: Cambridge University Press, 2000); Levi and Alam, eds., *India and Central Asia: Commerce and Culture, 1500–1800* (Oxford: Oxford University Press, 2007).

[6] Ron Sela, *The Legendary Biographies of Tamerlane: Islam and Heroic Apocrypha in Central Asia* (Cambridge: Cambridge University Press, 2013), 122.

[7] Anatoly Khazanov, *Nomads and the Outside World* (Madison, WI: University of Wisconsin Press, 1994 [second edition]). See also Khazanov and Andre Wink, eds., *Nomads in the Sedentary World* (New York, NY: Routledge, 2001).

certainly traded and sold in the cities. But the kinds of bustling slave-bazaars found in Istanbul or Timbuktu, in which hundreds or even thousands of individuals were displayed for purchase at any given time, simply did not exist in the region. While a city such as Khiva was a site of slave-trading and of slave labor, it was hardly the "core" of the slave trade; it was merely one possible transit point among many. In fact, as I will argue here, slaves were sold and traded at caravanserais and in rural settlements throughout the region. Rather than searching for a "core" or "periphery," it would be better to think of the slave trade in terms of "circulation."[8] Slaves and their sellers circulated in decentralized zones of commerce.

Two aspects of the Central Asian trade contributed to its decentralized character. First, a significant portion of the trade took place between nomads and other nomads. Second, the nature of slavery itself in the region was distinctly rural: Eyewitness accounts as well as studies of the region's urban economies have confirmed that the predominant type of work that slaves performed was agricultural.[9] The primarily rural character of slavery was a consistent trait over the course of centuries, although the trajectory of the trade in slaves shifted over time. The demographic of slaves from India, once prominent in the region, was fast disappearing by the end of the seventeenth century, with Iranian Shiʿite slaves from

[8] Claude Markovits, Jacques Pouchepaass, and Sanjay Subrahmanyam have recently offered an expansive definition of this term that touches upon the circulation not only of people and objects in trade-networks but also of "information, knowledge, ideas, techniques, skills, cultural productions (texts, songs), religious practices, even gods" ("Introduction: Circulation and Society under Colonial Rule," in Markovitz, Pouchepaass, and Subrahmanyam, eds., *Society and Circulation: Mobile People and Itinerant Cultures in South Asia, 1750–1950* (London: Anthem, 2003), 2–3. Here, I discuss only the circulation of people and merchandise, but where people go, their ideas, songs, and gods go with them, and one of the goals of this chapter is to reveal how people circulated, both with merchandise and as merchandise.

[9] For example, "Nevol'niki v Khive," *Vestnik Evropy* 80:7 (1815), 245; Major Blankenagel', *Zamechaniia maiora Blankenagelia, vposledstvie poezdki ego iz Orenburga v Khivu v 1793–94 godakh* (St. Pb, 1858), 13, 17; N. N. Murav'ev, *Muraviev's Journey to Khiva through the Turcoman Country, 1819–20* (Calcutta: Foreign Department Press, 1871), 144; N. Zalesov, "Pis'mo iz Khivy," *Voennyi sbornik* 1 (1859), 288; Georges de Meyendorff, *A Journey from Orenburg to Bukhara in the Year 1820* (Calcutta: Foreign Department Press, 1870), 62. R. K. Mukminova's study of sixteenth-century *waqf* documents has revealed that most of the slaves mentioned therein were used for agricultural labor or animal husbandry (Mukminova, *Sotsial'naia differentsiatsiia naseleniia gorodov Uzbekistana v XV–XVI vv.* [Tashkent, 1985], 122–123; see also Levi, "Hindus Beyond the Hindu Kush," 278n5). Other sources reveal, for example, large numbers of slaves working in agricultural on the estates of prominent Sufi leaders such as the Juybari shaykhs (ibid., 278).

Khurasan taking the Indian slaves' place.[10] The Turkmen deserts north of Khurasan became increasingly prominent zones of captivity, transport, trade, and sale. By the nineteenth century, Iranian Shiʿites would, by all accounts, constitute an overwhelming majority of the region's slaves. Through the northward trajectory of these trade networks, they came to form a significant demographic in Khwarazm and Bukhara. Estimates of the number of slaves in Khwarazm in the nineteenth century generally range from 30,000 to 60,000 individuals; similar numbers were estimated for Bukhara.[11]

EVIDENCE FROM THE LIVES OF SLAVES

As the region's slave traders have left us no ledgers or diaries, the best way to reconstruct the trade itself is through eyewitness accounts, as well as through the declared experiences of the slaves themselves. For much of the Muslim world, detailed information on the lives of individual slaves, and especially accounts authored by individual slaves, appear to be few and far between.[12] Based on the recent ethnographic literature on Ottoman

[10] Levi, "Hindus Beyond the Hindu Kush," 277–279.

[11] For example, among our nineteenth-century estimates for Khwarazm, A. P. Khoroshkhin, who had been involved in a Russian census project based at Orenburg after the conquest of Khiva, estimated that 29,291 Iranian slaves had been living in the khānate, along with 6,515 manumitted slaves (Khoroshkhin, *Sbornik statei: Kasaiushchikhsia do Turkestanskago kraia* [St. Pb., 1876], 486); Murav'ev estimated at least 33,000 slaves, 30,000 of them Iranians (Murav'ev, *Muraviev's Journey to Khiva*, 57–58); Blankenagel' estimated 25,000 slaves (Blankenagel', *Zamechaniia maiora Blankenagelia*, 12–13; Herbert Wood estimated 50,000 Iranian slaves and manumitted former slaves (Wood, *The Shores of Lake Aral* [London: Smith, Elder & Co., 1876], 219; Basiner estimated 52,000 Iranian slaves (see Emil Schmidt, *The Russian Expedition to Khiva in 1873* [Calcutta: Foreign Department Press, 1876], 12); Vambery estimated 40,000 Iranian slaves (ibid., 12); Alikhanov-Avarskii estimated 25,000–40,000 total slaves (M. Alikhanov-Avarskii, *Pokhod v Khivu (Kavkazkikh otriadov) 1873. Step' i oazis* [St. Pb, 1899], 280); and Ḥassan Muḥammad Amīn Oghlï, author of an unpublished Chaghatay tract on slavery from the early Soviet period, estimates that there had been 58,500 slaves and manumitted former-slaves in 1873, including Iranians, Kurds, Afghans, Azeri Turks, and Russians (MS IVAN Uz No. 12581, f. 51b). For Bukhara, estimates are scarcer; Meyendorff estimated 30–40,000 Iranian slaves, and the Greek metropolitan Khrisanf Neopatraskii, writing near the end of the eighteenth century, estimated 60,000 Iranian slaves (in S. G. Karpiuk, ed., *Puteshestviia po Vostoku v opokhu Ekateriny II* [Moscow: Vostochnaia literatura, 1995], 279). Joseph Wolff, the eccentric missionary and adventurer, estimated 200,000 slaves, though this figure seems unlikely (Wolff, *Narrative of a Mission to Bukhara in the Years 1843–1845*, Vol. 2 [London: J.W. Parker, 1845], 104).

[12] On the relative lack of firsthand slave narratives in the Ottoman context, see, for example, Y. Hakan Erdem, "Slavery and Social Life in Nineteenth-Century Turco-Egyptian

slavery, for example, it seems that there are precious few enslaved persons for whom we know the full complement of basic information: their birthplace; their age at capture, if captured, along with the location and circumstances of their capture and who captured them; their sale price and the location(s) of their sale(s); the length of their captivity; the sort of work they did; the identity and character of their owner(s); their treatment at the hands of their owner(s); their marital status; and the manner and means of their manumission, if freed, as well as what became of them afterwards.[13]

This was precisely the sort of data collected from Central Asian slaves and former slaves by the officials of the Orenburg Border Commission and other Russian border authorities,[14] however, and the scarcity of such information for the broader Eurasian world would render even a few such interviews precious. For the present work, I have collated data on forty-five of these slaves and former slaves for whom the documentary record is particularly rich; for each of these individuals, most or all of the above information was collected at the Russian border.[15] In some

Khartoum," in Terence Walz and Kenneth M. Cuno, eds., *Race and Slavery in the Middle East: Histories of Trans-Saharan Africans in 19th-Century Egypt, Sudan, and the Ottoman Mediterranean* (Cairo: American University in Cairo Press, 2010), 125; and Toledano, *As If Silent and Absent*, 52, 57.

13 Recent examples of an ethnographic approach to Ottoman slavery include Ehud R. Toledano, *As If Silent and Absent* (New Haven, CT: Yale University Press, 2007), and Eve Troutt Powell, *Tell This in My Memory: Stories of Enslavement from Egypt, Sudan, and the Ottoman Empire* (Palo Alto, CA: Stanford University Press, 2013).

14 Established in 1799, the Commission was tasked with extending legal and administrative control over the Kazakhs of the steppe; the Junior Horde was subjected to particular scrutiny, as its territories of migration abutted the Russian border. The reasons why border officials would have been tasked with recording former slaves' testimonies and autobiographical details are not entirely clear, but a couple possibilities come to mind. First, the former slaves, once they had arrived at the border, would either be received as citizens of the Russian Empire or returned to the steppe, and their testimonials, once written, would serve as proof that protocol had been followed in "processing" these individuals. Second, the testimony of the former slaves often contained details concerning violence and tensions between nomadic groups that could be of interest in formulating the Empire's steppe diplomacy and policies.

15 The information collated is found in the following documents held by the Central State Archive of the Republic of Kazakhstan (henceforth TsGAKaz): TsGAKaz 4.1.3646, ff. 45a–49b; ff. 73a–78a; TsGAKaz 4.1.198, f. 3a; ff. 19a-b; 36a–37a; 53a–54b; 104a; 137a; ff. 173a–b; TsGAKaz 4.1.195, ff. 10a–11a; TsGAKaz 4.1.3641, ff. 36a–38b; TsGAKaz 4.1.2821, ff. 2a–3a; 6a–b; TsGAKaz 383.1.89, ff. 14a–b; TsGAKaz 4.1.3573, ff. 40a–41b; 132a; 227a–b; TsGAKaz 4.1.197, f. 3a; 44a–b; 81a–b; TsGAKaz 4.1.3730, ff. 5a–b; 17a–18a; TsGAKaz 4.1.499, ff. 104a–b. Most of these documents date from between 1850 and 1861, with a few dating from as early as 1800. Some of these records are quite concise, comprising merely a few short sentences, while others are significantly more elaborate, but all of them provide much of the information listed in this section.

documents, their lives are recounted in the first person (albeit usually translated into Russian by interpreters, who were present and named). Most of these biographies and autobiographies follow a common formula, as if in response to a questionnaire, and the formula remained consistent throughout the nineteenth century. The accounts are short on sentiment, but the consistent nature of the information they provide lends itself well to a comparative assessment. With tens of thousands of slaves in the region at any given time, such a small sample cannot be taken for a comprehensive prosopography of Central Asian slaves in general. But certain striking commonalities that emerge from this small sample cannot be dismissed as mere coincidence; and at times, these commonalities defy common conceptions. The evidence provided by these biographies, when combined with evidence offered in other sources, points to a re-envisioning of the nature of nomadic trade in Central Asia, as well as to a revision of the standard narrative of how slavery came to an end in the region.

The origins of these forty-five slaves and former slaves are recorded as follows: thirteen were described as Persian; seven as Kalmyks; four as Afghans; three as Arabs; two as Hazaras; two as Turkmens; two as "Bukharans"; two as Kirghiz; two as Karakalpaks; two as "Central Asians"; one as a Tatar; one as an Uzbek; and four as of unknown origin.[16] These forty-five individuals – forty-one men and boys, and four women and girls – had lived a combined 683 years in captivity. It is claimed in some sources that slaves in the Muslim world could very often expect their freedom after a period of roughly seven years, since it was at this point that slaves became eligible to purchase their own freedom.[17] Indeed, this alleged peculiarity of slavery in the region has been used to argue that Central Asian slaves – and slaves in the Muslim world more generally – had an easier time of it than slaves elsewhere, as they were rarely held in perpetuity. Of the thirty-five slaves in the present cohort whose total

[16] Typically, those of unknown origin had been taken captive very early their childhood. Here, I have specifically selected accounts given by Muslim slaves, as these slaves formed the overwhelming majority of slaves in Central Asia as a whole. Russian slaves were likewise received, liberated, and interrogated, however, and some excellent recent research offers coverage of their fates as well as the (sometimes evidently "dramatized") accounts of their captivity: Smolarz, "Speaking about Freedom and Dependency," 44–71; Gao, "Captivity and Empire: Russian Captivity Narratives in Fact and Fiction."

[17] For example, Toledano, *As If Silent and Absent*, p. 91. William Gervase Clarence-Smith provides a comparative overview of slaves' periods of captivity throughout the Muslim world: *Islam and the Abolition of Slavery* (Oxford: Oxford University Press, 2006), 67–68. The period of seven years' captivity before manumission appears to have had deep roots as a tradition in the Judeo-Christian world; it is mentioned in the Old Testament (Deuteronomy 15: 1–18); Clarence-Smith, 222.

period of captivity is recorded, however, only three individuals had spent fewer than fifteen years in bondage. Only two had been enslaved for a period of fewer than seven years before gaining their freedom. (Both of these two had been presented at the Russian border by their owners after the circulation of Imperial decrees threatening punishment for all Kazakhs under Russian dominion who did not bring forward their slaves.[18]) Sixteen others, having been presented to the Russian authorities, requested to be sent back with their owners in order to continue in their present circumstances – their captivity was open-ended at the time of their interview, in other words. In all, the mean period of captivity among this cohort of slaves was 19.51 years, with a median of fifteen years. This tells us, among other things, that these slaves had substantial experience of captivity by the time they were interviewed.

Though nearly all of these forty-five slaves had come to the Russian authorities from among the Kazakhs, their generally long duration of captivity cannot be considered a trait unique to the Kazakh context: These statistics alone do not reflect the fact that a great many of these slaves had several owners over the years. Indeed, the prominence of traffic from owner to owner is another striking commonality that emerges in their biographies. This "horizontal" transit is especially pronounced among those slaves who were initially taken captive by the Turkmens: For this cohort of sixteen individuals, ten were sold more than once, and on the whole they were sold an average (mean) of 2.43 times per individual. This mobility from one owner to another is worth bearing in mind as we come to consider slaves' transit across the region. We will now turn to the autobiography of one of these slaves, whose story unfolds across a remarkably broad geographical and cultural range.

Received by Russian border authorities in November of 1852, a man named ʿAbdullāh, son of one Mullā Walī Yār, described himself as forty years old, a Shiʿite, and originally from Herat. Fourteen years prior, he had been living with his parents, his elder brother, his wife, his two sons (Begrashīd and Sayfullāh), and six servants (*prislugi*) on a farm the family owned near Herat. One day, they were attacked by a host of some 2,000

[18] On these policies and decrees, see, for example, TsGAKaz 383.1.184, ff. 11b–19a; TsGAKaz 383.1.89, ff. 10a–14b. The earliest of the decrees that ordered general manumission among Kazakhs under Russian dominion appears to have been issued in 1859, with similar decrees following in 1860, 1861, and 1869 (G. I. Semeniuk, "Likvidatsiia rabstva v Kazakhstane," repr. in Zh. O. Artykbaev et al., eds., *Raby i tiulenguty v kazakhskoi stepi* [Astana: Altyn Kitap, 2006], 238). Slaves manumitted at the border before this period were generally escapees.

Teke Turkmens, who were in some sort of relationship of dependency to Merv, and had been – according to ʿAbdullāh – at the command of Tabsad Khan [sic]. The attacking party robbed the family of their property, making off with 200 sheep, 60 horses, and 50 head of cattle. The Turkmens took the family captive, along with their servants, numbering thirteen people in all. (ʿAbdullāh's third son, Iskandar, and his daughter, A___,[19] had been living with his father-in-law, who was an official in Herat, so they were spared from the attack.) The captive family was taken to the Turkmens' camp, southwest of Merv, where they remained for four days. During that time, the Khan freed ʿAbdullāh's parents and sent them home, returning to them from among their stolen goods a carpet, some cattle, a cooking-pot, a blanket, and all of his father's books (his father had a reputation in the region, being a well-known *mullā*). ʿAbdullāh's brother was sold to some Turkmens for the very low sum of seven *tilla*s, and ʿAbdullāh was sold for eight *tilla*s to a Turkmen named Berdi-Kilich, who in turn sold him at a profit to a Khivan two months later, earning twelve *tilla*s. The sale evidently took place in the Turkmens' camp near Merv. The Khivan, named D___, immediately took ʿAbdullāh to the town of Urgench and sold him to another Khivan, this one named Palvān Niyāz, for eighteen *tilla*s. After five days, Palvān Niyāz sold him to another Khivan, identified as "*yuzbāshi* Yakub,"[20] for twenty-five *tilla*s. In less than three months, ʿAbdullāh had already been sold four times.

Soon after arriving at the *yuzbāshi*'s house, Abdullah received the news that his father-in-law, Arbab Zulfikar [sic], the Herati official, had written to Tabsad Khan regarding the manumission of ʿAbdullāh's wife and two sons, who had also been sold off. He learned also that their servants had been sold to Khiva, but he did not find out where they and his elder brother were currently residing.

ʿAbdullāh lived with the *yuzbāshi* for the next four years, evidently in Urgench, doing agricultural labor for him, and after four years his master sold him to a Khivan named Yusuf Khop-Khar [sic] for twenty-five *tilla*s,

[19] The Russian transliterations of non-Russian names that appear in these documents often appear strange or ambiguous to me, and, rather than continuing to garble these individuals' names for posterity, I have opted to use first-initials wherever I have had especially strong reservations about proper identification and rendering of a name.

[20] In Khwarazm, the title of *yuzbāshi* – literally meaning "head of one hundred" – did not, according to Murav'ev, indicate a formal position, but was rather an honorary title "bestowed by the Khan in war time on the officers commanding divisions of his forces" (N. N. Murav'ev, *Muraviev's Journey to Khiva through the Turcoman County, 1819–20*, trans. Philipp Strahl [Calcutta: Foreign Department Press, 1871], 50). Those upon whom this title was bestowed tended to retain it indefinitely, and not only at times of war.

earning back the sum he had initially paid for ʿAbdullāh four years prior. After five days, this Khivan sold ʿAbdullāh to a Karakalpak named Mullā Bishbay [sic] for thirty-seven *tilla*s, and he lived with the Mullā for the next seven years, performing domestic labor (*domashnaia rabota*) for him. At the end of seven years, the Mullā sold ʿAbdullāh for thirty *tilla*s to a Kazakh of the Tabïn clan who was a nomad in Khivan territory. He lived with this nomad for a month before being sold once again, this time for three horses and twenty sheep, to a Kazakh named Chin-Timur [sic], who was from the Shekti clan and lived as a nomad along the river Emba. He lived with Chin-Timur for a little over a year before this owner presented him to Sultan Arslan Jan-Turin [sic], who gave him over to the Russian authorities. ʿAbdullāh reported that seven of his owners subjected him to no manner of abuse or mistreatment – implying, however, that one of his eight total owners did mistreat him. He requested that the Orenburg Border Commission convey him back home to Herat, at long last.[21]

Over the course of fourteen years, ʿAbdullāh was enslaved by a remarkably diverse cross-section of Central Asian society. He was held and sold by Turkmen raiders, by Khivan traders, by a Karakalpak mullā, by an Urgench *yuzbāshi*, and by two different Kazakh nomads. We know that he worked both as a domestic servant and as an agriculturalist, and one can only imagine the range of households to which he became accustomed – from Turkmen camps to Kazakh tents to the *yuzbāshi*'s estate. His price ranged from seven *tilla*s, near the site of his capture, to thirty-seven *tilla*s as an "import" at an urban center. "Horizontal" mobility and demographic diversity characterize his ordeal, and in both of these traits ʿAbdullāh's narrative is no great exception in our cohort of forty-five. His story also follows a general pattern among our biographies in that a significant portion of his experience took place beyond the "urban" sphere.

The first half of ʿAbdullāh's story is quite in keeping with common perceptions of how the slave trade functioned: archetypically, Turkmens raided Khurasan and brought Iranian captives to the bazaars in Khiva or Bukhara, where they would enter the service of urban notables. Here we find the standard model of nomadic economic networks, with nomads supplying cities whose markets were the nexus of the slave trade. The nomadic and sedentary economies thus become inseparable, as in the widely repeated observations of Murav'ev: "The practice of catching human beings and selling them to the Khivans has become an absolute necessity to the nomadic tribes; that is to say, the latter have to depend for

[21] TsGAKaz 4.1.3646, ff. 75b–76b.

grain on Khiva, and grain cannot be grown there without extraneous labour, so that this abominable trade has become an institution for the mutual benefit of Khiva and the predatory tribes, without which neither could exist."[22]

Soon after, however, ʿAbdullāh passes from the cities back into the hinterlands, where he is traded among nomads. Rare indeed is the study that emphasizes trade among and within nomadic groups, and scholars attuned to the many reminders that nomadic and sedentary economies were inextricable may begin to wonder whether there was any such thing as an intranomadic economy, and whether there is any alternative model for nomads' trade-relations other than symbiosis (or, according to older models, parasitism) with respect to settled regions. For our purposes, two questions emerge in light of ʿAbdullāh's story: First, did a significant slave trade exist beyond the urban bazaars? And, second, could the slave trade persist without the bazaars?

At first glance, the travelers and diplomats who provide much of our data on the nineteenth-century slave trade do not give us much cause to depart from the standard "urban core/nomadic periphery" models sketched earlier, or even to elaborate on them. In source after source, we are told of a linear progression: captives were dragged from the peripheries to the urban bazaars of Khiva and Bukhara, with Turkmens – and, less commonly, Kazakhs – as their vector. The center of the trade was the urban bazaar, and the nomads themselves were ever the captivators, armed chaperons, sellers, and nothing more. Thus, we have it since the very earliest Russian appraisals of the slave-dealing economy, such as the following, dating from 1815:

> The Kirghiz [Kazakhs], marauding raiders in Russian lands, and the Turkmen in Persian lands, abduct no small number of people, and sell them as slaves to the Khivans, who, being squarely between Russia, Persia, and Bukhara, have for some time maintained for themselves a healthy trade. Without their mediation, the thieves would not be able to have so much success and [such a level of] dissemination; for the [Kazakhs], if they had not always such ready and generous bidders in the Khivans, would not be so eager to go and take captives, inasmuch as they are but little kept as slaves [for themselves].[23]

[22] N. N. Murav'ev, *Muraviev's Journey to Khiva through the Turcoman County, 1819–20*, trans. Philipp Strahl (Calcutta: Foreign Department Press, 1871), 148. He elsewhere observes, "The Turcomans buy their grain at the markets, and dispose of slaves, so useful in the cultivation of the land, as they are generally the ploughmen; were the trade with the Turcomans to cease, Khiva would lose the chief source of its prosperity, and probably sink back into insignificance" (ibid., 144).

[23] "Nevolniki v khive," *Vestnik Evropy* 80:7, (1815), 244.

The idea that Kazakhs and Turkmens kept few slaves among themselves plays into the notion that they were exclusively raiders, transporters, and dealers, and it is likewise a longstanding misconception. One can trace the idea from early Russian travel reportage through Soviet scholarship. A. I. Levshin, who traveled among the Kazakhs in the first half of the nineteenth century, was perhaps the earliest to propose that they kept no slaves among them – other than their women, who, Levshin characteristically claims, generally took the place of slaves, given the alleged laziness of Kazakh men.[24] In the many years since, some scholars have flatly denied that slavery could develop in nomadic societies in general, and particularly among the Kazakhs. Their reasoning usually concerns: (1) the relative lack of labor-intensity involved in herding; (2) the weak development of agriculture and crafts among the Kazakhs; (3) the availability of alternative sources of inexpensive or free labor; and (4) the prohibitive expense of slaves when compared with the average Kazakh's worldly holdings.[25]

The first three points presume that owning slaves was merely a matter of perceived labor necessity – a simplistically "rationalist" vision of slavery which overlooks the many tasks performed by slaves, throughout human history, which have been neither rational nor necessary nor always readily identifiable as "labor." This leaves us with the notion of prohibitive expense. Semeniuk, for one, argues that a slave typically cost, among the Kazakhs, an average of seventy-five sheep, while, according to my collation of his data, only 21.1 percent of Kazakh households in his sample (from mid-nineteenth-century Omsk) had more than fifty sheep, and only 9.6 percent had more than 100.[26] By considering ʿAbdullāh's biography, however, among others, we can see that prices fluctuated wildly. ʿAbdullāh's price rose by nearly 500 percent – from eight *tilla*s to thirty-seven *tilla*s – in different contexts and at different times. At a mere eight *tilla*s, ʿAbdullāh would have been an obtainable commodity for many. And some slaves were free: They could be captured, and they could reproduce.

[24] A. de Levchine, *Description des hordes et des steppes des Kirghiz-Kazaks ou Kirghiz-Kaissaks* (Paris: Impr. royale, 1840), 354.

[25] On these points, see Semeniuk, "Istochniki rabstva v Kazakhstane v XV–XIX vekakh," in *Raby i tiulenguty v kazakhskoi stepi*, 140–41, 151, 176; K. Kraft, "Unichtozhenie rabstva v kirgizskoi stepi," in *Iz kirgizskoi stariny* (Orenburg, 1900), 95. David Sneath has connected the claim that Central Asian nomads had few slaves to a more general preoccupation among scholars, especially in the Soviet Union, with the idea – one Sneath combats at length – that nomadic societies were fundamentally egalitarian (Sneath, *The Headless State: Aristocratic Orders, Kinship Society, & Misrepresentations of Nomadic Inner Asia* [New York: Columbia University Press, 2007], 152–154, 186).

[26] Ibid., 150–151.

If one is still inclined to question whether the Kazakhs kept significant numbers of slaves, the Border Commission's tally of freedmen – those who either fled captivity in the steppe or were freed by their masters, and arrived safely at the border – can be illuminating. The earliest numbers I have seen are already impressive: between 1749 and 1753, no fewer than 1,024 former slaves from among the Kazakhs turned up at Russian defensive posts.[27] Of these individuals, 862 claimed to have fled their owners.

The most compelling evidence concerning slavery among the Kazakhs, however, is the testimony of the slaves themselves. It is with this in mind that we return to ʿAbdullāh, whose journey eventually took him in precisely the opposite direction from the standard model of nomadic trade: he went from the city of Khiva to the domains of nomadic Kazakhs and Karakalpaks, rather than vice-versa. Here, his story is similar to the others in his cohort: all spent some portion of their captivity among the Kazakhs, as one might expect, given that they emerged from the steppe; more surprisingly, most spent nearly the entirety of their captivity among Kazakhs. The sedentary centers of Khiva and Bukhara emerge in these biographies as merely two transit-points in a series of sales. Generally, major towns are rarely mentioned in these documents. Another example will further illustrate the common feature of broad mobility beyond the bazaars and urban centers.

Like ʿAbdullāh, Kalbay Hamzin [sic] was interviewed by Russian border officials in November of 1852. He was then twenty-four years old, a Shiʿite from the town of Kalyan, one-and-a-half days' caravan journey from Mashhad, where his parents and brother were evidently living at the time of his interview. Six years prior, at the end of a winter night, Kalbay and twelve companions were grazing sheep about twelve versts (eight miles) from town, when they were attacked by forty Teke Turkmens who had been based at Ashgabat. These Turkmens took them captive and brought them to the town of Alkabad, where they were divided up, and Kalbay was sold to a Turkmen with whom he lived for one month. This Turkmen then sold Kalbay to another Turkmen, named Khwāja Bulak [sic], for thirty-seven *tilla*s. Khwāja Bulak was from one of the tribes which had accompanied the raiding party. He immediately took Kalbay to the Khivan village of Pars, two days' caravan journey from the town of Urgench, where he sold him to a Khivan named Kut-Muḥammad [sic] for thirty *tilla*s. He lived with Kut-Muḥammad in Pars for the next five years, serving him by

[27] "Iz istorii Kazakhstana XVIII v.," *Krasnyi arkhiv* 2:87, (1938), 167–168.

planting grain and working the land. Finally, he was sold by Kut-Muḥammad to a Khivan trader of Persian slaves named Palvān, for thirty *tillas*. This trader turned around and sold him for the same amount to a Kazakh of the Tabïn clan, living within the domain of Khiva. Kalbay lived with this Kazakh for two months before he was traded to another Kazakh, this one named Murat-Bek [sic], of the Karakesek, in exchange for ten large sheep, a camel, a horse, and three large felt carpets. Kalbay stayed with Murat-Bek for seven months, and he was then sold to a Kazakh named Butunbay [sic] of the Nazar clan,[28] with whom he lived for another four months. This last master finally presented Kalbay to the sultan of the Middle Horde. At the conclusion of this narrative, Kalbay adds the details that all of his masters treated him well, that they did not beat or abuse him, and that he possessed no livestock or holdings of his own, or of his former masters.[29]

As with ʿAbdullāh, Kalbay spent much of his captivity in the steppe. It is not clear that he ever passed through the urban bazaars of Khiva, Urgench, and Bukhara, and his time in the Khwarazmian khanate was evidently spent in remote, rural quarters. This rural orientation is, as mentioned, something his narrative shares with nearly all others in the cohort, and in order to appreciate the magnitude of this commonality, we will now step back briefly from particular narratives and have a look at trends related to acts of sale.

Of these forty-five slaves, seven were kept by their original captors, and the other thirty-eight were sold – so far as their biographies reveal – a total of sixty-seven times altogether. For sixty-three of these recorded sales, something of the origins of the buyer and seller is recorded, i.e. whether they were "Kirghiz" (Kazakh), "Khivan" (a category which seems to exclude Turkmens and Kazakhs within Khivan domains), Karakalpak, Turkmen, and so on. Given the urban-centered model offered by our eyewitness accounts and by later secondary literature, one would naturally expect that most of the sales took place between Turkmens and Khivans, between Khivans and other Khivans, and – because these slaves issued from the Kazakh steppe – between Khivans and Kazakhs. After all, the best-known sources are unanimous in emphasizing that the bazaars of Khiva and Bukhara served as the crux of the traffic in slaves. But in fact only five of the sixty-three detailed sales took place between Turkmens and sedentary Khivans. Another four

[28] The Nazars were a large subdivision of the Shektis, living along the Emba River. As of 1848 they reportedly numbered some 1,200 yurts. I am grateful to Allen J. Frank for providing this information.

[29] TsGAKaz 4.1.3646, ff. 74a–75a.

took place between Khivans and other Khivans. In other words, only 14 percent of the recorded sales involved a sedentary Khivan buyer, and only eleven sales (17 percent) involved a sedentary Khivan seller. Bukharans were involved in six of the sales, and in four of these cases they were recorded selling slaves to the Kazakhs. On both the buying end and the selling end, Turkmens and Kazakhs predominate. Sixteen of the sales involved Kazakhs selling slaves to other Kazakhs, with another eight being sales in which the buyers were Kazakhs and the sellers were, based on context clues, very likely other Kazakhs. Another eleven sales involved Turkmens selling slaves to Kazakhs. There were two sales by Turkmens to other Turkmens, two by Kazakhs to Karakalpaks, and two by Karakalpaks to Kazakhs. In all, among the sixty-three detailed sales, these sources document fifty buyers from nomadic or semi-nomadic groups (Turkmens, Kazakhs, Karakalpaks); at least thirty-six sellers from these groups; and no less than thirty-three cases in which both seller and buyer were from one of these (generally nonsedentary) groups. The predominance of urban centers – Khiva, Bukhara, or others – is nowhere in evidence, nor is the predominance of urban, sedentary traders.

Four brief examples, all of which will be drawn, like the biographies of ʿAbdullāh and Kalbay, from the autumn of 1852, will give some further idea of how these slaves changed hands beyond the urban, sedentary sphere: (1) A Turkmen whose name is recorded as Kul-Murat Sagdiev was twenty-five years old when he was interviewed by border officials. After the death of his parents, he passed into the care of his brother, who quickly sold him to a Kazakh for a camel and two horses. This owner surrendered him to the Russian authorities, and Sagdiev requested of them that he be sent back to his original homeland.[30]

(2) An Afghan, whose name was illegibly recorded, was forty-five years old when he was interviewed by border officials. He did not know the details of his original captivity, only that Turkmens sold him to a man named Khuday-Berdi for sixty *tilla*s, and that this man resold him, when he was four years old, to a Kazakh, for the same amount. He lived with this owner for the next thirty-seven years. He was married to a Kazakh of the Bayulï clan, and he had three sons, two daughters, and his own *kibitka* (yurt) among the Kazakhs. His owner presented him to the Russian authorities, who formally freed him, but he requested to be sent back to live with his present family among the Kazakhs.[31]

[30] TsGAKaz 4.1.3646, f. 47b. [31] TsGAKaz 4.1.3646, ff. 47b–48a.

(3) A Karakalpak whose name is recorded as Mamandat Imamaliev was thirty years old when he was interviewed by border officials. After the death of his parents, he likewise passed into the care of his brother, who sold him for 100 sheep to a Kazakh, with whom he "traveled" for ten years. At the time of interview, he had a wife and a son among the Kazakhs. His owner surrendered him to the Russian authorities, who granted him his freedom, but he requested that he be returned to his home among the Kazakhs.[32]

(4) An Afghan whose name is recorded as Midman was thirty-four years old when he was interviewed by border officials. He relates that he was originally from Herat. Nineteen years prior, he had been tending to some cattle when he was taken captive by Turkmens. These Turkmens carried him along with them for the next two years before finally selling him to a Kazakh for forty [?] sheep. He lived with this owner for the next fourteen years before being presented by that same owner to the Russian authorities. Midman did not wish to be returned to his original homeland, and requested that he be sent back among the Kazakhs.[33]

Despite the scarce mention of Khiva and Bukhara in these sources, it may be wise to assume that those sales involving sedentary Khivans and Bukharans took place in or near a town, for the simple fact that townsmen did not often venture out into the hinterlands unless joining a caravan. But in those cases when Kazakhs sold slaves to other Kazakhs (for example), it is equally likely that these sales took place in the steppe. Transport to a town prior to sale is never mentioned in such cases, nor would it be necessary: not only did neighbors trade with one-another beyond the bazaars, but it turns out that the bazaars themselves – and urban spaces more generally – were not as essential to the slave trade as they were elsewhere in the Muslim world. As we shall see, this hypothesis is borne out by the available descriptions of urban slave-trading in Central Asia.

THE SLAVE TRADE OBSERVED

Most of the eyewitness reportage on urban slave-trading in the cities of Khiva and Bukhara concern the latter, given the relative inaccessibility of Khiva (and Khwarazm as a whole) for European travelers. Notorious as it was as a hub of the slave trade, the city of Khiva remained fundamentally obscure to most Western explorers and diplomats well into the mid-nineteenth century.

[32] TsGAKaz 4.1.3646, f. 47a. [33] TsGAKaz 4.1.3646, ff. 48a–48b.

A powerful indication of this obscurity comes in the form of an annotated map of the town that was published in the Russian journal *Syn otechestva* in 1842. Here, this map, which in its sparseness resembles a Piet Mondrian painting *sans* color, is presented on the pretext that it should help provide some military knowledge in support of Russian expeditions, since the Russians knew so little of the layout of the town. The problem – such as it is – is that the map itself was drafted more than a hundred years prior, not long before Nādir Shah's troops caused significant damage to the city. The idea that this map from 1740 should offer valuable military intelligence to the armies of 1842 may lead us to suspect that few Russians had, in the intervening years, become intimate with the city (except under circumstances of captivity), and that fewer still would have personally observed slave-dealing there.[34]

The earliest eyewitness account which I have yet seen of an actual Khivan slave-bazaar is that of Murav'ev, published in 1822. His description is very concise indeed, and it is not clear if he is describing a scene he saw for himself. Of Iranian captives coming to Khiva, he writes, "On arrival at Khiva their owner sets himself down with them in the market, and purchasers surround him, inspecting and examining the poor wretches, and haggling about their prices, as if they were buying horses. Sometimes the Turcomans kidnap them out of Khiva and take them back to their parents in Persia, who are often able to pay them handsomely. During my stay in Khiva several such batches were brought into the market, sold, and taken off to the villages."[35] Though Murav'ev had much to say about the trade in slaves and their experience of captivity, he had nothing more to say about the spaces where they were sold. As far as I have seen, there would not be anything like another eyewitness report on a Khivan slave-bazaar for nearly four decades thereafter.

The next account I have found – and perhaps the first which truly resembles eyewitness reportage – is by N. Zalesov, from his 1859 "Letter from Khiva." The passage is striking for its luridness; for our purposes, it is still more striking for the modest scale of the bazaar itself, and its scant offerings:

> Not far from the court there is a small pool, bounded on all sides by high buildings, among which a narrow passage serves as the only throughway. Arriving at this pool,

[34] "Khiva za sto let nazad," *Syn otechestva* 1 (1842), 33–39. Many Tatars and Bashkirs from Russian dominions had been there, either as residents or traders, but I am not aware of any substantial written records of Khiva by nineteenth-century Tatar or Bashkir observers.

[35] Murav'ev, *Muraviev's Journey to Khiva through the Turcoman County*, 58.

you will find yourself in a slave-market, which is mostly supplied with Persian captives, male and female, recently delivered here by Turkmens, though the trade for this commodity decreased significantly during the Turkmen revolt, and throughout the period of our stay in Khiva, we saw in the market only an old women of around 60 years old, two boys between 9 and 12, and a lovely girl who was about 14 but already perfectly formed. All of these unfortunates sat in the aforesaid lane leading to the pool, which was fenced off with sticks. With the arrival of a purchaser for a male or female slave, [this purchaser] would be conducted to an inner [part of] the market, where, in specially-arranged rooms, they would undress and examine the goods in every detail. Among the male [slaves], attention is paid to the firmness of their muscles; among the women, to their beauty and litheness of figure. When we examined the market, the girl for sale looked at us coquettishly and it seemed that she wanted very much to strike the fancy of the young "Urus" [Russian] rather than some old Uzbek. The girl was assigned a price of 30 *tilla* (60 silver rubles), but the acquisition of her – as with the other slaves – was permitted only for a Muslim.[36]

Another decade would evidently pass before any traveler offered further observations about the specifics of a Khivan slave-bazaar, and we have reason to doubt that the traveler in question – Arminius Vambery – actually saw the market with his own eyes. While listing the various bazaars of Khiva in his *Travels in Central Asia*, Vambery writes: "I must also class amongst the bazaars the Kitchik Kervanserai, where the slaves brought by the Teke and the Yomuts are exposed for sale. But for this article of business Khiva itself could not exist, as the culture of the land is entirely in the hands of the slaves."[37] This is all Vambery has to say about the bazaar, though he elsewhere dedicated ample space to discussing the plight of Iranian captives in the region. Indeed, he is one of our most impassioned commentators on the subject. Had he seen the bazaar for himself, we can be sure he would have provided more detail than this. His comment is helpful nevertheless, as it identifies the site of sales not as a typical bazaar, but rather as a caravanserai – a hint, perhaps, that slave-trading was the sort of thing which tended to take place in venues with interior rooms and out-of-the-way dwelling spaces.

Amazingly, this appears to be the full extent of our eyewitness reportage on Khiva's slave-bazaars. In all, firsthand evidence regarding the nature of those market-spaces is inconclusive – despite a general sense of certainty among sources (especially those who never saw the bazaar) that, as V. A. Tugan-Mirza-Baranovskii put it, "Until 1873, the main locale for

[36] N. Zalesov, "Pis'mo iz Khivy," *Voennyi sbornik* 1 (1859), 285.
[37] Arminius Vambery, *Travels in Central Asia* (New York: Harper & Bros., 1865), 380.

the sale of slaves was in Khiva, in whose markets one could always meet with Tekes trafficking in this commodity."[38]

We are more fortunate when it comes to eyewitness reportage on the slave-bazaar of Bukhara. One of the earliest accounts of the bazaar, offered by the English explorer Alexander Burnes, gives a wealth of detail:

> I took an early opportunity of seeing the slave-bazar of Bokhara, which is held every Saturday morning. The Uzbeks manage all their affairs by means of slaves, who are chiefly brought from Persia by the Toorkmuns. Here these poor wretches are exposed for sale, and occupy thirty or forty stalls, where they are examined like cattle, only with this difference, that they are able to give an account of themselves viva voce. On the morning I visited the bazar, there were only six unfortunate beings, and I witnessed the manner in which they are disposed of. They are first interrogated regarding their parentage and capture, and if they are Mahommedans, that is, Soonees. The question is put in that form, for the Uzbeks do not consider a Shiah to be a true believer; with them, as with the primitive Christians, a sectary- is more odious than an unbeliever. After the intended purchaser is satisfied of the slave being an infidel (kaffir), he examines his body, particularly noting if he be free from leprosy, so common in Toorkistan, and then proceeds to bargain for his price. Three of the Persian boys were for sale at thirty tillas of gold apiece; and it was surprising to see how contented the poor fellows sat under their lot. I heard one of them telling how he had been seized south of Meshid, while tending his flocks. Another, who overheard a conversation among the by-standers, regarding the scarcity of slaves that season, stated, that a great number had been taken. His companion said with some feeling, "You and I only think so, because of our own misfortune; but these people must know better." There was one unfortunate girl, who had been long in service, and was now exposed for sale by her master, because of his poverty. I felt certain that many a tear had been shed in the court where I surveyed the scene; but I was assured from every quarter that slaves are kindly treated ...[39]

In this account, it sounds as if the bazaar in question was capable of accommodating a fair amount of merchandise, with thirty or forty stalls available. But again, as with the extant descriptions of the Khivan markets, our eyewitness saw just a few captives for sale. We see not the faintest glimmer of the kinds of teeming slave-bazaars for which Istanbul (for example) was known. As with Zalesov's visit to Khiva, it appears that Burnes visited Bukhara during a low point in the trade, a season when slaves for sale were generally scarce.

[38] V. A. Tugan-Mirza-Baranovskii, *Russkie v Akhal-Teke* (St. Pb, 1881), 71.
[39] Alexander Burnes, *Travels into Bokhara*, Vol. 2 (London: John Murray, 1839), 241–242.

Another traveler of the early 1830s – P. I. Demaisons, sent to Bukhara to secure the release of Russian captives – offers some further information about the structure of a Bukharan slave-bazaar, though there is no indication that he saw one for himself. He writes: "In the dirty yard by the Registan there is a slave-market. It is open at dawn on Mondays and Thursdays, usually [staying open] for no more than three hours. Here they merely exhibit the slaves, and the commercial transactions are almost always concluded in the caravanserais, where those who come to Bukhara to sell these unfortunates reside."[40] Demaisons later identifies the caravanserai by name: the Sarāy-i pā-yi astāna (literally, "Palace at the Foot of the Threshhold," or simply "Gateside Palace").[41]

Concise as it is, the information Demaisons offers here is significant: slaves, he tells us, were not actually sold at the bazaar, which served merely as a showroom. The fact that much of the trade took place in peripheral spaces, beyond the public eye, is likewise confirmed by Vambery, who writes:

> The sale [of slaves] takes place either in the dealers' magazines, or in some market-place outside the town, to which place the goods are removed some days previous. The most important depots are to be found in the Khanat of Khiva, first of all at the capital, then in Hezaresp, in Gazavat, in Giirlen, and in Kohne. Besides these, every place of any pretensions has a retail dealer, who is in connection with the large wholesale dealers, or sells goods on commission. In Bokhara is to be mentioned first of all Karakul, and next the capital; besides these, Karshi and Tchihardjuy.[42]

The cumulative impression here is of a trade which was perhaps deliberate in its remove from the public eye. The general absence of slave traders from the main bazaars is nowhere more palpable than in the account of Mohan Lal, the brilliant Kashmiri *munshī* who served as an aid to Alexander Burnes during his voyage to Bukhara. Lal, like Burnes and Vambery, was repulsed by the trade in Iranian slaves, and dedicated extensive commentary to the subject in his travelogue. He too interviewed a number of Iranian slaves, and he extensively describes the circumstances of their captivity, both in specific and general terms. He was also

[40] P. I. Demezon and I. V. Vitkevich, *Zapiski o Bukharskom khanstve*, N. A. Khalfin ed. (Moscow, 1983), 57. (The French-born Demaisons and the Polish-born Witkiewicz published their travel accounts in Russian, and their reportage can thus be found under their "Russified" names, Demezon and Vitkevich.)

[41] *Zapiski o Bukharskom khanstve*, 59. This information was confirmed in the account by Demaisons' contemporary, Witkiewicz: *Zapiski o Bukharskom khanstve*, 101.

[42] Arminius Vambery, *Sketches of Central Asia* (London: W.H. Allen & Co., 1868), 217.

a connoisseur of Central Asian bazaars: in the course of his travels, Lal visited bazaars in nearly every major town he passed through; he comments on the bazaars of Charjui, Mashhad, Bala Khayaban, Turbat, Herat, Shikarpur, Ghazni, Jalalabad, Balahisar, Kabul, Kulum, Balkh, Karasan, and, of course, Bukhara. But for all his time in the bazaars, he reports only a single eyewitness experience of slave-dealing, which he observed in Qarshi, a town identified by Vambery as one of the major slave "depots" of the region. Lal writes:

On my return from the bazar, I asked my companion to shew me the house of a slave-dealer; so I was conducted through numerous hot streets, and after a short walk, I got into the caravansarae where the merchant resided. He received me with courtesy and sent for three women from the room next to his own. They sat unveiled, and their master asked me which of the three I liked the best. I pretended to select the younger one; she had regular features and most agreeable manners, her stature was elegant, and her personal attractions great. On my choosing her, the others retired to their lodgings, and she followed them, but sat in a separate room guarded by an old slave. The merchant told me to go to her, speak to and content her. After a good deal of conversation, she felt pleased with my choice; but told me to swear not to sell her again. She was thirteen years of age, and an inhabitant of Chatrar, a place near Badakhshan. She said that she belonged to a large family, and had been carried off by the ruler of the country, who reduced her to slavery. Her eyes filled with tears, and she asked me to release her soon from the hands of the oppressive Uzbeg. As my object was only to examine the feelings of the slave-dealer, and also to gratify my curiosity, and not to purchase her, I came back to my camp without bidding farewell to the merchant.[43]

In this account too, we find the trade based not at the bazaars, but in the chambers of a caravanserai, seemingly well out of the public eye. Again, the scale of the trade is strikingly small: here, only three women for sale.

One might expect to gain further details on Khivan and Bukharan slave-markets from freed Russian slaves, many of whose biographies were preserved either in the Russian press or in Russian travelogues. But here too, eyewitness reportage is scarce, and by the early 1840s the trade in captive Russians had subsided so much that the Russian officer I. F. Blaramberg wrote of it in his journals as a distant memory: "August 21st, [1843]. I went to Orsk. Upon arrival at that place, I visited the exchange yard, the hospital, and the Cossack settlements, and I met Major Lobov, who was for many years a slave in Bukhara. When he was just a young man, he was abducted by the Kirghiz and sold into slavery. He told me horrifying details

[43] Mohan Lal, *Travels in the Panjab, Afghanistan, and Turkistan, to Balk, Bokhara, and Herat; and a Visit to Great Britain and Germany* (London: W.H. Allen, 1846), 122.

about the treatment of Russian slaves in Bukhara and Khiva in those days. Thank God those days are long gone!"[44]

In the 1860s and 1870s, the Russian conquests further reduced the visibility of slave-trading. Captain L. F. Kostenko, reporting on the Russian mission to Bukhara in 1870, evidently learned that the slave-market there was no longer in existence: "There had previously in Bukhara been a slave-bazaar, in which male and female Persians were sold like beasts of burden. But with the Russian occupation of Samarkand, when many slaves fled from Bukhara to this city, where they were freed by the Russian government, the slave market in Bukhara has been discontinued, owing to bidders' fears that whatever goods they purchase can escape."[45] Emil Schmidt reported a similar state of affairs in Khiva, where slavery was formally abolished in 1873: "Latterly … the slave trade had considerably diminished, and a thousand individuals per annum were no longer brought to the Khivan markets."[46] The open trade in slaves, then, which had evidently never been especially visible to foreign travelers in the region, was by the late nineteenth century assured to remain mostly out of sight.

THE SLAVE TRADE CONTINUES

According to some Russian officials as well as foreign observers, the conquest of Khiva in 1873, which resulted in a proclamation of abolition jointly prepared by General Kaufman and the Khivan khan, signaled not only the emancipation of Khwarazm's slaves but the effective end of the region's slave trade. In fact, the reality was not so simple.

First, we must observe that, although the Russian conquest of Bukhara in the late 1860s had resulted in a number of Bukharan concessions rendered in ambitious treaties, an order of general emancipation was not among them. It was only in the autumn of 1873 – some five years after Bukhara's conquest – that, by Russian demand, the universal emancipation of slavery became a law in the territory. The enforcement of the law involved a striking concession on the part of the Russian Empire, however: General Kaufman, the architect of the treaty, allowed the Bukharan Amīr an entire decade to provide complete emancipation, during which time all

44 I. F. Blaramberg, *Vospominaniia* (Moscow: Glavnaia redaktsiia vostochnoi literatury; Tsentral'naia Aziia istochnikakh i materialakh XIX-nachala XX veka, 1978), 252.

45 Kostenko, *Puteshestvie v Bukharu russkoi missii v 1870 godu* (St. Pb, 1871), 94.

46 Schmidt, *The Russian Expedition to Khiva in 1873*, trans. P. Mosa (Calcutta: Foreign Department Press, 1876), 122.

slaves would stay with their present masters. Attempts to escape to freedom were punishable by death.[47] In all, we find here a remarkably hesitant approach to emancipation for an "abolitionist" Empire.

Moreover, while it was the liberation of specifically *Russian* slaves that, as Morrison observes, was frequently evoked to justify military expansion, multiple eyewitness accounts confirm that Russian slaves were already quite scarce in the khanates by the mid-nineteenth century. Jan Prosper Witkiewicz wrote that "There are not many Russians in the Khanate; perhaps one could count up to 50 of them, and these ones are elderly, imported some time ago." Some twenty of them, he estimated, belonged to the Khan.[48] Alexander Burnes, who likewise visited the khanate in the 1830s, put the number of Russian slaves at not more than 130.[49] The Russian officer L. F. Kostenko, reporting on Bukhara circa 1870, wrote: "Aside from fugitives, there are still Russian captives in Bukhara, but now they are not many – two or three people. Previously there had been many more. In 1869 the Amīr sent them to Charjui where they all died, due to the swampy climate and foul accommodations."[50] As for Khwarazm, as Kaufman and his forces approached the city, the Khan made a desperate attempt to placate him and stave off invasion by rounding up and sending to the General what he claimed to be all of the Russian slaves that remained in the khanate. They totaled twenty-one people in all.[51]

Notwithstanding the scarcity of Russian slaves to liberate, popular opinion that conquest was necessary to end Russian enslavement in the khanates was rooted in a widespread feeling in Russia of perennial victimhood on the frontiers. This feeling manifested itself, as Bruce Grant has shown, in a vast popular literature, consisting of everything from short stories and novels to popular songs and ballads, all concerning Russian captivity in the East, generally among Muslims.[52] To the extent that these captivity narratives had historical roots, these roots might be found in the long, traumatic period during which Russians were regularly captured and

[47] Seymour Becker, *Russia's Protectorates in Central Asia: Bukhara and Khiva, 1865–1924* (New York: Routledge, 2004 [1968]), 67–68.

[48] Ia. P. Vitkevich, *Zapiski o Bukharskom khanstve* (Moscow: Nauka, 1983), 115.

[49] Alexander Burnes, *Travels into Bokhara*, Vol. 2 (London: Carey & Hart, 1835), 115.

[50] L. F. Kostenko, *Puteshestvie v Bukharu russkoi missiiv 1870 godu* (St. Pb, 1871), 107.

[51] MS IVAN Uz No. 12581, f. 42a; cf. also MacGahan, *Campaigning on the Oxus, and the Fall of Khiva* (London: Sampson Low, 1874), 20.

[52] Bruce Grant, *The Captive and the Gift: Cultural Histories of Sovereignty in Russia and the Caucasus* (Ithaca, NY: Cornell University Press, 2009); see also Kurtynova-D'Herlugnan, *The Tsar's Abolitionists*, 37–72.

carried off by the soldiers and raiders of the Crimean Khanate. Up to 200,000 Muscovites were estimated to have been taken into slavery by Crimean Tatar and Noghay captors between 1600 and 1650.[53] The total number of Ukrainians, Russians, and Poles captured by Tatars between 1468 and 1694 has been estimated at 1,750,000.[54] As recently as the eighteenth century, Russians were frequently captured along the steppe frontier and the eastern Caspian shores; many were ransomed, but some were sold into slavery.

By the mid-nineteenth century, the age of Russian enslavement had mostly passed. Meanwhile, as we shall see, the trade in Iranian slaves, who constituted the vast majority of slaves held in the khanates, seems to have continued in some quarters even after the fall of Khiva. Nevertheless, Russian military presence in the sedentary heartland of Central Asia does appear to have occasioned some changes in the volume of the slave trade. One significant change evidently concerned the demographics of the highest registers of power in Bukhara, as many functions of state were carried out by slaves. P. Shubinskii described the alleged inconveniences the Bukharan Amīr 'Abd al-Aḥad (r. 1885–1910) occasioned for himself in proposing general abolition:

> Sayyid 'Abd al-Ahad passed this measure, and brought upon himself some very significant challenges, since a considerable portion of the Bukharan military and almost all of the minor court officials and palace servants were slaves. Receiving their freedom, all of these people hastened to return to their homeland, and in their place unfamiliar salaried people had to be recruited, the maintenance of whom brought about substantial new expenditures.[55]

It is unlikely that "all" of the slaves who had been serving as court officials – however minor – would have departed upon receiving their freedom, and we have no further evidence, so far as I have seen, to support the claim. Nevertheless, it is plausible that manumission, if it had really been effective, would have had a cumulatively dramatic effect on the military, on the government, and on the domestic sphere among the nobility. But a trade that occurred largely in out-of-the-way spaces – rural nomadic settlements, backrooms in caravanserais – must have been difficult to abolish while demand for slaves still existed. Indeed, according to N. P. Stremoukhov,

[53] Brian L. Davies, *Warfare, State and Society on the Black Sea Steppe, 1500–1700* (New York: Routledge, 2007), 25.

[54] Alan W. Fisher, "Muscovy and the Black Sea Slave Trade," *Canadian-American Slavic Studies* 6:4 (1972), 575–94; see also Clarence-Smith, *Islam and the Abolition of Slavery*, 13.

[55] Shubinskii, "Ocherki bukhary," *Istoricheskii vestnik* 7 (1892), 125.

who traveled to Bukhara in 1873, demand still existed, and it was still satisfied:

Officially, the trade in slaves was banned in Bukhara by the command of the Emir, and the caravanserai where slaves used to be sold is now permanently closed. Violators of this command are subject to punishment, a fine of 1000 *tenga*, and six months in prison. Even so, a large number of people (mostly merchants) engage secretly, in their own homes, in the buying and selling of slaves. As before, the main suppliers of slaves can be identified as Turkmens, whose raids have not stopped. Most of those who fall into captivity are Persians (I have already said that there are very many Persians among the troops of the Bukharan Emir, and these are all unfortunate ones who had been captured by Turkmens). But especially vast is the traffic in women: even those from within our own borders are taken by Bukharans [sic], by means of deception, using all sorts of tricks; and they are secretly sold in Bukhara, and this is done so discretely that there is absolutely no way to keep track of them. The traffic in women is conducted predominantly by Tatars.[56]

Given the occult nature of the practices Stremoukhov describes, it is unfortunate that he provides no hint as to how he gathered the foregoing information. He testifies, in any event, that the trade continued not only among merchants, but at the highest levels of state:

Although a formal ban exists, it exists only nominally, as the very Emir himself patronizes this despicable trade. Two things impel him in this respect: first, this trade provides him with recruits for the army; and second, by these means he can acquire for himself young and beautiful women, and get rid of those of whom he's grown tired. For the purchase and sale of slaves, Muzaffar maintains certain secret agents, who he pays very handsomely.[57]

Along with these bold claims, Stremoukhov provides one anecdote concerning the continuance of the trade which was drawn from his own personal experience:

On the morning of the 6th of June, some poor old man dressed in rags . . . ran to my tent and began asking for my protection. He turned out to be an Uzbek, and complained that two of his daughters, despite the publicized prohibition against selling slaves, had been forcibly captured and sold to a wealthy Bukharan who, paying no attention to the order of the kadis and the command of the Emir, did not want to return them to freedom at any cost.[58]

Elsewhere in Central Asia, travelers, military personnel, and other eyewitnesses were turning in similar reports. In Badakhshan, where Shiʿites

[56] N. P. Stremoukhov, "Poezdka v Bukharu," *Russkii vestnik*, 6 (1876), 690.
[57] Stremoukhov, "Poezdka v Bukharu," 690. [58] Stremoukhov, "Poezdka v Bukharu," 655.

had long been taken into captivity, and where groups of them had long been sent off into slavery as tribute to local Afghan rulers, the announcement of abolition from Kabul evidently had mixed effects. According to Thomas Edward Gordon, the more visible forms of trafficking had ceased, but the trade went on:

Slavery still continues to be the curse of many of the Shiah states round about Badakhshan. Notwithstanding its prohibition by the Amir of Kabul, the disgraceful trade in human beings, with all its attendant crime and cruelty, still flourishes ... The open slave-market certainly is closed, but beyond that nothing seemingly is done to suppress the shameful and horrible traffic, which is otherwise carried on as briskly as ever. The Affghan occupation of Badakhshan has had the good effect of abolishing the tribute in slaves which used to be demanded and enforced by the ruling Sunni Mirs from their feudatories with subjects professing the heretical Shiah creed. Futteh Ali Shah of Wakhan told me that the tribute he paid in September 1873 was the first ever given of which slaves did not form a part.[59]

It would not be long before a traveler attempted to conduct a more intensive and personal investigation into the persistence of the slave trade. The traveler in question was the American diplomat Eugene Schuyler, who visited Bukhara in his Central Asian travels, having departed St. Petersburg for the region in March of 1873. He made his first attempt to observe the trade when he arrived at Qarshi, the town whose slave-dealing had been noted by Vambery and Mohan Lal. Here, he saw nothing: "I asked to see the slave market and was shown the sarai, but saw no slaves, though I was told that the next day (Tuesday), being bazaar day, some would probably be brought in for sale."[60] He apparently never had a chance to return the next day, but in the town of Bukhara he would resume his search. His curiosity was piqued by a disparity between the claims of some Russian officials and those of local merchants and others he had met in the region. He writes:

In visiting Bukhara I was especially anxious to learn something about the slave trade, and if possible to see for myself what was going on. The Russian authorities had expressed their desire that the slave trade should cease, and had been of course informed by the Bukharians that it had long since come to an end. Nearly all the Russian officials who had been in Bukhara had been deceived in this respect, and an official report had been made to General Kaufmann that the slave trade no longer

[59] Edward Gordon, *The Roof of the World: Being a Narrative of a Journey over the High Plateau of Tibet to the Russian frontier and the Oxus Sources on the Pamir* (Edinburgh: Edmonston and Douglas, 1876), 147.

[60] Schuyler, *Turkistan: Notes of a Journey in Russian Turkistan, Khokand, Bukhara, and Kuldja* (New York: Scribner, Armstrong, 1876), 79.

existed there. Merchants, however, told me that they had frequently seen public sales of slaves in the bazaar, and my interpreter said that, on two visits to Bukhara during the preceding year, he had seen the slave market filled with Persians who were dying of cholera and hunger, for, in the panic caused by the epidemic, they had not been fed; and the Agent of the Ministry of Finance had been able, in the spring of 1872, to see slaves publicly exposed for sale. He had made a report of this, but the matter had been passed over without notice by the Russian authorities.[61]

Schuyler knew that he could not reveal his intentions to the Bukharan officials around him, since they would be likely to deny the existence of the trade. Seizing an opportune moment, he asked someone less beholden to the Bukharan government whether he might be shown a slave-market, and he was promptly taken to "a large sarai," where he proceeded up the stairs into a gallery and found "several rooms, some of which were locked, and a number of slaves – two little girls of about four years old, two or three boys of different ages, and a number of old men – all Persians." Schuyler reports that there were no women in sight, as both young women and old – excepting, apparently, the very young girls – were purchased immediately upon their arrival in Bukhara. The slaves were shown off by "an old Turcoman, who acted as a broker," and who explained to Schuyler that "the market was rather dull just then, but that a large caravan would probably arrive in the course of a few days." At this point, curious to learn about how such sales were conducted, Schuyler began bargaining for a "lively looking lad of fifteen" who, he was told, had been taken captive near Astarabad five months previously.[62]

The ensuing negotiations drew a small crowd: "I was immediately asked to take a seat on a mat," Schuyler writes, "and the room soon filled with people, all of whom seemed to take much more interest in the sale than did the boy himself, who did not understand what was being said, the conversation being in Turki. The first price asked was more than 1,000 tengas, which I gradually reduced to 850 tengas; the seller constantly dilating on the good points of the boy, what an excellent jigit he would make, and so on, the bystanders joining in on one side or the other."[63] At first, Schuyler vacillates on the price, and searches the building's other rooms for other

[61] Schuyler, *Turkistan*, 100–101. [62] Schuyler, *Turkistan*, 100–101.

[63] The comparatively astronomical price of the slave will be noticed: unless we can assume severe currency depreciation in 1870s Bukhara – the likes of which I have not heard – the price of 1000 *tengas* for a slave is roughly thirty-three times greater than the historical market norm. Perhaps the dealer was relying on Schuyler's unfamiliarity with the usual price-range. Schuyler shows at least some awareness of the odd pricing, however: "I thought that 850 tengas was too much to pay for the lad, especially as I had no desire to buy him; at the same time, the wistful looks of the boy, who seemed very anxious to be

slaves. When he and his guide find none, he finally agrees to buy the boy, evidently for 850 *tenga*, planning to take him to Russia and, eventually, to secure his safe return to Iran. At this point he is confronted with "a broker, a swarthy, thick-set fellow from Kara-kul, a well-known slave dealer," who tells him that a rival bidder had agreed to pay 900 *tenga* for the boy, along with two "gowns" on top of that. An additional complication, according to this "broker," was that the boy's real owner was not present, so that he himself had no right to part with the boy on his owner's behalf – the result being that Schuyler agreed to pay a portion of the price to the man as an advance in order to secure the later delivery of the boy, whom he failed to take with him.

In short, Schuyler was swindled. He never received the boy, nor, apparently, did he ever get back the money he had already paid for him. He sent an acquaintance back to the place of sale two days later in order to seek out the boy, but this man found only two very young girls and one other boy for sale.[64] Later, Schuyler mentions his adventure to a Bukharan official, who insists that the slave trade had indeed been ended, and that these few items of sale were nothing more than remnants. "I told him," Schuyler writes, "that I did not doubt his words, although, at the same time, it appeared very strange to me in this case, that when a caravan of sixty slaves had arrived at Bukhara the night before, at nine o'clock, he himself had given order that it should remain outside the Kara-kul gate, in order that I should not see it." Schuyler did not see it, nor would he ever see it, but by his own account the official did not deny the accusation.[65]

Undeterred, Schuyler resolves to buy another slave. He sends his wagon-driver, Pulat, to search the town for one to buy. Pulat spends the day searching, and returns the same evening with the news that he had found a boy for sale, about seven or eight years old, offered for 700 *tenga* "and a good gown." Schuyler buys him, and he turns out to be "very small and feeble, although intelligent," a Persian from Maymana who had been taken captive by Salar Turkmens some three years earlier. According to Schuyler, the boy had little recollection of his parents, and seemed not to know his own name, in light of which he "took the liberty, which in these countries is always allowed on the purchase of a slave, and named him Hussein." He managed to retain this boy, despite the efforts of the boy's former owner to steal him back (fearing, after the sale, that he would be

bought, smote my conscience a little, and I asked for the refusal of him at that price, which was given" (Schuyler, *Turkistan*, 102).

64 Schuyler, *Turkistan*, 105–106. 65 Schuyler, *Turkistan*, 104–105.

punished by officials for selling a slave to a foreigner who could expose the ostensibly illegal trade).[66] Schuyler later tells us that his purchase caused a stir in Samarqand and Bukhara, with some notables further denying the existence of the trade and others glad to have it exposed.[67] Ultimately, Russian authorities seem to have taken the reports of slave-trading in Bukhara seriously: after the fall of Khiva, the Russian Court Councilor K. V. Struve negotiated a treaty with the Amīr, which resulted in a new injunction, signed in the autumn of 1873, that the slave trade be ended in Bukharan domains. This action, according to Schuyler, was still insufficient: "Unfortunately, the Russians have always found it more easy to make treaties in Central Asia than to enforce their observance, and I have received information from Russians as well as from natives that since this treaty the slave-trade has rather increased than diminished, although slaves are no longer sold publicly in the open market, as was done when I was in Bukhara."[68]

Schuyler was perhaps the most deeply invested among foreign observers investigating the persistence of the slave trade. There is likewise, however, significant evidence from native Central Asian sources that confirms the continuation of the trade after the Russian-fostered "official abolitions" of the 1870s. When it comes to Bukhara, for example, we can observe the persistence of slavery through the lens of Islamic law, thanks to a document collection published by Turgun Faiziev. This collection comprises some fifty-two documents, most of a legal nature, including everything from bills of sale to manumission contracts and correspondences among Bukharan notables concerning slaves. The compilation contains no fewer than seventeen such documents dating from the year 1886 alone.[69] One document contains a brief register of the names and jobs of slave-boys – fifteen in all – owned by the Amīr, some serving in the royal household and some in the government chambers.[70] In another document, two Muslim notables write to the Amīr notifying him that one Sardar Ishāqjān, residing along with "several households" of people in Qubadiyan province, remains in possession of three male and seven female slaves, despite the fact that these slaves had been freed by official decree. Evidently, the slaves had come before

[66] Schuyler, *Turkistan*, 108–109. Later, he brought "Hussein" back to Russia, where he saw to his education.
[67] Schuyler, *Turkistan*, 310. [68] Schuyler, *Turkistan*, 310–311.
[69] T. Faiziev, *Buxoro feodal jamiyatida qullardan foydalanishga doir hujjatlar (XIX asr)* (Tashkent: Fan, 1990), 115–127, documents no. 26–42.
[70] Faiziev, *Buxoro feodal jamiyatida qullardan foydalanishga doir hujjatlar (XIX asr)*, 117–118, document no. 30.

a Bukharan general and a Russian official and explained that their masters had agreed to set them free, but that these masters were declining to issue them manumission documents in order to make their freedom legitimate within the context of Islamic law. The masters were duly ordered to issue the necessary paperwork.[71] The implications are remarkable: the official decree was not enough; for these slaves, and perhaps also for their owners, in order for manumission to be valid, it needed to issue – in the traditional fashion – from legitimate Islamic juridical authorities.[72]

Other documents preserve petitions requesting that the Amīr validate and ensure the release of slaves, in keeping with his general manumission decree. There are two ways of understanding such petitions: on the one hand, the fact that denizens of Bukhara felt that they could affect change by appealing to the highest authority might hint at a degree of action on the part of the Amīr and other high officials when it came to enforcing manumission; on the other hand, the fact that these same residents felt they needed to address their petitions to the royal court indicates the failure of more "local" organs of change, and for each petition naming a particular slave, we must wonder how many other slaves went unmentioned by any appeal.

CONCLUSION

Acknowledging that the slave trade appears to have persisted after the period of "official abolition," it is nevertheless difficult to get a sense of the scale of the commerce. As we have seen, even Schuyler – who, among our eyewitnesses, sought it out most intensively – saw no more than a few slaves being sold, and, like many others before him, he was informed that he had chosen an inauspicious day if he had wished to see many slaves for sale. Better that he should come back the next day; better that he should have come earlier. Not a single eye-witness, so far as I know, reported seeing a caravanserai or marketplace overflowing with victims of the trade. And yet none denied that the region itself was flush with slaves: However

[71] Faiziev, *Buxoro feodal jamiyatida qullardan foydalanishga doir hujjatlar (XIX asr)*, 127 (document no. 43).

[72] Similarly, concerning the French-sponsored abolition of slavery in the Comoro Islands in 1904, Gill Shepherd writes that "slaves were not freed, in Comorian eyes, by European emancipation decrees, but only by the individual action of their masters." Shepherd, "The Comorians and the East African Slave Trade," in James L. Watson, ed., *Asian and African Systems of Slavery* (Oxford: Basil Blackwell, 1980), 96; see also Clarence-Smith, *Islam and the Abolition of Slavery*, 147.

invisible their sale and exchange, they were visible at all levels of society, from the royal court to the nobles' estates to the tents of nomads.

In this disparity between the low visibility of the trade and the evident wealth of slaves, we can ascertain something of why the commerce would have been so difficult to stop. First, it appears that slave-selling did not tend to take place openly, in public markets and bazaars. Slaves were sometimes exhibited in such spaces, but it appears to have been more common for sales to take place in out-of-the-way spaces: in backrooms, or in the chambers of caravanserais. Granted, a shipment of sixty slaves may indeed have been waiting beyond the gates as Schuyler did his shopping, but the balance of our evidence points to the conclusion that slave-dealing took place predominantly in caravanserais, at least some of which were specially appointed for this sort of business.

If the trade in slaves was a business for caravans and their members – a proposition which makes intuitive sense, given the great distances the "merchandise" had to travel between, say, Khurasan and Bukhara, and the dangers of the road in between – then we might look to caravanserais, rather than the main bazaars of major towns, as our nexuses and points-of-sale as we attempt to recreate a "geography" of the slave trade in Central Asia. The region, moreover, was traversed by caravan routes, and dotted with so many caravanserais that, in the last decade, the United Nations Educational, Scientific and Cultural Organization (UNESCO) launched a multi-national project to inventory all of the caravanserai structures that can still be found there.[73] A map released by UNESCO reveals, by my count, more than two dozen known caravanserais stretching from Khurasan across the territory of the Khanates.[74] Presumably, dealers in slaves – or any other merchandise – could have stopped at any one of these that may have been operational in the nineteenth century, and plied their trade while in residence. This could help explain the dispersal of slaves across the rural landscape observed by Burnes as he traveled through a small village in the region: "Though the village in which we were now residing could not boast of more than twenty houses, there were yet eight Persian slaves; and these unfortunate men appear to be distributed in like proportion throughout the country."[75]

[73] *Inventory of Caravanserais in Central Asia* (UNESCO / Ecole d'Architecture Paris Val de Seine EVCAU Research Team, 2004).

[74] www.unesco.org/culture/dialogue/eastwest/caravan/countries.htm.

[75] Burnes, *Travels into Bokhara*, 342.

We may now recall the former slave Kalbay Hamzin whom we met earlier in this chapter. He was held for some time at the Khwarazmian village of Pars, which he describes as a two-day caravan journey from Urgench. Kalbay never mentions having been sold at Urgench, however, and when he was resold by his owner at Pars – to another "Khivan," and then to a Kazakh – we may ask ourselves whether it seems likely that each subsequent owner needed to travel to a major town in order to buy or sell him, when caravans of slave-dealers and other merchants were passing through the hinterlands all the while. The more likely site of sale would have been the caravanserai closest to where the owner lived, and only for some owners would this have meant towns like Khiva, Urgench, and Bukhara. All caravanserais were sites of commerce, and there is no reason to believe that slaves were different than any other commodity in terms of where they could be sold. Stopping the trade in slaves, in other words, would have involved, at the very least, patrolling the caravanserais. Beyond the caravanserais, moreover, there was slave-trading among nomads. Kazakhs of the remote steppe evidently exchanged slaves with other nomadic Kazakhs, and Turkmens did the same further south.

In short, the generally accepted view that the Russians ended the slave trade by enforced decree from the towns of Khiva and Bukhara becomes still harder to believe in light of contrary eyewitness evidence, and especially in light of native documents, dating from well beyond the 1870s, which prove that Islamic jurists were still receiving cases concerning slaves at that time and dealing with slavery in the familiar legal framework. When we turn to the geography and mobility of the trade itself, we can cast further doubt on the effectiveness of Russian-sponsored abolition. In light of the evidence that caravanserais served as points where slaves were trafficked, and in the absence of any evidence that the vast network of Central Asian caravanserais was patrolled by any "abolitionist" force (whether Russian or native), we should wonder how probable it is that dealers would have been caught with any frequency. Finally, in light of evidence suggesting that nomadic groups traded and sold slaves among themselves, we can easily understand why Russian authorities had to rely increasingly on native informants to track down offenders and free captives. While we cannot accept, for the reasons set out in this chapter, the proposition that Russian and locally fostered abolition actually stopped the slave trade, we cannot dismiss the numerous reports which suggest – contrary to Schuyler's claim – that the volume of the trade did indeed decline. To find the reasons for this decline, however, we must look beyond the bazaars, turning our attention from the urban centers and markets to those steppe and Iranian borderlands from which the supply of captives had long been taken.

Here, we have considered some major aspects of the trade in slaves across Central Asia. In the next chapter, we will explore the experience of slavery in the region through the eyes of a man who spent a decade in bondage.

3

From Despair to Liberation

Mīrzā Maḥmūd Taqī Āshtiyānī's Ten Years of Slavery

When Mīrzā Maḥmūd Taqī Āshtiyānī, an Iranian scribe, artist, and accountant (*karguzar*), arrived at his family home in Tehran in 1870, his loved ones may have thought they were looking at a ghost. Mīrzā Maḥmūd had been away for nearly a decade. He had fallen into captivity among a group of Sarïq Turkmens while accompanying the Qajar military in a campaign against Merv in 1860–61, and had spent the next ten years as a slave. After making his way back to freedom, he authored the richest firsthand account of Central Asian slavery in existence.[1] Having been enslaved both as a laborer in a Turkmen desert village and as a well-compensated servant of Bukharan elites, his decade-long ordeal offers us a window onto the remarkable diversity of experiences possible for slaves in the region. As we shall see, the many clever strategies Mīrzā Maḥmūd used in guiding his own fate, whether by manipulating his owners or by shrewdly deploying his artistic talents, likewise reveal something of the individual initiative slaves could exert to survive their ordeals and better their positions.

For the study of slaves' experiences in Central Asia, there is no better point of entry than Mīrzā Maḥmūd's account. Rather than breaking up the momentum of his narrative with analytical asides, this chapter will provide

[1] The first half of the work has been the subject of a recent paper by Arash Khazeni and Abbas Amanat: "The Steppe Roads of Central Asia and the Persian Captivity Narrative of Mahmud Mirza Taqi Ashtiyani," in Nile Green, ed., *Writing Travel in Central Asian History* (Bloomington, IN: Indiana University Press, 2014), 113–133. The authors highlight several important aspects of Mīrzā Maḥmūd's early ordeals, although they offer no discussion of the eventful years he spent in and around Bukhara, which constituted the majority of his time as a slave.

a detailed, uninterrupted retelling of Mīrzā Maḥmūd's ordeal, concluding with some thoughts on what his experiences can tell us about slavery in the region more generally.

MĪRZĀ MAḤMŪD'S STORY

Soon after taking Mīrzā Maḥmūd into captivity, the Sarïq Turkmens take his clothes. His proper hat is swapped for an ill-fitting hat that hangs over his eyes, and he is given an old green shawl – the shawl of a *sayyid* (an esteemed direct descendant of the Prophet Muḥammad). At first he declines to wear it, on the grounds that donning the attire of a *sayyid* is inappropriate for a man of a lesser lineage. For several days he attempts to make do without any covering at all, but eventually he caves in to the elements and takes to wearing the shawl, leading many of his fellow-travelers to assume – notwithstanding his vehement denials – that he is of sacred lineage.[2] As he marches through the desert in his green shawl, he has no way of knowing his ultimate destination. He knows only that slaves were sent off to all parts, urban and rural: Bukhara, Shirgen, Urgench, Labab, Khiva, Balkh, Qaraqul, and "other, worse places." Day by day, 200 or 300 individuals were sent off to slavery as if they were "ugly wares and dirty commercial goods."[3] For the time being, he would be the property of a Sarïq named Khan Muḥammad, who is determined to ransom him back to Iran for no less than 100 *ṭilla*s, a very large sum for any slave.

Khan Muḥammad refuses lesser offers, and he begins tormenting Mīrzā Maḥmūd in order to force him to correspond with Iranians in Mashhad to secure a higher ransom. Mīrzā Maḥmūd is shackled at night with stocks (*bukhaw-i pā*) on his legs, weighted ring-cuffs on his hands (*ṭās-i ḥalqa*), and a chain on his neck (*zanjīr*). The chains wound him where they dig into his skin, and he cannot sleep due to the excess of filth and lice (*chirk o shipish*). He is given no carpet or blanket to use at night, and his hat, which blackens from the smoke of the dwelling's wood-fire, is all he has with which to cover himself. He is given stale barley bread to eat, bread so hard that it cuts his mouth, though he observes that the Turkmens themselves partook of the same.[4]

[2] Āshtiyānī, *'Ibratnāma*, 27–28. To one supplicant he objected, "Do not call me a *sayyid*; for both you and me it is a sin" (*mārā sayyid magūyīd ke az barā-yi man o shomā har du taqsīr o gunāh ast*), but, despite his objections, some among the Sarïqs took to calling him "Sayyid Taqi."

[3] Āshtiyānī, *'Ibratnāma*, 28–29. (*kālā-i zisht va mutā'-i kaṣīf.*)

[4] Āshtiyānī, *'Ibratnāma*, 29–30.

Mīrzā Maḥmūd soon begins planning his escape. He and six others pool their resources to hire a guide, figuring that it is too dangerous to try to make their way alone to Herat, Mashhad, or Sarakhs. Mīrzā Maḥmūd secures a loan of 14 *ṭilla*s from his master, promising to pay him back 20 *ṭilla*s in one month's time – a hint of the privileges that could be enjoyed when a slave convinced a master of his or her talents. Altogether, the group of seven slaves gather over 90 *ṭilla*s, and a man named Rustam agrees to guide them. At the captives' prompting, Rustam swears on a Qur'ān and vows to divorce his own wife (*sawgand-i zan talāqī*) if he fails to live up to his end of the bargain. He receives 82 *ṭilla*s with which to buy horses for all involved, and another 10 *tilla*s as payment for his services. He returns with the horses, and the group sets off toward freedom. Just a few miles down the road, however, Rustam stops them. He asks for more money, for reasons that Mīrzā Maḥmūd cannot ascertain. Then Rustam disappears into the desert, leaving the group stranded. They return to their masters, who are fortunately unaware of the attempted escape.[5]

A month passes, and Mīrzā Maḥmūd's debt to his master comes due, but – to the slave's good fortune – Khan Muḥammad is thoroughly distracted: He is enraptured by a "beautiful" ten- or twelve-year-old slave boy named Shahbāz, whom he had recently purchased. Khan Muḥammad dresses the boy in such fine clothes that it is impossible to tell that he is a slave (*hālat-i asīrī dar u hīch ma'lūm nabūd*). He takes the boy everywhere, and, in Mīrzā Maḥmūd's words, intended to "tame" him and use him for sodomy (*livāṭ*). He prepares the boy's bedding close to his own, and sleeps beside him. Mīrzā Maḥmūd, meanwhile, finds it difficult to sleep more than a couple of hours a night, and on one sleepless night he hears the boy weeping. He attempts to comfort the boy, but suddenly Khan Muḥammad arrives and beats Mīrzā Maḥmūd for bothering his beloved slave. The next morning, Shahbāz comes to Mīrzā Maḥmūd and explains how Khan Muḥammad mistreats him at night (*shabhā-rā bā man 'amal-i bad nimāyad*), and that he sometimes suffers punishment when he refuses his master's advances.[6]

Mīrzā Maḥmūd's heart aches for Shahbāz, and he hatches a plan to liberate him from their master. He conspires to inform Khan Muḥammad's wife of her husband's doings. One night, while Khan Muḥammad is busy abusing the boy, his wife rushes in and yanks the blanket from them. In Mīrzā Maḥmūd's words, she "saw his pantless ass and gave him a kick" (*kūn-i bī-shalvār dīda lagadī bar u zāda*). She shouts at him, pulls

[5] Āshtiyānī, *'Ibratnāma*, 32–34. [6] Āshtiyānī, *'Ibratnāma*, 36–37.

his beard and rips his clothes. In the end, Khan Muḥammad sells Shahbāz to a man from another village.[7]

Soon after, Mīrzā Maḥmūd would come to the aid of a fellow slave held in the village. The slave, named Muḥammad, was purchased by a wealthy shepherd named Aqqi who, despite his wealth, was so stingy that his usual meal was nothing more than an onion and a dish of water. This tight-fisted master had turned down multiple offers of ransom for Muḥammad, and it was clear that he – like Mīrzā Maḥmūd's own master – was holding out indefinitely for an unrealistically high price. This inspired anger among the people from Muḥammad's native village, and in the meantime Muḥammad was made to herd sheep and work the land. One day, a Sarïq named Baylï tells Mīrzā Maḥmūd of his intentions to rob the stingy slave-owner. Baylï was famous for his thieving, but he evidently had disdain for the slave trade; he was also competent in shoemaking (*kaffāshī*), and he earned his keep both as a shoemaker and as a thief. At dawn, he robs Aqqi's residence and carries off the goods to Herat in order to sell them. When Baylï returns, he announces to Mīrzā Maḥmūd that he has come out 100 *ṭilla*s richer than expected, and that his next plan was to free Muḥammad from his master. He provides the slave with money, bread, food, and water, and Muḥammad prepares to make his getaway.[8]

On the night of his escape, Muḥammad meets Baylï at an agreed-upon place and they ride off to Herat. It is a windy night, with dust blowing all around, and Aqqi shouts out to Muḥammad, reprimanding him for failing to close the tent-flaps. He soon realizes that his slave is gone. A month later, Mīrzā Maḥmūd receives a letter from Muḥammad, who reports that he managed to make it safely back home to Mashhad. His successful escape has the incidental effect of worsening Mīrzā Maḥmūd's own servitude, however: Khan Muḥammad, paranoid of losing his valuable slave in a similar manner, keeps a stricter watch on him, rising twice each night to check the tightness of Mīrzā Maḥmūd's chains.[9]

With the coming of summer, the Turkmens spend their time working the land, and Mīrzā Maḥmūd is forced to lug stones and tend to the chickens. He suffers terribly from the heat and from his shackles, and finds that he cannot endure the labor. He cries out behind Khan Muḥammad's residence at night like a man possessed, and at one point he throws himself to the ground and faints (*khod-rā be zamīn afkānda va bīhūsh shoda*). Khan

[7] Āshtiyānī, *'Ibratnāma*, 37–38. [8] Āshtiyānī, *'Ibratnāma*, 39–41.
[9] Āshtiyānī, *'Ibratnāma*, 42.

Muḥammad and his brother come and carry Mīrzā Maḥmūd into the house, where he behaves as if insane, striking out at anyone who comes near and bashing his head against the ground. His master, understandably, laments that he had not sold Mīrzā Maḥmūd when he had the chance.[10]

Mīrzā Maḥmūd soon realizes the benefits of madness: He is excused from lugging stones. He keeps up the act for twenty-three days, and word spreads among the village children about the "crazy" slave. He frightens them away whenever they gather to see him. He also takes to scaring Khan Muḥammad's wife away from her meals, snatching the bread she leaves behind. With the extra sustenance and exemption from labor, Mīrzā Maḥmūd's health improves, and he hatches a new plan to escape. He takes advantage of his free access to the "postal" system, by which his master had formerly made him contact possible ransom-payers, as well as his connections to other slaves and former-slaves he had met in the village. One of these slaves was a Qandahari named Mullā Riżā, who had done *taqīya* (claiming to be a Sunni rather than a Shiʿite) in order to improve his lot, but was still treated harshly by his master. Mullā Riżā's captivity came to the attention of the Afghan chieftain Dost Muḥammad Khan, and he was ransomed for 44 *tilla*s. Mīrzā Maḥmūd contacts the liberated Mullā Riżā, and makes an unusual request: He asks him to send some arsenic (*sam al-fār*) and a file (*sūhān*). Mullā Riżā sent him two *misqāl*s of arsenic.[11]

It would not be long before Mīrzā Maḥmūd gets his chance to deploy the poison. One day, Khan Muḥammad asks Mīrzā Maḥmūd to prepare some tea for him. Seizing the opportunity, he poisons the tea-water with half a *misqāl* of arsenic. But just as he is adding it to the water, Khan Muḥammad's brother arrives and requests milk-tea instead. Mīrzā Maḥmūd pours out some of the water, since milk-tea requires less of it, and then adds milk to the poisoned water remaining in the pot. Mīrzā Maḥmūd had no intentions of poisoning Khan Muḥammad's brother along with Khan Muḥammad himself, but soon enough the situation becomes still more complicated: His master's sister, son, brother, wife, and one daughter all arrive to enjoy some of the freshly made tea.[12]

Khan Muḥammad and his sister sip the poisoned tea, and they complain about its strange flavor. Khan Muḥammad's brother echoes the complaint, and spills his cup on the ground. The others, too, declare it to be bad tea, and soon enough a change comes over them all. They go pale, grow weak,

[10] Āshtiyānī, *ʿIbratnāma*, 44. [11] Āshtiyānī, *ʿIbratnāma*, 45–46.
[12] Āshtiyānī, *ʿIbratnāma*, 47.

and begin to vomit. They all complain of suffering great thirst, and they begin to speculate that they have been poisoned.[13]

Khan Muḥammad accuses Mīrzā Maḥmūd of trying to kill the lot of them, and the *ḥākim* of the Turkmens is summoned along with a Herati Jewish doctor, who examines the tea and tests it with instruments. In response to their accusations, Mīrzā Maḥmūd objects that he had been a slave there for some two years and lacked both the money and the means to get hold of any poison. He claims that the dirty copper teapot was to blame for the poisoning, and he wins enough support for this hypothesis that his life is spared. He is nevertheless beaten brutally (for good measure), and he is never again permitted near the cups and pitchers. His master learns to fear him, and Mīrzā Maḥmūd reaps the benefits of being feared: for two or three months, he is exempted from some of his former labors.[14]

Not long after, a number of slaves from the village would make another attempt to escape. After spending the night hiding in a pit that had been dug at a local residence, the group ventures toward Balamurghab along with a group of Turkmens. They are intercepted in the desert by a band of *alamanchis* (raiders), however, and after a fierce fight in which several Turkmens are killed, the slaves are dragged back to Panjdih. Although Mīrzā Maḥmūd is not among them, he again suffers incidentally from the escape-plans of other slaves; once again, Khan Muḥammad grows paranoid about losing his slave, and he tightens Mīrzā Maḥmūd's chains.[15]

One of Mīrzā Maḥmūd's duties had been to give fodder to Khan Muḥammad's camel, a task he seems usually to have performed within sight of his master. One day, however, Khan Muḥammad gives him a rope and a sack, unchains him, and instructs him to go retrieve more fodder on his own. Mīrzā Maḥmūd seizes the opportunity: once he is out of sight, he sets off toward Balamurghab. He ties his shoes on backwards in order to deceive any pursuers (*kaffashī ki dar pā dāshtam ān-rā vārūna pūshīda*). Eventually, the cord with which he had strapped on the shoes frays, and he continues barefoot through the desert. He soon loses his way. That night, he finds himself at a Salar settlement. He stays out of sight, and attempts stealthily to steal a horse. He cannot get the animal untethered, however, and so he travels on, still barefoot. By morning he is tired, hungry, and terribly thirsty. He comes to a deep canyon with a river at its bottom, but the river is unreachable. Mīrzā Maḥmūd climbs a hill to get his bearings

[13] Āshtiyānī, *'Ibratnāma*, 47–48. [14] Āshtiyānī, *'Ibratnāma*, 49.
[15] Āshtiyānī, *'Ibratnāma*, 49–51.

and sees, in the distance, the village of Murghab; with freedom in sight, he resolves to press on toward the village under the cover of night.[16]

Suddenly, he sees five Turkmens some distance down the hillside – three on horseback, two on foot. They see him too. Mīrzā Maḥmūd's hair had grown long, "like an Afghan's," and the Turkmens on foot take him for an Afghan from Balamurghab. But the horsemen knew better: They were from Panjdih, and they recognize Mīrzā Maḥmūd, shouting out to the others that he is an escaped slave. They capture him and Mīrzā Maḥmūd pleads that they not bring him back to the village; he promises a reward if they sell him instead in Balamurghab. The Turkmens on foot immediately agree, but the horsemen from Panjdih at first refuse. Eventually, however, they too consent to the idea. Settling in for the night, they swear an oath that they will sell Mīrzā Maḥmūd somewhere nearby the very next day.[17]

Their promise turns out to be a ploy, probably intended to placate their prisoner. Khan Muḥammad is informed of Mīrzā Maḥmūd's recapture, and the slave is taken to the Salar settlement of Marchaq, where Khan Muḥammad is waiting to retrieve him. There, Mīrzā Maḥmūd finds his master "sitting like an angry boar" (*chūn gurāz-i khashmgīn nishasta*). Mīrzā Maḥmūd is beaten and chained. The next morning he is taken back to Panjdih, where he is beaten yet again until a local resident intervenes, counseling Khan Muḥammad that there is no point in beating a slave, since a caged bird will inevitably think of flying to freedom.[18]

Not long after, Mīrzā Maḥmūd, remarkably undeterred, makes yet another attempt to gain his freedom. He slips from his chains one night while Khan Muḥammad is asleep, and heads again toward Balamurghab. He stays some distance from the main road, hoping to stay out of sight, but once again he loses his way. Wandering without water in the brutal heat of the day, the elements push him to the brink of death. Dazed from thirst, he finds the bones of a sheep and tries ravenously to break them open, hoping to find some blood with which to wet his parched mouth. The effort serves only to weaken him further, and he begins to speculate that living in slavery is better than dying of thirst in the desert. He scrambles up a hill to get his bearings, and, from on high, he sees the glitter of water some distance away. By night, he travels toward it.[19]

Suddenly, in the night, he hears the bark of a dog, followed by two or three gunshots. He would later learn that the dog belonged to a shepherd, who had fired into the air to scare off what was assumed to be a thief. Khan

[16] Āshtiyānī, *'Ibratnāma*, 51–53. [17] Āshtiyānī, *'Ibratnāma*, 52–54.
[18] Āshtiyānī, *'Ibratnāma*, 55–56. [19] Āshtiyānī, *'Ibratnāma*, 56–57.

Muḥammad later came upon the shepherd in his hunt for Mīrzā Maḥmūd, and the shepherd described the runaway's footprints: They must belong to a fugitive, the shepherd shrewdly reasoned, since if they had been the footprints of a Turkmen they would not have passed through Egyptian thorn (*khar-i mughīlān*).[20]

Meanwhile, Mīrzā Maḥmūd had made his way down to the river that he had seen from the hilltop. Thanking God that he had not died of thirst, he went down to the waterside. Just as he is about to drink, he hears a voice behind him, warning him that the water is bitter and salty. He turns to see Khan Muḥammad, who greets him with brutal blows from a horse-whip (*qamchī*). Khan Muḥammad drags him into the water and bids him to drink it; Mīrzā Maḥmūd vomits from a single sip. His master then gives him some bread and clean water, and brings him to a Turkmen tent where he is given a yogurt drink (*dūgh*). Khan Muḥammad assures him that if he had not consumed the bread, fresh water, and yogurt, the foul river-water would have killed him.[21]

When they return together to Panjdih, Khan Muḥammad beats Mīrzā Maḥmūd once more and shackles him so tightly that escape is impossible. In his manacled state, Mīrzā Maḥmūd assumes, at the very least, that he would no longer be made to work the hand-mill (*dastās*) or graze the camels. But he is made to graze the camels anyway, though he is no longer much use in this line of work. Khan Muḥammad's wife, noticing his poor work with the camels, insists that Mīrzā Maḥmūd be starved, so that he can suffer the same fate as the camels he looks after. He goes hungry until, in a stroke of luck, he finds two small melons (*kharbūza*) and a watermelon (*hindivāna*) along with two discs of bread out in the fields.[22]

One day, Mīrzā Maḥmūd hears a local Turkmen crier (*jarchī*) announce to the people of Panjdih that a raid was being organized in the direction of Mashhad, and that any who wished to partake should begin preparing provisions and readying their horses (literally, keeping the horses "raw" [*khāmī*]). Khan Muḥammad is not up for raiding himself, but he has a fine horse and he plans to lend it to a raider in exchange for one-half of any spoils the raider earns. Mīrzā Maḥmūd is assigned to look after the horse in the meantime. The thought that the animal might be used to drag another human being into slavery is more than he can take; he fetches his arsenic. The horse dies that very night from the poisoned barley Mīrzā Maḥmūd

[20] Āshtiyānī, *'Ibratnāma*, 57–58. [21] Āshtiyānī, *'Ibratnāma*, 58.
[22] Āshtiyānī, *'Ibratnāma*, 59.

puts in its feedbag, and Khan Muḥammad seethes with rage, cursing anyone who comes near.[23]

The raid, as it turns out, ends in disaster for the two hundred horsemen who gathered to take part in it. They encounter strong resistance on the way, and ninety-six of them perish in the resulting battle. Another eighty-two are taken prisoner and dragged to Mashhad, where, according to Mīrzā Maḥmūd, they are all beheaded, and their heads are sent to Tehran (*majmūʿa-i ānhā-rā sar burīda ravāna-i dār al-khilāfa namūdand*). A number of Turkmens flee to the mountains, saving themselves, and after eight or nine days they return to Panjdih, describing their ordeal to their townsmen.[24]

Mīrzā Maḥmūd still has some arsenic left, and it is not long before he comes up with yet another plan to torment his cruel master. One day, a Turkmen trading caravan passes through Panjdih, and Khan Muḥammad plans to make some money by paying a camel-driver to convey a load of grain to Herat using his camels. Mīrzā Maḥmūd mixes arsenic with their doughy fodder (*khamīr*), and when the camel-driver comes to collect the camels they are already dead. Khan Muḥammad loved his camels more than any son or brother, Mīrzā Maḥmūd recalls, and he is bitterly saddened by their deaths.[25]

Sometime thereafter, Mīrzā Maḥmūd falls terribly ill for a period of several weeks, nearly dying from his mysterious sickness.[26] When his condition finally improves, he learns something intriguing from the members of a Bukharan caravan passing through the village: In Bukhara, slaves are neither chained nor injured by their masters; those with skills in calligraphy, composition, and crafts are respected. Mīrzā Maḥmūd wishes intensely to make his way to Bukhara, although he cannot help but recall an ominous verse from Rumi: "If you're going to Bukhara then you're insane / worthy of the dungeon and the chains." Poetic advice notwithstanding, he begins to gather information on the Iranian merchants who trade and live in Bukhara, and he gradually develops a plan of action.[27]

The plan that materializes is a brilliant one. Mīrzā Maḥmūd forges a letter to Khan Muḥammad from three known merchants trafficking goods between Bukhara, Panjdih, and parts south: Āqā Muḥammad Kāzim, Āqā Mīr Taqī, and Qāsim Bay. The letter says, among other things, that the merchants would give Khan Muḥammad 250 *ṭilla*s for Mīrzā

[23] Āshtiyānī, *ʿIbratnāma*, 63–64. [24] Āshtiyānī, *ʿIbratnāma*, 65–66.
[25] Āshtiyānī, *ʿIbratnāma*, 66. [26] Āshtiyānī, *ʿIbratnāma*, 66–72.
[27] Āshtiyānī, *ʿIbratnāma*, 73–74.

Maḥmūd, as the elites of Bukhara had use for a highly literate slave like him. To make the forged letter more realistic, Mīrzā Maḥmūd steals some soap and carves a seal for each of the three merchants. All that remains is to make sure the letter is delivered to Khan Muḥammad by someone ostensibly unrelated to Mīrzā Maḥmūd, so as to avoid any suspicion of his role in the ruse. The perfect man for the job was a Turkmen named Niyāz Qul whose father was a surgeon. Mīrzā Maḥmūd tasks him with delivering the letter to Khan Muḥammad at the bazaar, and he tells the young man to explain that he had received the letter from a Salar Turkmen who was traveling from Bukhara to Herat. In return, Mīrzā Maḥmūd agrees to knit Niyāz Qul a pair of socks for the winter.[28]

The ruse works. Khan Muḥammad receives the letter and is ultimately convinced of its veracity. He reads it in front of Mīrzā Maḥmūd and exclaims, "I've struck it rich!" (*ganjī yāfta!*). Instead of his usual nickname of "Demon" (*ghol*), Khan Muḥammad begins calling Mīrzā Maḥmūd the respectful "Āqā Mīrzā." Before long, the news arrives that "Āqā Mīrzā" is to leave on a caravan for Bukhara. He is introduced to a caravan-leader named Qara Bay, who chains him by the neck to a camel, and when they leave Panjdih on the long road to Bukhara, Mīrzā Maḥmūd is forced to march shackled and on foot during the night. Khan Muḥammad sends along a reply to the merchants' fabricated letter, saying that he was sending along his slave, and that he himself would follow in some ten days' time, but that he would not sell Mīrzā Maḥmūd for any less than 300 *ṭilla*s.[29]

The road to Bukhara brings fresh tortures for Mīrzā Maḥmūd. He is put to work driving the camels, collecting firewood, and cooking for the other members of the caravan. Qara Bay beats him repeatedly, and Mīrzā Maḥmūd sees no rest. Passing through the hinterlands, he observes other Iranian slaves: He sees many of them occupied with working the land (*dehqānī*) in places like Lubāb and Ghanjū. When the caravan comes to Qaraqul, news spreads that a literate slave has arrived, and Mīrzā Maḥmūd is brought before a potential buyer. He is taken to a *majlis* with a number of Turkmens arranged around a felt carpet, and he is invited to drink with them. But he is warned, mysteriously, not to point his feet toward the verses of the Qur'ān that are in their presence, nor to drink before them. Mīrzā Maḥmūd looks around in confusion, seeing no verses

[28] Āshtiyānī, *'Ibratnāma*, 76–77. Mīrzā Maḥmūd observes with surprise that scarcely any of the Turkmens in the village knew how to make a decent pair of socks. He had previously taught one of them the craft in exchange for a handsome payment: nearly a maund of bread and some quantity of dried beef jerky (*qāq*).

[29] Āshtiyānī, *'Ibratnāma*, 80.

anywhere in sight, and he remarks that he can see nothing of the Qur'ān around them. His hosts reply that a group of "*qizilbāsh* feltmakers" (*namadmālān-i qizilbāsh*)[30] had added Qur'ānic verse inscriptions to the margins of the felt carpet before them. Mīrzā Maḥmūd glances at the felt and observes that it is only poetry, and not scripture, that is woven there, and he teases his hosts for the error. Hoping to save face, one of the inquisitors engages him in a debate on the subject of ritual ablutions, and Mīrzā Maḥmūd – to the discomfort of the Turkmens around him – quickly proves his superior erudition on matters of Islamic ethics.[31]

The debate soon turns to the relative merits of Shiʿites and Sunnis, and whether it is licit for Sunnis to take Shiʿites into slavery. Mīrzā Maḥmūd proposes to his hosts that they are contravening their own religion by holding Shiʿite slaves, but they dismiss the idea. Man-selling, they say, was a custom from ancient times (*ādamfurūshī az qadīm rasm būda*). Why else, after all, did the sons of Ya'qūb sell their own brother Yusūf? (And Mīrzā Maḥmūd, they scoff, is no more honorable than Yusūf.) Why else, moreover, do Shiʿites themselves sell the Qur'ān, when they are no dearer than the holy book? At this moment, it dawns on Mīrzā Maḥmūd that he is talking to Sarïqs, who, he writes, have no other trade besides thievery (*duzdī*). He jokingly observes aloud to them that they themselves are mentioned by name in the Qur'ān: *al-sāriq*, in the scripture, means "thief." At this taunt, the party grows openly hostile, and Mīrzā Maḥmūd hastens away.[32]

Mīrzā Maḥmūd accompanies the caravan to the city of Bukhara without further incident, and upon arrival there Qara Bay takes Mīrzā Maḥmūd to the man he was perhaps least eager to see: Āqā Muḥammad Kāzim, whose name and seal he had forged. Naturally, Āqā Muḥammad is flabbergasted to meet his supposed purchase, having no knowledge of any alleged correspondence with the slave's owner. His predictable objection leaves Mīrzā Maḥmūd histrionically heartbroken, and Āqā Muḥammad reassures the poor slave that he needs only to have patience; the merchant agrees to liberate him from Khan Muḥammad. Āqā Muḥammad's plan is that a man named Shāhrukh Khan would buy Mīrzā Maḥmūd and send him off to Mashhad.[33]

Mīrzā Maḥmūd is also permitted to stay at Āqā Muḥammad's residence while awaiting his master Khan Muḥammad's arrival in Bukhara, and the

[30] The phrase "*qizilbāsh*" was long used as a generic term for Shiʿite Iranians in Central Asia.
[31] Āshtiyānī, *'Ibratnāma*, 83–84. [32] Āshtiyānī, *'Ibratnāma*, 84–85.
[33] Āshtiyānī, *'Ibratnāma*, 86.

merchant allows him to venture out on an errand, giving him some money to fetch ice from the bazaar. On his way there, Mīrzā Maḥmūd finds a blackened coin on the ground. The occasion provides the perfect catalyst for a display of his keen entrepreneurship. At the bazaar, Mīrzā Maḥmūd finds a man selling dyed eggs, and he uses the found coin to buy a red egg (*bayza-i qirmizī*) from him. Returning home with the ice in his hands and the egg under his arm, he borrows a pen-knife from Āqā Muḥammad's retainer, Qāsim, and sets to work making fine engravings (*naqash o hakākī*) in the egg. When the work is done, he returns to the bazaar, showing off the egg to great acclaim. One onlooker buys the egg for 14 *pul* – fourteen times what Mīrzā Maḥmūd had paid for it in its plain form. He uses the money to buy fourteen more eggs, which he engraves and sells for 8 or 10 *pul* each. From his earnings, he keeps no more than 20 *pul* and gives the rest to Qāsim, both in payment for the use of his pen-knife and, perhaps, in the expectation that he would prove to be a valuable ally later on.[34]

Mīrzā Maḥmūd takes his remaining earnings to a bathhouse, where he meets another potential ally: an elderly barber and bath attendant who reveals that he is likewise a Shiʿite, but that he has been practicing *taqīya* (pretending to be a Sunni) for many years in Bukhara. He reassures Mīrzā Maḥmūd that he never fails to help his Iranian brothers who are enslaved in Bukhara, and Qāsim later confirms the old man's claims. Within just a few days, Mīrzā Maḥmūd has already begun to establish a network of friends and admirers.[35]

The next day, Mīrzā Maḥmūd returns to the bazaar and finds a paper-dealer's shop selling fine Samarqandi paper. He engages the shopkeepers in conversation and again quickly proves his erudition. They ask him for a lesson in Qur'ānic study and *naḥv* (reading and grammar in Arabic), and he corrects their mistakes as they practice recitation. Ashamed of their blunders, they ask for the chance to evaluate a sample of Mīrzā Maḥmūd's calligraphic skills, and in *nastaliq* he pens a verse from Saʿadi: "Skill is the greater fault in the eyes of the opponent / Saʿadi is a rose, but in the enemies' eyes a thorn." He then produces lines in a variety of classical calligraphic forms: *naskh, thuluth, shekasta*, and *taʿliq*. Students gather around to observe him, and they all notice his poor state of dress: Mīrzā Maḥmūd goes barefoot. "If this man was not a Shiʿite," one student remarks, "I would pay all the money in the world for him" (*agar īn mard shīʿa nabūd man u-ra be har qīmatī ke bāvad mī-kharīdam*). The student reflects that it is for the best that he remains in slavery: If Mīrzā Maḥmūd is

[34] Āshtiyānī, *ʿIbratnāma*, 88. [35] Āshtiyānī, *ʿIbratnāma*, 88–89.

ever to be emancipated, according to the young man's logic, he will never become a Sunni (*hargiz sunni nakhwāhad shod*).[36]

Mīrzā Maḥmūd continues the very next day with his energetic networking. He meets the Shiʿite barber at the bazaar, where the latter introduces him to a man named Ḥajji Muḥammad Sāliḥ, who quickly proposes to be Mīrzā Maḥmūd's patron. The man offers him some money as a stipend. Mīrzā Maḥmūd replies that it would be wrong of him to accept charity, but that he would be happy to go to work as an employee.[37]

With new friends and new prospects of employment, Mīrzā Maḥmūd returns to Āqā Muḥammad's residence, where, unfortunately, a complication had arisen: his master, Khan Muḥammad, had arrived from Panjdih, eager to collect his expected payment. Khan Muḥammad quickly learns from Āqā Muḥammad that he will get nothing like the price he had anticipated. This was not to say, of course, that there was no demand for Mīrzā Maḥmūd: Khan Muḥammad learns that his slave had indeed stirred up some interest in Bukhara. A slave-dealer (*ghulām-jallāb*) named ʿAẓīmbay is summoned to appraise Mīrzā Maḥmūd, and – likely in collusion with Āqā Muḥammad – he estimates the slave's value at the low sum of 20 *tumans*. At this, Khan Muḥammad is speechless. Without another word, he returns to the caravanserai that served as his lodging place.

Two or three days later, a Jewish man named Musa negotiates with Khan Muḥammad and Āqā Muḥammad to buy Mīrzā Maḥmūd for 22 *tumans*. Thus begins a curious series of transactions. Mīrzā Maḥmūd lives at Musa's *hujra* for no more than two days before Hajji Muḥammad, his would-be patron, buys him from Musa. Hajji Muḥammad explains himself by saying that it is not acceptable for a Muslim to be the servant of a Jew (*rāẓī nashod ki musulmān khidmatkār-i yahūdī bāshad*). Two days later, he turns around and sells Mīrzā Maḥmūd to a man named Ḥājjī Raḥīm Herātī, who buys Mīrzā Maḥmūd for 20 *tumans*, and then promptly re-sells him to Āqā Muḥammad, who promises once again that eventually Mīrzā Maḥmūd would become a free man.[38] In the meantime Mīrzā Maḥmūd goes to work as an accountant for an acquaintance of Āqā Muḥammad.

Soon enough, Khan Muḥammad appears once again at the merchant Āqā Muḥammad's residence, accompanied by two or three Bukharans. He grabs Mīrzā Maḥmūd's collar, announcing that he still owns him,

[36] Āshtiyānī, *ʿIbratnāma*, 91. [37] Āshtiyānī, *ʿIbratnāma*, 92.
[38] Āshtiyānī, *ʿIbratnāma*, 93–94.

regardless of the present circumstances. At that moment, all of the injuries Mīrzā Maḥmūd had suffered under that cruel master rush into his mind, and he grabs Khan Muḥammad's beard and gives it a yank, punching him in the face with his other hand and knocking out the two or three decaying teeth which remained in his mouth. Khan Muḥammad, helpless, can do nothing more than complain to Āqā Muḥammad, who declares that the Turkmen no longer has any business with his former slave, as his ownership had been terminated when he agreed to sell Mīrzā Maḥmūd some days previously. Taking stock of the intensity of Khan Muḥammad's agitation, however, the merchant must have wondered if swindling this man out of his property would really be worth the effort: Āqā Muḥammad, in the end, shows some willingness to negotiate with Khan Muḥammad for the eventual return of Mīrzā Maḥmūd to Panjdih.[39]

Upon hearing this, Mīrzā Maḥmūd flees the merchant's residence, and he eventually makes his way to the home of a man named Mīr ʿĀsad, who was rumored to have freed several slaves and to have aided them in their journeys to elsewhere. Arriving at his door, however, Mīrzā Maḥmūd learns that the man is out shopping at the bazaar, and he is told to return later. Terrified of being found by Khan Muḥammad, Āqā Muḥammad, or any of their helpers, Mīrzā Maḥmūd takes refuge for some time among the worshippers in a nearby mosque. He later returns to Mīr ʿĀsad's house once more, only to find that he still had not returned home. With nowhere else to go, Mīrzā Maḥmūd heads back to the mosque – "there is," he writes, "no better hiding-place than that."[40]

Mīrzā Maḥmūd pretends to sleep at the mosque until the crowd gathers once more for their prayers. As he prays with them, Mīrzā Maḥmūd wonders what he will do if Mīr ʿĀsad has not returned by nightfall. On his way back to the man's residence, he runs into one of Āqā Muḥammad's retainers – evidently a fellow slave, and a man with whom Mīrzā Maḥmūd had become friends. He learns from this man that Khan Muḥammad, enraged, had taken his case to the *ḥākim* of Bukhara. The retainer's best suggestion for Mīrzā Maḥmūd is that he take refuge with Mīr ʿĀsad. They go to his residence together, and they wait for him for some time, but he does not appear. Unable to wait indefinitely at the stranger's house, Mīrzā Maḥmūd realizes – surely with profound sorrow – that he has nowhere else to go, and no better option than to return to Āqā Muḥammad and hope for the best.[41]

[39] Āshtiyānī, *ʿIbratnāma*, 95–97. [40] Āshtiyānī, *ʿIbratnāma*, 98–99.
[41] Āshtiyānī, *ʿIbratnāma*, 99.

When he arrives at Āqā Muḥammad's residence, he finds Khan Muḥammad sitting there, eyeing him with rage "like a shot bear" (*misl-i khirs-i tīr khwārda*). Mīrzā Maḥmūd attempts to explain his disappearance by claiming that he had needed to attend the wedding of a friend. Khan Muḥammad insists that Mīrzā Maḥmūd must return with him to Panjdih that same day. Mīrzā Maḥmūd replies simply that there is a problem with this plan. "What is the issue?" Khan Muḥammad asks. Mīrzā Maḥmūd replies: "That I must either drown you or drown myself in the waters of the Jayhūn" (*bāyad tū-rā dar āb-i daryā-yi jayhūn ghurq o halāk kunām yā khodam-rā*). Āqā Muḥammad, meanwhile, understandably wanting nothing more to do with the conflict, declares simply that Mīrzā Maḥmūd is Khan Muḥammad's slave, and that he can do with him whatever he wishes.[42]

With Mīrzā Maḥmūd's sad fate seemingly sealed, the news comes that Shāhrukh Khan – the man who was initially expected to purchase Mīrzā Maḥmūd and, eventually, to free him – has returned to Bukhara. As quickly as the news arrives, Mīrzā Maḥmūd is spirited off to Shāhrukh Khan's residence by his friend Qāsim, unbeknown to Khan Muḥammad and Āqā Muḥammad, and Shāhrukh interviews him about his background and his past work for the Iranian military. Mīrzā Maḥmūd stays there for two or three days. Eventually, Āqā Muḥammad arrives to investigate, and he and Shāhrukh Khan hatch a plan together to convince Khan Muḥammad that Mīrzā Maḥmūd had fled to Kabul.

For once, however, Khan Muḥammad is not to be fooled, and he arrives, furious, at Shāhrukh Khan's door, demanding the release of his slave and threatening to take the matter to the Amīr of Bukhara himself. Shāhrukh Khan replies that Mīrzā Maḥmūd is a *sayyid*, and that he never should have been bought or sold in the first place; moreover, if Khan Muḥammad insists on bringing the case before the Amīr, Shāhrukh would describe Mīrzā Maḥmūd's high birth and talents before the court and observe that such a gifted slave belongs only in the service of His Majesty. In that way, Khan Muḥammad could expect to end up with no slave and no payment.[43]

Khan Muḥammad sees that his case had become hopeless, but Āqā Muḥammad, perhaps mindful of the Turkmen's unpredictable temper, negotiates with Shāhrukh Khan to offer a settlement of 30 *tillas* in exchange for the slave. He counsels Khan Muḥammad that it would be wise to take the offer. Khan Muḥammad replies that he had paid 14

[42] Āshtiyānī, *'Ibratnāma*, 99–100. [43] Āshtiyānī, *'Ibratnāma*, 103.

*ṭilla*s when he bought Mīrzā Maḥmūd; that the slave had outstanding debts to him totaling 18 *ṭilla*s; that on two of the occasions when he had run away, Khan Muḥammad had paid a 3 *ṭilla* reward leading to his capture; that he had covered the 3–4 *ṭilla* customs toll for transporting his slave to Bukhara, along with another 3 *ṭilla*s to rent the camel that conveyed him there. Why, then, after all this, should he sell Mīrzā Maḥmūd for 30 *ṭilla*s? Āqā Muḥammad answers bluntly: because, he says, there would be no higher offer. Khan Muḥammad agrees to the deal, announcing that, henceforth, he intended to quit the business of slave-dealing (*man ba'd tark-i asīrfurūshī-rā khwāham*), repenting of the fact that he had ever gotten involved in it and vowing never again to buy or sell a slave (*tawba kardam ke dīgar asīr nikharam va nifurūsham*).[44]

Shāhrukh Khan immediately shows Mīrzā Maḥmūd his hospitality, as does his brother, Muḥammad Ḥassan Khan, and Mīrzā Maḥmūd impresses them in the days to come such that he is assigned to oversee their household's kitchen and stables. He is provided with a stipend equivalent to three Iranian *tuman*s per month. In his spare time, he is given the freedom to work in other occupations, some of which prove quite lucrative: In just five months, Mīrzā Maḥmūd reports earning 70 *tuman*s from his labors as well as six or seven suits of clothing. Meanwhile, Mīrzā Maḥmūd's erroneous reputation as a *sayyid* reasserts itself thanks to Āqā Muḥammad Khan, who spreads rumors of his noble birth and urges him to maintain the charade, which, he says, could come to benefit him in Bukhara. Mīrzā Maḥmūd soon finds himself dubbed "Āqā Sayyid Taqī," an honorific he does little to shake off, despite his guilty conscience.[45]

Some two months later, Mīrzā Maḥmūd finds himself on his way to Samarqand, tagging along with his master's retinue. His trip to the ancient city offers him an opportunity to reflect on the region more generally, revealing some of his thoughts on nature and society in Turkestan. He observes that the climate in Samarqand is vastly superior to that of Bukhara, and that it is generally free from the ravages of guinea worm, a problem that in Bukhara had reached epidemic proportions. Mīrzā Maḥmūd describes Bukhara's guinea worm crisis with a palpable horror – and in sickening detail – and reveals another of the jobs he worked while living in that city: He had been tasked many times with drawing guinea worms from the bodies of unfortunate victims. He is understandably relieved to find that the ailment hardly exists

[44] Āshtiyānī, *'Ibratnāma*, 104. [45] Āshtiyānī, *'Ibratnāma*, 105–106.

in Samarqand, which he attributes to the good quality of its air and water.[46]

Less appealing in his eyes, however, is Samarqand's social climate: He describes Samarqand as a city of hedonists (*ʿayyāsh*), strewn with multiple opium dens (*kūknārkhana*), in each of which could be found a "simple youth with curly hair" (*javānī-i sāda ba gīsūvān-i mujaʿad*) serving tea and passing around the opium pipes. Smoking cannabis mixed with tobacco (*chars*) and opium-eating (*taryāk-khurdan*), he claims, are also exceedingly common in the city, and as a result the men of Samarqand are generally lazy, timid, sickly, lacking in energy, and yellowish in pallor.[47]

With unrest growing in the region on the eve of the Russian conquest of the khanate of Kokand, Mīrzā Maḥmūd soon finds himself headed to the capital city of Kokand itself as his master, Shāhrukh Khan, is appointed to oversee the Bukharan armory (*tupkhana*). Shāhrukh Khan is welcomed by many of the city's elites, but he and his retinue are soon on the move again in the face of hostilities from the forces of a Kazakh leader named Mullā Qulī Khan (ʿAlimqul).[48] It seems that Mīrzā Maḥmūd did not see much of the city of Kokand, as he offers a scant description of it, noting only the presence of esteemed burial sites along with his impression that the city's men are yellowish and lean, while its women are ravishing (*dilrubā*) and lively (*rūḥparvar*). With this, Mīrzā Maḥmūd heads back on the road again, journeying with his master and his retinue to the mountains near Osh as violence engulfs the region. Mīrzā Maḥmūd here offers valuable reportage on local struggles that destabilized Kokand on the eve of the Russian conquests, as the population of the capital city was split in their allegiances between Khudāyār, the incumbent ruler, and Mullā Qulī Khan.[49]

Mīrzā Maḥmūd stays at Shāhrukh Khan's side even as the latter begins to slander his own ruler, the Amīr of Bukhara (out of jealousy, Mīrzā Maḥmūd alleges), calling him a traitor. The Amīr does not take kindly to these slights, and rumors soon surface that the Amīr plans to place Shāhrukh Khan under arrest. This revelation must have come as a traumatic one for Mīrzā Maḥmūd, who under Shāhrukh Khan's stewardship was considered a retainer of the court (*nökar-i dīvān*) and had even been confirmed as *chur-aqasi*, a title, in Mīrzā Maḥmūd's telling, higher

[46] Āshtiyānī, *ʿIbratnāma*, 109. [47] Āshtiyānī, *ʿIbratnāma*, 110–111.

[48] I am grateful to Alexander Morrison for identifying this figure for me. Amazingly, ʿAlimqul's memoirs are available to us in English translation: Timur Beisembiev, *The Life of Alimqul: A Native Chronicle of Nineteenth Century Central Asia* (New York: Routledge, 2015).

[49] Āshtiyānī, *ʿIbratnāma*, 111–119.

than that of *yuzbāshi*.[50] When Mīrzā Maḥmūd goes to Shāhrukh Khan's residence one day to discuss the frightening rumors going around, he finds that he is too late: His master's place is swarming with men tasked by the Bukharan Amīr with emptying it. Mīrzā Maḥmūd's own goods were expropriated, his master's horses were gathered in the yard, and all of the women and servants of his mobile estate had been stripped "as naked as captives" and carried off, weeping.

Mīrzā Maḥmūd is taken to a government dungeon (*maḥbūs-i ḥukūmatī*) in the citadel of Sar Teppe. The citadel is home to multiple prisons, each heinous in its own characteristic way. One is called the "Damphouse" (*narm-khana*), so called because of its intolerable humidity. Another is called the "Tickhouse" (*kana-khana*), where prisoners would suffer ticks "as big as camels" that would suck their blood so vigorously that they would be dead within just two days. Prominent prisoners, such as Shāhrukh Khan and his brother, were held in one of two or three small, private yards. The grave of Siyāvush Dāmād Afrāsiyāb was also said to be in the dungeon.[51]

Within three days, the Amīr of Bukhara ordered that all of the goods and prisoners should be sent onward to Bukhara, and that all of Shāhrukh Khan's horses should be sold for profit. Mīrzā Maḥmūd gains at this point a preview of his most likely fate, as two Iranian slaves that Shāhrukh Khan had bought and freed were resold to buyers elsewhere. Some employees of the Amīr then demand money from Mīrzā Maḥmūd, offering him his freedom in return, but he assures them that all of his worldly holdings had already been taken; Mīrzā Maḥmūd figures that the hope of extorting money from him is all that delays his inevitable fate of being sold.

Soon enough, for reasons that are unclear to him at the time, Mīrzā Maḥmūd is told that he is to have a personal audience with the Amīr. He finds himself being led to a caravanserai, within which he is taken to a room illuminated with dozens of candles. He realizes that he has been taken to some secret cell, and asks his captors where they have taken him. One laughs, and replies that he is in the "house of pain" (*manzil-i ta'b*) – another of the Amīr's dungeons. In this dungeon he sees just one other man: a Jew, who shares a water-pipe with him and says that he was imprisoned after a quarrel over silk with two men who later requested his detainment. Mīrzā Maḥmūd requests that the guards move him to

[50] It seems unlikely that his position was really so lofty as this, however: Mīrzā Maḥmūd reveals that his main job at this point of his captivity was to supervise his master's horses and stables, a job of considerable responsibility but hardly equal to that of a *yuzbāshi*.

[51] Āshtiyānī, *'Ibratnāma*, 122.

a more hospitable place, and they consent, shifting him to a room where some of Shāhrukh Khan's men were being kept.[52]

Mīrzā Maḥmūd is not imprisoned there for long before he learns that the time for his audience with the Amīr has come. He is brought out before the Amīr and some of his men, and he realizes upon being brought into the light that his place of detainment was in fact part of a complex of stables. The Amīr's men demand money from Mīrzā Maḥmūd, but he replies once more that whatever he had was already taken from him "except for this depressed body and oppressed heart" (*savā-yi īn jism-i afsarda va jān-i sitam rasīda*). This answer does not satisfy the Amīr, who orders that Mīrzā Maḥmūd be stretched between two posts and branded (*dāgh kardan va ʿuqābayn kashīdan*). Before the hot brand can touch the slave's flesh, however, the Amīr changes his mind, and instead of proceeding with the torture he tells Mīrzā Maḥmūd of his intentions to take ownership of him. Mīrzā Maḥmūd, perhaps dazed from his ordeal, replies that he would never consent to this, and asks to be sold to some other owner instead.[53]

The Amīr, angered, has Mīrzā Maḥmūd turned over to his vizier, who receives him kindly and, offering to purchase him with a payment of 30 *ṭilla*s to the state treasury, plans to put Mīrzā Maḥmūd to work tutoring his son. Mīrzā Maḥmūd goes to work, and he soon proves his talents as a scribe as well, so that the vizier gives him over to work as an accountant for his brother, a merchant at the silk bazaar. Mīrzā Maḥmūd likewise performs admirably in his new position, earning the esteem of the silk merchants and settling into a comfortable new routine. He later learns that his former master, Shāhrukh Khan, has not been as lucky: On the Amīr's orders, both he and his brother were beheaded, their bodies buried dishonorably.[54]

Some days later, an international scandal is precipitated as the Amīr orders the imprisonment of some English travelers and the confiscation of their goods. A spy of Armenian descent named Mīrzā Yaʿqūb Khan is dispatched to investigate this and other matters, posing as a merchant. This secret agent soon learns of Mīrzā Maḥmūd and endeavors to interview him as a possible source and ally. Mīrzā Maḥmūd passes on the news of Shāhrukh Khan's brutal murder, along with details concerning the military and finances of Bukhara. According to Mīrzā Maḥmūd, Mīrzā Yaʿqūb Khan records this information in a letter to officials in France.

[52] Āshtiyānī, *ʿIbratnāma*, 124. [53] Āshtiyānī, *ʿIbratnāma*, 125.
[54] Āshtiyānī, *ʿIbratnāma*, 128.

The spy manages to extract covert information from several others too before arousing the suspicion of some individuals loyal to the Amīr, who inform the vizier of his activities. Mīrzā Yaʿqūb is imprisoned in a small, dark room, and his possessions are scoured for evidence. (Fortunately, Mīrzā Maḥmūd reports, the Amīr's henchmen were unable to read his letter to France.) Mīrzā Yaʿqūb claims to his interrogators that those he had met with privately in the khanate, including Mīrzā Maḥmūd, were simply old acquaintances. But this is not enough to secure Mīrzā Maḥmūd's safety: He is beaten so brutally that he fears for his life, and he learns that the vizier has ordered his execution as a punishment for talking with the spy.[55]

Mīrzā Maḥmūd's life is saved only through the intervention of Iranian friends and acquaintances, who convince the vizier to sell him instead of having him killed. A slave-dealer (*barda-furūsh*) is summoned, but because Mīrzā Maḥmūd is still badly bruised from his beating, the vizier decides to imprison him until he heals enough to be sold. Thus Mīrzā Maḥmūd finds himself in a dungeon for the third time. This time, he is held in a small room "darker than night and more dreadful than the heart of the aggrieved" (*tārīktar az shab-i dījūr va mūḥishtar az dil-i ranjūr*).

Once more, Mīrzā Maḥmūd manages to improve his situation by using his wits. Each day, after evening *namāz*, the vizier would pass by Mīrzā Maḥmūd's cell, and Mīrzā Maḥmūd would perceive the light of his lantern moving past the cell door. One evening, as he passes by, evidently unaware that Mīrzā Maḥmūd knew he was near, the prisoner shouts out prayers and lamentations to the effect that God knows of his innocence and that he has committed no betrayal. The vizier comes closer to his cell, listens for a time to Mīrzā Maḥmūd's cries, and then leaves. A half-hour later, the cell door opens; the vizier's servants bring Mīrzā Maḥmūd a candle and a carpet, telling him that their master's heart ached for his predicament and that he had been forgiven.[56]

Mīrzā Maḥmūd is freed from the dungeon, interrogated once more about his connections with Mīrzā Yaʿqūb Khan, and for some time held in Ghijduvan, and afterwards in a smaller settlement some distance from Bukhara. In the meantime, the Amīr of Bukhara was facing one of the greatest crises in the khanate's history: The armies of the Russian Empire, having subjugated the town of Kokand, were now headed for Tashkent, the Kokand khanate's most important city. In the midst of the long siege that followed, Mīrzā Maḥmūd claims that his master, the vizier, occupied

[55] Āshtiyānī, *ʿIbratnāma*, 129–133. [56] Āshtiyānī, *ʿIbratnāma*, 134–135.

himself with a lavish circumcision ceremony for his son, for which he paid the outrageous sum of 4,000 *tumans*. Mīrzā Maḥmūd explains that the manumission of slaves often served as a key element in circumcision ceremonies among Sunni elites (*chūn qaʿida-i ahl-i tisnan dar chūnīn jashn azād kardan-i usārā hast*), and that the vizier had intended to liberate twelve Iranian slaves during the course of the event. The Amīr of Bukhara, however, evidently desperate for revenue, forbids him on the grounds that the slaves could be sold and the proceeds given over to the treasury.[57]

Mīrzā Maḥmūd, noting the vizier's disappointment over the Amīr's greed, attempts to convince the vizier to free him and allow him to return to his homeland. It is no use, however, and soon enough Mīrzā Maḥmūd receives an unusual new assignment: The Amīr arranges to have a room in his residence elaborately painted, and he orders Mīrzā Maḥmūd to join eight artists from Bukhara for the task. Among them, Mīrzā Maḥmūd recalls, three – Nāẓim and Aḥmad Kalla, and ʿAbd al-Qādir Khwāja – were quite famous in the khanate. The walls of the residence were to be decorated with human and animal figures as well as floral motifs. Here, Mīrzā Maḥmūd provides a window onto the workings of decorative artists in Bukhara. Observing that drawing human likenesses was prohibited in Bukhara (*ṣuratkashī-ra mamnūʿ o mażmūm būd*), Mīrzā Maḥmūd relates that his fellow artists were unskilled at it and relied on old images by Iranian artists that they had carried with them under their arms. They traced these images through the process of pouncing and then outlined the images in black with a brush before adding color. Mīrzā Maḥmūd allows that they had considerable skill in drawing arabesque designs (*islīmī*) as well as flowers and other elements from nature, though he cannot help but add that their skill in these areas was still inferior to his own. In his own telling, they soon recognize this fact as well, referring to him as "master of masters" and seeking his guidance on their own work.[58]

The Amīr likewise praises Mīrzā Maḥmūd's artistry, and rewards him generously. At one point, the Amīr asks him about his circumstances, wondering whether Mīrzā Maḥmūd considered himself a slave or a free man while under the vizier's dominion. Mīrzā Maḥmūd cleverly – if evasively – replies that "the free people of the world all wish to be slaves to Your Excellency" (*āzādān-i jahān hama-hama ārzū-yi bandagī-i janābli dārand*). The Amīr, pleased with his answer, thanks Mīrzā Maḥmūd. "I will give you a family and make you a man of the house [i.e. one of my own servants]," he tells him. "I will give you a wife from among my slave-girls"

[57] Āshtiyānī, *ʿIbratnāma*, 139–140. [58] Āshtiyānī, *ʿIbratnāma*, 140–142.

(*az chūrīhā-yi andarun zan be tū mī-deham*). The offer would surely have thrilled many slaves, but Mīrzā Maḥmūd realizes that if he marries a woman from the household of the Amīr then it will become all the more unlikely that he can ever be freed. He obsequiously demurs and, delicately, asks the Amīr for his freedom instead. His evident ingratitude angers the Amīr, who remarks on how inappropriate it would be if a Shiʿite was sent back to live among his fellow "infidels" after having passed into the "abode of Islam." Mīrzā Maḥmūd reports (perhaps dubiously) that he offered a tart reply to this insult, and the enraged Amīr storms off, leaving Mīrzā Maḥmūd's fellow artists wondering over his audacity, which seems to them like a death-wish.[59]

Mīrzā Maḥmūd continues to prove his worth as an artist, however, and he suffers no punishment for his impudence. But he cannot find a means to free himself, even after he manages to receive a letter of manumission sealed by a chief judge in Bukhara. In the months to come he petitions the Amīr repeatedly for his freedom. He does this so often that the Amīr, finally losing patience, tells him that if he brings one more petition then he would end the conversation by killing him (*ay ghulām agar yakdafaʿa dīgar ʿariża-i tū be ḥużūr-i man bī-āyad bedūn javāb o savāl koshta khwāhī shod*).[60]

Distraught as the prospect of gaining his freedom through official channels slips away, Mīrzā Maḥmūd nevertheless continues to put his many talents to work in Bukhara. One evening at the vizier's house, after hearing a recitation by a poet favored among Bukharan elites, Mīrzā Maḥmūd is asked teasingly by the Amīr if he likes the poet's work. He replies that he does not, much to the amusement of the gathering, and proceeds to offer insightful critiques of its failings. The poet too appreciates his corrections, and soon enough Mīrzā Maḥmūd finds himself in the role of a minor court poet, occasionally writing verses that he would submit to the Amīr or have others recite for him. Mīrzā Maḥmūd complains bitterly about the paltry remuneration he receives for his work – no more than a few ceremonial robes. (We, however, as observers, are more likely to be struck simply by his progression from a field-slave distributing camel fodder in a Turkmen village to a court-poet among Bukharan royalty.[61])

Meanwhile, Mīrzā Maḥmūd uses some of his savings to help fellow slaves on their journeys home. He offers 60 *tumans* toward the price of

[59] Āshtiyānī, *ʿIbratnāma*, 143–144. [60] Āshtiyānī, *ʿIbratnāma*, 143–147.
[61] Āshtiyānī, *ʿIbratnāma*, 147–150.

freedom for a slave-woman from Mashhad, and he assists with the travel expenses for three other manumitted slaves on their way to Herat. He also finds work as a calligrapher, working on several copies of the Qur'ān. During this period of steady work but limited prospects for freedom, he hangs his hopes on the only possible means of emancipation he could still imagine: If the Russians conquered Bukhara, he reasons, he could potentially find himself a free man amid the chaos.[62]

In the months to come, this once-distant possibility starts to seem increasingly likely. After the fall of Tashkent, Mīrzā Maḥmūd observes the Russians advance into Bukharan territory, while the Amīr of Bukhara declines opportunities to ease tensions and to forestall a conquest that seems increasingly inevitable. Desperate to increase his fighting force, the Amīr issues an order that all Iranian slaves in his domains must be brought to Bukhara, where any of them willing to enter military service would be purchased by the Amīr and outfitted for war. Within three weeks, 4–5,000 slaves had gathered at various caravanserais, and from among them 1,000 entered the armed forces. These new troops fought the Russians at Ura-Teppe, but their assistance could not secure the city, which fell to the Tsar's army.[63]

With the Amīr increasingly panic-stricken before the Russian onslaught, Mīrzā Maḥmūd's thoughts turn again to the possibility that he might gain his freedom simply by requesting it, figuring that his poetic and artistic talents would be little use to the Bukharan elites amid the present chaos. He contacts the vizier, who replies that both the Amīr and the city of Bukhara were indeed in dire straits. Finally, he agrees to grant Mīrzā Maḥmūd his freedom.[64]

The vizier gives Mīrzā Maḥmūd a letter to help secure his free passage back to Iran. The letter states that Mīrzā Maḥmūd is the vizier's slave and that no Turkmens should block his way at the river-crossings or otherwise interfere with him on the way to Mashhad. Mīrzā Maḥmūd receives letters from Mullā ʿAbd al-Karīm and some other well-known merchants as well, and he readies his belongings and prepares a horse for the journey home. He pays 70 *tumans* to a guide who promises to convey him safely to Iran, and two days later he joins a Turkmen caravan bound for Merv. The party suffers an attack on the way, but Mīrzā Maḥmūd and some of his fellow travelers finally arrive in the town, where Mīrzā Maḥmūd finds lodging with a merchant who had made his fortune shipping goods between Mashhad and Bukhara.[65]

[62] Āshtiyānī, *ʿIbratnāma*, 150. [63] Āshtiyānī, *ʿIbratnāma*, 161–166.
[64] Āshtiyānī, *ʿIbratnāma*, 169–170. [65] Āshtiyānī, *ʿIbratnāma*, 172.

A few days later, Mīrzā Maḥmūd leaves the merchant's house in the company of four soldiers, all headed for Sarakhs. They lose the road, however, and wander for a few days, trying to find their way. At night, they resist the urge to make fires for fear of Turkmen thieves. Finally, they see Sarakhs before them in the distance. In celebration, they make tea and share a water-pipe.[66]

Mīrzā Maḥmūd stays in Sarakhs for forty-five days, likely fearing to continue onward because of the presence of raiders from Merv said to be decamped not far outside the city, at the shrine of ʿUlaq Bābā. This saint, also known (according to Mīrzā Maḥmūd) as Luqman Sarakhsī, was held in such esteem by the Turkmens that runaway captives who managed to reach his shrine were permitted to remain free, and that if a Turkmen hunting party chased prey into the vicinity of it, the hunters would give up the chase. Finally, Mīrzā Maḥmūd joins a large party for the three-day journey to Mashhad, where he finds lodging at an Uzbek caravanserai. He remains in Mashhad for twelve days before heading home to Tehran. Home at last, he sees his mother and his brother for the first time in a decade.[67]

REFLECTING ON MĪRZĀ MAḤMŪD'S ORDEAL

Mīrzā Maḥmūd's narrative is, above all, a story of how one slave managed, through the force of his own ingenuity, to influence his fate against extraordinary odds. Nevertheless, it would be naïve to see Mīrzā Maḥmūd's story in purely optimistic terms, stressing nothing more than his triumph over adversity. Notwithstanding the gains in quality-of-life that Mīrzā Maḥmūd gradually achieved, desperation was the driving force behind his audacity and his creativity. If we are to speak of his "agency," we must remember that he was his masters' agent in most things. Meanwhile, in matters where he seized some personal initiative, danger was ever-present, and his efforts to improve his circumstances sometimes left him brutally beaten. More than once, he reports being beaten so badly that he expected to die from his injuries. Good luck was as much a factor in Mīrzā Maḥmūd's eventual success as his own considerable genius: He was lucky that he was not beaten to death; he was lucky that Khan Muḥammad did not conclude with certainty that Mīrzā Maḥmūd had poisoned him and his family; he was lucky to find his way while lost in

[66] Āshtiyānī, *ʿIbratnāma*, 174. [67] Āshtiyānī, *ʿIbratnāma*, 175–179.

the desert; and he was lucky that the unusual trick he deployed to get himself to Bukhara worked as well as it did.

Mīrzā Maḥmūd deserves much credit, however, for making expert use of the freedoms available to him. In Panjdih, these freedoms were much more limited than in Bukhara, but even while shackled, Mīrzā Maḥmūd evidently had access to a rural postal system – a concession that Khan Muḥammad allowed, we may assume, because he hoped his literate slave would use it to negotiate for his own ransom. Mīrzā Maḥmūd also appears to have enjoyed free social exchanges with his fellow slaves as well as with various townsmen and visitors, and he made key allies. He draws on the postal system and his village alliances to effect his escape, as well as to torment his master. In Bukhara, he enjoys much more extensive freedoms: Here, he even has the time and the liberty to earn a living above and beyond the support offered by his various masters. At times, he also has the freedom to travel around the city on his own. He improves his position much more quickly here than he had among the Turkmens. He reveals himself to be an entrepreneur, a skilled artist, and a valuable companion to Bukharan elites.

The range of different jobs and roles Mīrzā Maḥmūd occupies during his time as a slave is revealing on two counts. First, it reveals how the author's many talents could, given the right setting, serve to define the nature of his captivity. Second, it reveals the many sorts of jobs that could be delegated to slaves in Central Asia. Mīrzā Maḥmūd worked as a herdsman, a domestic servant, a water-bearer, a stable-keeper, a doctor, a painter, a calligrapher, a craftsman, an Arabic instructor, an accountant, and a poet. Single-handedly, he reveals the social mobility that could be available to talented, fortunate slaves in an urban environment like Bukhara. He also reveals the veritable dead end of slavery in the hinterlands: For all his talents, there was no work available to him in the village of Panjdih other than the meanest physical labor. Given that most slaves in Bukhara and Khwarazm worked in rural settings that were more similar to Panjdih than to the capital cities, we can assume that his experiences in Panjdih were closer to the norm. The nature of Mīrzā Maḥmūd's survival strategies, moreover, differed in either location: In Bukhara, he exercised productive talents; in Panjdih, where those talents were useless to him, he exercised trickery. Instead of craftwork and poetry, he feigns madness and plots his escape. His talents define the nature of his captivity, but the nature of his captivity defines which talents he can use.

Mīrzā Maḥmūd frequently meets with other Iranian slaves, and we find them working as messengers, domestic servants, soldiers, and agriculturalists.

We never meet another slave who had attained such high stations as he himself achieved in Bukhara, however. The scarcity of educated slaves in Bukhara factored into his easy mobility, but also played a part in the perpetuation of his captivity: His kind were always in demand, such that letting a slave with his talents get away was unthinkable. His skills were a blessing and a curse.

Along with information on slaves' jobs and conditions of labor, Mīrzā Maḥmūd also reveals much about the inner workings of the slave trade. He shows clearly how the slave trade followed caravan networks from cities like Mashhad to Bukhara. We learn that the trade in Iranian slaves was sometimes conducted – at least in part – by Iranian merchants, who financed caravans and loaded them with diverse shipments of goods for sale. It was by these same caravan routes that manumitted slaves were conveyed back to their homelands. Mīrzā Maḥmūd provides evidence of merchant-specialists who may have dealt predominantly in slaves, but upon his arrival in Bukhara, when he is bought and sold repeatedly by various individuals in quick succession, only one of these individuals is identified as a "slave-dealer." This series of sales also hints at a trait slaves shared with any other commodity: They were sometimes bought and sold purely in the interests of market speculation. It was easy to find buyers for Mīrzā Maḥmūd, both because his initial liaison in town was a well-connected merchant and because his literacy made him a relatively safe investment.

To what extent can we believe Mīrzā Maḥmūd's narrative? Even if we allow that some of the episodes Mīrzā Maḥmūd recounts seem far-fetched, the remarkable level of detail accompanying his most memorable achievements lends the narrative an overall atmosphere of earnest documentation. When he claims to have accompanied Shāhrukh Khan across the region, for example, he provides extremely specific details concerning shrines and other major sites that they pass by. When he claims to have been imprisoned in multiple dungeons, he takes the time to recount conversations and particulars that are not directly related to the development of his narrative. Throughout the text, in other words, Mīrzā Maḥmūd provides details that one would be unlikely to include merely as fabrications. It is also worth noting that not all of the tactics Mīrzā Maḥmūd describes having used to better his situation cast his wits in a positive light; especially while in Panjdih, his ploys were more likely to fail miserably than to succeed.

Nevertheless, Mīrzā Maḥmūd's skilled prose alone suggests an author who may be acutely aware of his audience and their expectations. Such an erudite man would not have been unaware of genre conventions that were then prevalent in the realm of "adventure" literature. One particular area in which embellishment seems likely is in the invariably witty, audacious repartee that Mīrzā Maḥmūd delivers at every opportunity. Did he really insult the Sunni tradition while standing amid a hostile (and probably armed) group of Sunni Turkmens? Did he really mock the religiosity of Bukharans in the presence of the Bukharan Amīr himself? It is possible, but seems unlikely. We can be sure, meanwhile, that such dialogue would have earned appreciative laughs from readers in Iran.

As we shall see in the chapters to come, the best indication of Mīrzā Maḥmūd's reliability is in the numerous instances in which later travelers – who would never have read his unpublished account – confirm and corroborate his claims about the workings of the Central Asian slave trade. Mīrzā Maḥmūd himself is remarkable in every respect, but his experiences, for all their inherent drama, are not altogether unique. He was not the only Iranian slave to have gained a high station in Bukhara; to have earned a good living for himself through his talents; to have served the Amīr. And he is certainly not the only slave to have suffered miserably in the desert, to labor in the hot sun for months on end, and to be beaten and abused by a cruel master. His account is valuable in part because his ordeal shares so much with that of other slaves: He provides something like a voice for those who suffered a similar fate.

4

The Slaves' World

Jobs, Roles, and Families

Mīrzā Maḥmūd's narrative reveals the remarkable range of occupations a slave could hold in different parts of Central Asia, but slaves in the region played many other parts as well. In this chapter, I will show something of the diversity of slaves' jobs and roles, along with the various environments in which they lived and performed their work. Some types of work were designated especially for slaves, while other types of work appear to have been off-limits to them. Slaves' origins and capabilities often played a part in defining the kind of work they did: Russian slaves, for example, were much more likely to be found doing certain types of labor, while other types were largely the purview of Iranian slaves. In light of slaves' varied labor roles, I will argue that a limited and contingent degree of social mobility could be available to seemingly any slave, though elite political posts were reserved exclusively for men. I will also explore slaves' marriages, examining a variety of possibilities and outcomes related to family life among slaves.

Considering the diverse roles and environments occupied by slaves reveals that they were ubiquitous in many parts of the region. They constituted a fundamental aspect of Central Asian societies down to the late nineteenth century.

LEGAL FRAMEWORKS

The Hanafi Muslim legal lexicon of Central Asia in the nineteenth century recognized at least six distinct types of slave, distinguished by the means of their acquisition and by certain circumstances of their use. Each category carried with it particular legal obligations on the part of a slave's owner. The *Sharḥ-i mukhtasar-i viqāya-i turkī*, published in 1901 in Tashkent, describes these categories, all of which are familiar (though sometimes under different names) in the broader context of Hanafi law on slavery:[1]

(1) *Zarkharīd*. This is the category of slave that, ostensibly, enjoyed the lowest number of protections. The word literally means "bought for gold," and presumably applies to most of those slaves bought in Central Asian bazaars and caravanserais. Such slaves could be given by their masters as gifts; pawned; left as an inheritance; rented out for use by others; or made to constitute part of a dowry.

(2) *Khanazād*. This category encompasses the children of slaves; the word means, roughly, "house-born."[2] These slaves could not under any circumstances be sold at the market. Vambery observed that the law, in this case, had pervaded social mores as well: "The sale of a khanezad is regarded as a disgraceful action, and one who commits such an act is branded as a thief and a robber."[3]

(3) *Mukātab*.[4] Slaves in this category could not be sold, given as gifts, pawned, left as inheritance, or made part of a dowry, because the terms of their servitude included a contract (*kitāba*) stipulating that they would be able to buy their own freedom after a certain period. To accomplish this, the slave would be allowed to save whatever proceeds he or she could manage to earn during the period of servitude. (In the context of ancient Roman slavery, such proceeds were called the *peculium*.) Vambery explains that these proceeds often came directly from the slave's owner: many slaves, he writes, "receive after a certain time either monthly wages, or else a share of the produce of the land or cattle committed to their

1 Faiziev, *Buxoro feodal jamiyatida qullardan foidalanishga doir hujjatlar*, 34–35. This author adds a seventh category to the six described here, which he calls the *shartli qul* (conditional slave). This slave was, according to Faiziev, distinguished by undergoing a fixed period of service, at the end of which he was freed – presumably without having to buy his manumission (see Faiziev, 35). We might add a further category to the list if we offset those slaves given special permission by their owner to transact business on their behalf. Naturally, we might expect all categories of slave that appear in the traditional Hanafi canon of *fiqh* to appear in use in Central Asia in the nineteenth century.

2 Other terms describing the same category include *qin* and *khālis qul* (cf. *Buxoro feodal jamiyatida qullardan foidalanishga doir hujjatlar*, 34).

3 Vambery, *Sketches of Central Asia*, 226.

4 This and several other categories in evidence in our Central Asian sources can easily be found in the traditional Hanafi *fiqh* canon. See, for example, ʿAlī ibn Abī Bakr Marghīnānī, *The Hedaya*, trans. Charles Hamilton (London: Allen & Co., 1870), second edition, 267; 637.

care."[5] Petrushevsky, writing about slavery in Iran, adds that a female slave under such a contract (the *mukātaba*) would traditionally be exempted from the necessity to submit to sexual intercourse with her master.[6] Interestingly, Vambery seems to conflate all Central Asian slaves other than the *khanazād* with this category: "As the Iranian is generally more active and frugal than his Turanian neighbour, the slaves in Turkestan, in a remarkably short time, get together a little capital. This is employed by most of them in ransoming themselves from slavery, *which they have the right to do after seven years' service*."[7]

(4) *Mudabbar.*[8] Slaves in this category, as with the *mukātab*, could not be sold, given as gifts, pawned, left as an inheritance, or made part of a dowry. This is because the terms of their contract included a *tadbīr* (pledge) from their master that they would be freed upon their master's death.

(5) *Umm walad.*[9] Slaves in this category (which means "mother of the child") had borne children by their master. Such a slave likewise could not be sold, given as a gift, pawned, left as an inheritance, or made part of a dowry; like the *mudabbar*, her manumission was guaranteed upon the owner's death. We can find at least one famous example of an *umm walad* in a proximate context: the Bukharan Amīr Muzaffar's own mother had been a slave, purchased at the public market.[10]

(6) *Istīlād.*[11] A slave in this category has been impregnated by her owner. Upon the child's birth, she will become an *umm walad*. A slave in the category of *istīlād*, like an *umm walad*, cannot be sold, given as a gift, pawned, left as an inheritance, or made part of a dowry, and is automatically manumitted upon the death of her owner.

These, at least in theory, were the Hanafi Muslim legal categories that governed the slave system in Central Asia. It must be remembered that the existence of such legal categories as those above reveals only legal norms, and not necessarily observable phenomena. The social ideals and customs indicated by these norms are not often clearly evident in other kinds of sources – eyewitness reports and autobiographies, for example – that concern slaves' experiences. However, the existence of dozens of legal

[5] Vambery, *Sketches of Central Asia*, 223.
[6] I. P. Petrushevsky, *Islam in Iran* (Albany, NY: State University of New York Press, 1985), 157.
[7] Vambery, *Sketches of Central Asia*, 226. Emphasis added.
[8] See *Hedaya*, 488; 267; 637. [9] *Hedaya*, 32; 120; 267; 637.
[10] Faiziev, *Buxoro feodal jamiyatida qullardan foidalanishga doir hujjatlar*, 27.
[11] *Hedaya*, 274; 488; 514.

documents on slavery – such as those compiled by T. Faiziev and discussed earlier – provides strong evidence that contestations pertaining to slaves were raised and adjudicated in the region's Islamic courts. Extant bills of sale and deeds of manumission signed by Hanafi Muslim judges, meanwhile, suggest that the formal Islamic legal system was used to define who should be considered a slave.

SLAVES' ROLES AND OCCUPATIONS

One of the earliest European sources on slavery in Khiva, published in 1815, focused exclusively on the agricultural labor performed by its slaves, and noted differences between the mechanics of labor in urban and rural contexts:

> The usual work of slaves is as follows: 1) to fertilize and cultivate the available lands, gardens, and orchards. Land is plowed by a small two-ox plow; in the cities it is plowed with pickaxes. 2) To sow and harvest grain; in the cities, to plant vegetables in the gardens, clean the canals and channels, and prepare them for [the] irrigation [waters]; 3) daily, to grind flour in the hand-mill (*ruchnyi zhernov*) and pound grains in the "leg" (*nozhnyi*) mortar; 4) to carry out [the necessary work involving] the wagons and agricultural implements; in a word, to bear all domestic burdens. Thus we have the exercise of the captives, which continuously occupies them, such that they have not the slightest leisure time during the day, save for a few minutes to take their nourishment and a few hours of calm sleep. The slightest mistake or pause in their labor is punished severely.[12]

As we will see, the "usual work" of slaves extended far beyond the agricultural sphere, but the field-labor and grain-processing of slaves appears to have played a very significant role in Khwarazmian agriculture. Major Blankenagel', who traveled to Khiva in 1793–1794, presented the field-labor done by slaves as a central element in the cycle of production and trade: "The fields are in large part cultivated by slaves. [Any] one of these [slaves] succeeds so much in this that he can provide for more than a large family through his field-cultivation, and not a small fraction of that [surplus] produce is sold off. In this way, regardless of the small number of people put to work cultivating the land when compared to the total number of residents, [the Khwarazmians] have sufficiently abundant fruits and produce that the surplus can be sold to

[12] "Nevol'niki v Khive," *Vestnik Evropy* 80:7 (1815), 245.

neighboring Kirghiz [i.e. Kazakhs] and Turkmens."[13] He elsewhere hints that these fieldworkers were generally Iranian, noting that a "large part" of the 20,000 Persian slaves he estimated to be in Khwarazm "tend the fields."[14] Some twenty years later, Murav'ev would make a similar observation, claiming that Iranian slaves brought into the region by the Turkmens were "generally the ploughmen."[15]

Many slaves worked the land on the large estates and gardens owned by Uzbek elites. Zalesov reports that some of these wealthy Uzbeks owned "lots of lands and gardens," which were "worked almost exclusively by Persian slaves."[16] The situation was similar in Bukhara, of which Meyendorff writes: "There is not, I think, a single Bokharian citizen who is in easy circumstances that does not possess a garden and a villa outside the town, in which he spends the hot days of the summer. Owners of land let their property, or else have it worked by slaves."[17] An individual landowner could keep a great number of Iranian slaves for this sort of business: "The wealthy Bokharians," Meyendorff writes, "possess generally about 40 slaves, but some of the most distinguished, as, for instance, the Kooshbeghi, have about a hundred, for they require a large retinue, and have, besides, many gardens and much land, demanding a greater number of hands to labour."[18] Some Iranian slaves interviewed by Russian border officials reported that their duties included grain-planting and other agricultural labor, though they generally offered no other information about the nature and conditions of their work.[19]

Muḥammad Raḥim Khan, ruler of Khwarazm, evidently put some of his slaves to work on the irrigation canals, and Murav'ev's description of the khan's labor-force hints at the diverse backgrounds of the workers involved in this aspect of agriculture: "[The khan's] estates are full of canals, and are carefully cultivated by slaves, and by Sarts and Karakalpaks, who have settled and built villages on them, and whose contribution to the kettle-tax has in consequence been remitted."[20] Lieutenant Gladyshev, visiting Khwarazm nearly a hundred years prior,

13 Blankenagel', *Zamechaniia Maiora Blankenagelia vposledstvii poezdki ego iz Orenburga v Khivu, v 1793–94 godakh* (St. Pb., 1858). 13.

14 Blankenagel', *Zamechaniia Maiora Blankenagelia*, 17.

15 Murav'ev, *Muraviev's Journey to Khiva through the Turcoman Country*, 144.

16 Zalesov, "Pis'mo iz Khivy," *Voennyi sbornik* 1 (1859), 288.

17 Meyendorff, *Journey of the Russian Mission from Orenbourg to Bokhara* (Madras: Spectator Press, 1840), 62.

18 Meyendorff, *Journey of the Russian Mission from Orenbourg to Bokhara*, 62.

19 See, for example, TsGAKaz 4.1.3646, ff. 74a–76b; TsGAKaz 4.1.2821, 6a–b.

20 Murav'ev, *Muraviev's Journey to Khiva through the Turcoman Country*, 139.

likewise reported on diverse laborers cleaning the canals, though he identified them exclusively as slaves, witnessing "Russians, Kalmyks, and foreigners numbering three thousand people, of whom he became aware because in the spring they were put to work cleaning the canals around the city."[21] It was not only among the Khwarazmians and Bukharans that slaves were employed in agriculture; we find mention of slaves working the land for Turkmens too, as Mīrzā Maḥmūd occasionally had done, though evidence for agricultural slavery among Turkmens is not very extensive.[22]

We rarely find reports of Russians working in agriculture, though Witkiewicz met one Russian in Bukhara who had previously worked in the Khwarazmian khan's garden. This man, named Igor', seems not to have liked the work – or the khan: "[Igor'] escaped from Khiva, where he had lived with the khan, and he says that he repeatedly planned to use the hoe with which he worked the khan's garden to bash the khan's brains in [lit. 'chop the khan's forehead'], but he would rather not give himself up to the torture which would inevitably await him thereafter, and so he fled to Bukhara."[23]

Herding and livestock-raising were sometimes undertaken by slaves, though the scholar Semeniuk cautions that this would have been a rare occupation for them among pastoral nomads, who had the greatest volume of herds, and his claim is supported by the relative scarcity of sources that mention slaves engaged in herding.[24] Nevertheless, some slaves mention in their own autobiographical accounts having served Kazakh masters by herding livestock.[25] Mīrzā Maḥmūd, likewise, cared for his Turkmen master's camels. The Scottish explorer Alexander Burnes met an Iranian slave who had been put to work herding sheep;[26] and the English governess Lucy Atkinson, while adventuring in the region with her architect husband, met a Russian enslaved by Kazakhs who had been engaged as a cowherd among them.[27]

The military was another sphere occupied by both Iranian and Russian slaves, though the lower-ranking soldiers were, it seems, more likely to be

[21] Ia. V. Khanykov, *Poezdka iz Orska v Khivu i obratno, sovershennaia v 1740–1741 godakh Gladyshevym i Muravinym* (St. Pb, 1851), 18.
[22] See Turgan-Mirza-Baranovskii, *Russkie v Akhal Teke. 1879 g.* (St. Pb, 1881), 71.
[23] Vitkevich, *Zapiski o Bukharskom khanstve* (Moscow: Nauka, 1983), 116.
[24] Semeniuk, "Likvidatsiia rabstva v Kazakhstane," 168–169
[25] See, for example, TsGAKaz 4.1.2821, 2a–3a; 6a–b.
[26] Burnes, *Travels into Bokhara*, Vol. 1, 256.
[27] Lucy Atkinson, *Recollections of Tartar Steppes and Their Inhabitants* (London: J. Murray, 1863), 289–290.

Iranian (some Iranians held higher military posts, however). The general predominance of Iranians in the military appears to be a common trait of both Khwarazm and Bukhara. While travel-reports rarely distinguish among Central Asian soldiers except in terms of rank, our efforts to ascertain the military roles of slaves are aided greatly by Central Asian narrative chronicles, such as the Khwarazmian chronicle *Firdaws al-iqbāl* by Shir Muḥammad Mīrāb Munis and Muḥammad Riẕa Mīrāb Agāhī.[28] Slave soldiers are mentioned under several names in Munis and Agāhī's history. They sometimes appear simply as "*qul*" (apparently the most neutral and general term for a slave in Khwarazm).[29] We also find reference to a "*mamlūk*" engaged in battle,[30] and slaves in the personal retinue of the *khaqan* are referred to as *mamālīk-i khāṣṣa*.[31] Several slave soldiers grouped together are referred to as *qullar nökari* ("slave retinue").[32] Another group is referred to as consisting of *qullar sipāhi*, a term that seems to have denoted more specifically an organized military detachment.[33] A military detachment of slaves is also called, at one point, *qullar dastasi*.[34] We also find slaves working as envoys, dispatched by powerful *amīrs* – in this capacity, the slave is referred to as *toghma*.[35] Finally, Khwarazmian khans frequently made use of a private corps of slave bodyguards; these individuals were called *altun-jilaw* ("golden bridle"), and Yuri Bregel notes that they could on occasion hold posts in the khan's court.[36] It was perhaps this sort of access that allowed for one of the most significant acts of rebellion in the annals of Khwarazmian slavery: the assassination, in 1727, of Shīr Ghāzī Khan by his own slaves. (The *Firdaws al-iqbāl* notes an interesting chronogram of this khan's death-date: "*Dād az ghulāmān*" – "Help against the slaves!")[37]

Our European eyewitnesses also confirm the prominent role of Iranian slaves in the Khwarazmian and Bukharan militaries. Zalesov, approaching

[28] Shir Muhammad Mirab Munis and Muhammad Riza Mirab Agahi, *Firdaws al-iqbāl*, trans. Yuri Bregel (Leiden: Brill, 1999). In the course of the work, Munis cites a slave in his own family's employ as a source: "When [I], this humble [author], was a child, [we] had a decrepit Mashhad-born [slave] inherited from my [great-]grandfather Ishim Biy. He would tell: 'When Mashhad was raided by Shir Ghazi Khan, more than five thousand men and women were taken into captivity. I was one of them'" (*Firdaws al-iqbāl*, 58).

[29] *Firdaws al-iqbāl*, 427, 464, 491. [30] *Firdaws al-iqbāl*, 307. [31] *Firdaws al-iqbāl*, 317.

[32] *Firdaws al-iqbāl*, 473. [33] *Firdaws al-iqbāl*, 426. [34] *Firdaws al-iqbāl*, 317.

[35] *Firdaws al-iqbāl*, 465, 468. However, one further reference to *toghma* (p. 477) leaves it open to speculation whether this term could apply also to slaves working in other capacities, or to slaves generally.

[36] *Firdaws al-iqbāl*, 584n381. Bregel also speculates that they may have been identical with the *qullar dastasi* (slave military detachments) mentioned earlier (*Firdaws al-iqbāl*, 633n847).

[37] *Firdaws al-iqbāl*, 61.

the town of Khiva after an arduous journey through terrible heat and a veritable fog of dust, arrived at the city walls to find it ranged with Iranian guardsmen: "At the entrance to Khiva, we saw for the first time the khan's regular army, arranged in a row on either side of the gate. Its guards were up to 50 men, being without exception Persian captives."[38] The army was not exclusively Iranian, however: Murav'ev reports that Khwarazmian artillerymen were generally Russian slaves, while Witkiewicz met a converted Russian slave who served as high-ranking Bukharan artillery officer, though he notes that the head of the Bukharan artillery – the *töpchibashi* – was an Uzbek.[39] P. M. Stremoukhov, who had served as director of the Asiatic Department for the Russian foreign ministry (among other positions), claims that the Bukharan infantry was recruited almost entirely from the Iranian slave population, of whom there were more than 10,000 in the armed forces.[40] The Russian officer P. Shubinskii similarly observed that "a considerable portion of the Bukharan military" were slaves.[41]

According to Witkiewicz, who met with a *yuzbāshi* of Bukhara in the 1830s, the Bukharans occasionally made an active effort to recruit fugitives and slaves into the military, though their efforts were, around the time of Witkiewicz's journey, meeting with mixed success:

> He [the *yuzbāshi*] said that they are recruiting an army made up of runaway Tatars and Russian captives, and would soon punish the troublemakers; that after Kurban Bayram, the Khan himself planned to ride on Shahrisabz. We note that the Khan actually did recruit into his army a man from among 10 of our Tatar fugitives (in this case we speak of soldiers), keeping him by means of deception and without pay; and besides this he unveiled a firman by which all captives in private hands were invited to run away from their masters and come to the Ark, to the palace, where they would promptly be recorded as sepoys, as soldiers. This challenge was taken up by some 25 people, who were held in a most pitiable condition.[42]

Russian slaves often served the Bukharan and Khwarazmian militaries through craftsmanship and blacksmithing as well, the latter work being, according to Murav'ev, nearly monopolized by the Russians in Khiva.[43] In Bukhara too Russians were often tradesmen: Burnes met a Russian slave

[38] Zalesov, "Pis'mo iz Khivy," 277.
[39] Murav'ev, *Muraviev's Journey to Khiva through the Turcoman Country*, 153; Vitkevich, *Zapiski o Bukharskom khanstve*, 120.
[40] Stremoukhov, "Poezdka v Bukharu," *Russkii vestnik* 6 (1875), 651.
[41] Shubinskii, "Ocherki Bukhary," *Istoricheskii vestnik* 7 (1892), 125.
[42] Vitkevich, *Zapiski o Bukharskom khanstve*, 108.
[43] Murav'ev, *Muraviev's Journey to Khiva through the Turcoman Country*, 144.

employed as a carpenter,[44] and Witkiewicz, who interviewed a number of Russians in the city, met several others working in this trade. One of these craftsmen, named Ivan, may have been a freedman who chose to settle in the khanate. He had previously lived in Astrakhan and had been taken captive on the Caspian Sea. He reported living in Khiva for three years, and then fleeing to Bukhara, where he worked as a carpenter "for the khan," making gun carriages for the Bukharan army.[45] Another Russian slave had likewise escaped his master and come to the attention of the khan, being conscripted into the Bukharan army as well as serving as a shoemaker and carpenter; at the time Witkiewicz met him, this man intended to build carriages under Ivan's supervision.[46] A Pole named Mikhal'skii, who Witkiewicz interviewed, was also working as a craftsman in Bukhara, having arrived there by a very roundabout route. He had been taken prisoner in 1812, but somehow escaped to Orenburg, where he evidently served as a guard along the border from 1816 to 1817. "Here they wanted to punish him," Witkiewicz writes, "for the fact that his gun discharged during a hunt and badly injured his hand; they suspected that he wanted to make himself ineligible for duty." Rather than face his punishment, he fled into the steppe, where he was captured by Kazakhs and sold to the *kushbegi* of Bukhara. When Witkiewicz met Mikhal'skii, he was sixty years old, and was serving as "a shoemaker, carpenter, mechanic, and whatever else." He had previously set up a cobbler's shop in Bukhara along with a Tatar acquaintance, "but it was a catastrophe: they couldn't sew a decent pair of galoshes." Sometime after this, he cast a pair of guns for the khan. He was a convert to Islam and had married a Bukharan wife, with whom he had three children.[47]

Being a slave of a Bukharan *kushbegi* could come with notable benefits. At the time of his visit in 1820, Meyendorff reported that the "whole of the administration" of the domain was in the hands of the *kushbegi*'s family and slaves, a state of affairs Meyendorff considered less than ideal for the development of civic morale: "Thus we find Bokhara presents a repetition of the comedy eventually played by every despotic country, having a Prime Minister possessing unlimited powers, which he either can exercise

[44] Burnes, *Travels into Bokhara*, Vol. 1, 294.

[45] Vitkevich, *Zapiski o Bukharskom khanstve*, 115–116.

[46] Vitkevich, *Zapiski o Bukharskom khanstve*, 115.

[47] Vitkevich, *Zapiski o Bukharskom khanstve*, 115. Demaisons appears to have met this man too; he writes of him: "This Pole, after many years working for the *kushbegi*, was quite fluent in Uzbek and Persian. Like the rest of the slaves in Bukhara, he had to work all day for his master, who often left him without even any bread" (Demezon, *Zapiski o Bukharskom khanstve*, 39).

himself or by his subordinates, who do not possess the noble feeling which we call patriotism."[48] We may indeed question the "patriotism" of even highly promoted slaves, but generalized patriotism was surely less important than specific loyalty within the administration, a quality which the appointment of family and personal slaves was probably intended to foster. As elsewhere in the Muslim world, it was not uncommon to find slaves occupying administrative posts, as well as undertaking other court duties. Murav'ev notes some such cases in Khiva,[49] while, in Bukhara, Shubinskii writes that nearly every minor court official (as well as every palace servant) was a slave.[50]

The spheres of Islamic jurisprudence and prayer-leading, meanwhile, serve as examples of trades in which slaves were given little, if any, place. A child of slaves could take on these kinds of leadership roles, but the ranks of Islamic jurists, imams, and other high positions within religious institutions seem to have been closed off to converted slaves. One powerful case-study in the alienation of slaves and former-slaves from the higher echelons of the region's religious life can be seen in the social bifurcation of Khwaja-Eli, a Khwarazmian town known for consisting in large part of *sayyids*, who were exempt from most obligations to the khan. M. Alikhanov-Avarskii visited the town around 1873, and observed its social composition:

> In order to maintain their privileged position, Khwajas [*sayyids*] give their daughters in marriage to, and themselves marry, only the descendants of Muhammad, and carefully guard their city from any foreign elements. In spite of this, there are several hundred ordinary mortals in Khwaja-Eli – the descendants of slaves who were released or ransomed themselves, being [therefore] descendants of Persian captives sold here. These latter ones, of course, do not enjoy the privileges of the city; they live in a special quarter [of town] and annually contribute about 1,000 rubles to the khan's treasury.[51]

Does this mean that those among the manumitted converts to Sunnism and their descendants converted back to Shiʿism after gaining their freedom? This is one possibility, but another is simply that the ranks of the religious elite were closed to them; they may have been regarded with suspicion as "foreign elements" or – still more likely – held in lower regard due to their non-*sayyid* ancestry.

[48] Meyendorff, *Journey of the Russian Mission from Orenbourg to Bokhara*, 51.
[49] Murav'ev, *Muraviev's Journey to Khiva through the Turcoman Country*, 50; 130; 133.
[50] Shubinskii, "Ocherki Bukhary," 125.
[51] M. Alikhanov-Avarskii, *Pokhod v Khivu (Kavkazskikh otriadov)*, 196.

Slaves could, however, sometimes be found working as servants for religious institutions. They could even be permanently "attached" to religious institutions by formal endowment contracts. In one *waqf* deed dating to 1693, for example, it is stipulated that two families of slaves were to remain constantly in residence at a large Bukharan mausoleum complex, and that their responsibilities to the shrine were to pass from generation to generation. Likewise stipulated in the document is the right of each subsequent generation of slaves to draw their compensation from funds established by the *waqf*.[52]

The fact that slaves and former-slaves are rarely, if ever, seen among the class of Islamic jurists and imams does not mean that slaves never served as educators, broadly considered. On the contrary, the education of children among nomads was not infrequently entrusted to slaves, and it is not unreasonable to presume that this included some measure of religious education as well. One Tatar slave among the Kazakhs reports that he spent his time among them teaching his owner's children to read and write.[53] Russians also served in this capacity; one Russian slave described having been treated well by his Teke Turkmen mistress, who tasked him with educating her children.[54] In other contexts, historians have considered the ways in which slaves' educating children of a different background can result in cultural transmission, and it is tempting to assume that Kazakh children who received some education from Tatars, or Turkmen children who received some education from Russians, would glean from them more than just literacy. In the diverse cultural environment of Central Asia, though, it is difficult to isolate those aspects of culture that may have had "slave-mentors" as their vector. Even so, tentative hypotheses along these lines are possible in certain, specific areas: given the prominence of Russian slaves in Central Asian ironworking and military technology in the nineteenth century, for example, we might expect these fields to show a significant Russian imprint.

Slaves could also be used to provide musical entertainment, and we may assume that these slave-musicians were typically Iranian, as we have no evidence of Russian slaves performing such a role. It is likely that this use of slaves was a phenomenon particular to the elite, though we have strikingly little evidence either way. We lack any sources from Central Asia which would allow us to reconstruct an environment akin to that of

[52] *Vakf Subkhan-Kuli-Khana Bukharskogo 1693 g.*, 213; 230–231.
[53] TsGAKaz 4.1.197, 81a–b.
[54] A. Rzhevuskii, "Ot Tiflisa do Dengil'-tepe," *Voennyi sbornik* 9 (1884), 173–174.

the famous "singing girls" of the medieval Middle East – an environment in which slaves (and particularly slave-girls) provided the best-known form of spectator entertainment. Twentieth-century accounts of so-called *bachcha bāzī* ("boy play") in Afghanistan, which often involves effeminately clothed boys dancing and singing for small audiences, may describe a practice that existed also in nineteenth-century Central Asia, but there are few reliable reports of slave-entertainers of any age or gender that we can date to that period. Meyendorff offers one of the few accounts along these lines, providing his evidence mostly as a template for expressing a more generalized moral outrage of the kind so common in the era's travel literature: "I once asked a young Bokharian of good family," he writes, "of what his amusements consisted; he said that he gave midday dinner parties accompanied by the music of his slaves; further, that he sometimes attended the chase; and, lastly, that he kept Jawanis or boy favourites. The calm and unhesitating way he told me this astonished me, and proved to me how well acquainted they are here with the most horrible of all vices."[55]

In any event, slaves' work was often defined by what they were capable of, and we may assume that a slave who was a competent musician or dancer would have been put to work doing what he or she did best. That personal talents and perceived competencies could define a slave's sphere of action is well-evidenced by the predominance of Russians among military engineers, and by that of Iranians working in the royal court (the stereotype of Iranians as savvy bureaucrats and court attachés was long-held throughout the Muslim world). But it would be wrong to assume that most slaves performed only one role, or that they occupied only one sphere of action (agriculture, say, or the military). For example, any slave, given their owner's consent, could perform work beyond what was assigned to them if they had the time and the inclination, and they could even legally keep the additional income they earned if their owner allowed them to do so. A slave put to work predominantly as a planter could work as a shepherd on the side, and vice-versa. A slave could also be delegated as his or her owner's agent in matters of business, acting in the owner's place and enacting the rights of a free person only as a proxy (such a go-between in the Islamic legal context is typically called a *vakīl*). In Hanafi legal tradition, slaves could even be charged to speak on behalf of their owners in court cases, though I have not yet seen any direct evidence of this occurring in early modern Central Asia.

[55] Meyendorff, *Journey of the Russian Mission from Orenbourg to Bokhara*, 61–62.

Slaves could also serve as their masters' agents in ventures whose legality was more dubious, and indeed they would have been ideal candidates for illicit work (at least from their masters' perspective). Major Blankenagel' recalled the experiences of a Russian slave who was profitably employed in illegal labor:

> A Russian named Maksim, who had been slave at Khiva ... told me that he was briefly acquainted with a slave named Ivan belonging to a Bukharan kazi, who told him that, with his owner's consent, he secretly extracted the metals from gold and silver ores and got the proceeds from this, and that in half a year he had accrued the amount – totaling 30 silver coins – [necessary] to buy himself [from his owner, i.e. to purchase his own freedom] ... Maksim had often helped Ivan in his work, sorting the crushed ore and alloying the metals ... Maksim had also been in the mines which Khivan Sarts used to work in olden times, where he had found many [more] of those inexhaustible lumps of ore similar to the ones he had seen [while working] with Ivan. Though it was strictly prohibited to work in the Khivan mines, greed compels some to secretly extract the ore and take it back to Bukhara, where they sell it as a commodity much in demand. Maksim was at Khiva for 20 years, and he had amassed many skills for enriching himself by means of the land. I tried to convince him to come back to Russia with me, but he did not agree, fearing that he would not make it back to Khiva, where he had a wife and children in slavery. All the same, I promised him both a dual passport and the funds, allotted by Her Imperial Majesty, [necessarily] to buy these slaves, and he agreed to my proposal.[56]

Maksim's experiences underscore the degree to which cultivating skills could enhance a slave's circumstances. His account is also remarkable as an example – a unique one, as far as I have seen – of cooperation and sociability among slaves from different domains: here, we find a Bukharan slave teaching a trade to a Khwarazmian slave, with the two then working side-by-side. The illegal nature of the work in question, as well as the slaves' shared Russian background, likely facilitated this ostensibly rare kind of partnership.

Slaves' talents could also directly affect their sale-price, and Meyendorff claimed that competency in a craft could even double their market value: "The price of a well-built man is about 40 or 50 Tellas (600 to 800 Francs). Should he be acquainted with any profession, such as turning, making shoes, or the work of a blacksmith, then his value increases to about 100 Tellas (16,000 Francs)."[57] Beyond this, facility in a trade most certainly played a part in life beyond manumission. Those former slaves who chose

[56] Blankenagel', *Zamechaniia Maiora Blankenagelia*, 14–15.

[57] Meyendorff, *Journey of the Russian Mission from Orenbourg to Bokhara*, 61. Thus, professional skills could also make it more difficult for a slave to purchase their own

to remain in the region had to find their own way – and often did – using either the skills that they had before their capture, or those they acquired during their captivity. From this we can hypothesize that those manumitted slaves who voluntarily chose to stay in Khwarazm, Bukhara, or the steppe after their release were more likely to be skilled laborers, or at least laborers who had found a niche, such as the Russian slave Ivan, mentioned earlier, who continued working in the Khwarazmian mines after buying his own freedom, or the Persian slaves who stayed on as court functionaries after spending much of their captivity at work in a similar capacity.

THE ROLES AND POSITION OF ENSLAVED WOMEN

The literature on enslaved women in Central Asia is quite meager when compared to that concerning male slaves. Elsewhere in the Near East, enslaved women were extensively involved in agricultural labor, so that we might expect to find a similar trend in Central Asia, but mentions of enslaved women working in the fields are scarce in the sources I have seen. Nevertheless, some important features concerning enslaved women's spheres of action emerge from the scattered evidence available, and a number of women left their own accounts of their captivity in the form of interviews at the Russian border.

The most commonly discussed subject in our sources concerning enslaved women in the region, particularly in travel literature and eyewitness reportage, is marriage: enslaved girls and women were purchased to be married to male slaves, and they were sometimes married by free men. They could also serve as concubines, particularly for elites. That enslaved women in the Muslim world could occupy intimate and central roles within their owners' household, even to the extent of bearing and raising their owners' children, has inspired some historians to hypothesize that they were liable to enjoy better treatment and a greater permanency of position than their male counterparts.[58] In particular, the legal status of *umm walad* ("mother of the child"), by which an enslaved woman who bears her owner's child is free upon the owner's death, has often been cited

freedom if these skills were demonstrated before the slave was sold, since the price of buying one's own freedom was never less than one's sale-price.

[58] See, for example, Anthony A. Lee, "Enslaved African Women in Nineteenth-Century Iran: The Life of Fezzeh Khanom of Shiraz," *Iranian Studies* 45:3 (2012), 426–427; 437.

as a key advantage, the likes of which naturally was not available to male slaves. Permanency of position did not necessarily equate to better treatment, however, and our sources on the Central Asian context often serve to emphasize elements of social instability and misfortune that were unique to enslaved women, and from which even bearing their owners' children served as scant protection. While marriage served to incorporate them into the household and – especially among nomadic Kazakhs – into the local community, the death of a husband could spell disaster for an enslaved woman and reveal the tenuous nature of the bonds her marriage had forged with the larger society around her. The following two examples, drawn from the testimony of escaped, formerly enslaved women themselves, will illustrate this point.

On March 30, 1800, a woman who had fled the steppe arrived at the Russian border and was interviewed by border officials. She told these officials that she did not know her own age or precisely where she had originally come from. She had been with the Kazakh Baybakt clan since her early childhood, living with a man whose name is recorded as Tulagan Khudaynazarov. When she had come of age, she learned from this man that she was a Kalmyk, and that Tulagan had been among a group of Kazakhs that had taken her and some other Kalmyks captive near the town of Ural'sk. This group of captives was then divided up, and Tulagan became her owner. According to the woman, Tulagan eventually came to value her above his own Kazakh wife. She bore him three sons and three daughters; two of the sons and two of the daughters died in childhood. In 1790, ten years before she arrived at the Russian border, Tulagan died, and the woman and her children fell upon hard times. Five years later, in poverty, she sold her only surviving son to another member of the Baybakt clan, named Baymirza, and her daughter was given in marriage to a Kazakh from the Alachin clan, among whom the woman and her daughter both went to live. There, they were both pressed into servitude (*upotrebili v prislugu*) and suffered abuses whose harshness they could not bear. Finding an opportune moment, the woman fled to the Russian border at the Nizhni-Ural'sk Line, from which she was transferred to the Orenburg Border Commission offices. The officials there, as per usual, asked her if she wished to be baptized. She declined, and was permitted to reside among the Muslims living at Orenburg.[59]

On the very same day, another former slave from the steppe was processed by border officials, and her story, though different in most

[59] TsGAKaz 4.1.198 ff. 36a–b.

details, bears some striking resemblances to the previous one. Her name was recorded as Chiben, and she was forty-four years old at the time of her interview. She was a Kalmyk, born and raised near the Chinese border, and she had been taken captive along with her mother and several other Kalmyks of both genders by a number of men from the Kazakh Middle Horde. She was taken, along with her mother and sister, to their captors' *ulus* and, soon after, she was traded to a Kazakh from the Little Horde for nine horses, a fleece-and-fur coat, and a gun. Her mother and sister remained with the Middle Horde.

When Chiben came of age, she became the concubine (*nalozhnitsa*) of her new owner, bearing him two sons and a daughter. Her daughter had been married off some five years previously – in 1795 – to a Kazakh of the Jabaltay (?) clan. In the winter of 1799–1800, Chiben's owner died, and Chiben (who is referred to at this point in the document as the man's wife) remained among the Kazakhs along with her sons. She claimed that, after the death of her owner, the others in the tribe began to inflict "intolerable oppression" upon her and her children. She fled to the Nizhni-Ural'sk Line along with her youngest son, who was then thirteen years old. Her other son, fifteen years old, remained among the Kazakhs. She too declined to be baptized, and asked that she might be given leave to visit the daughter mentioned previously, who had married into another Kazakh clan.[60]

We find striking common elements in these narratives: Both of these women were Kalmyks, and both had been taken captive at a young age; both evidently grew up with the owners whose children they would eventually bear; both saw their daughters married off to different Kazakh clans; and, most strikingly, both reported suffering abuse and mistreatment starting from the time their owners died. It is not clear whether either woman was given the traditional rights of an *umm walad* – that is, the right of manumission after their owners' death – though the fact that the first woman was able to sell her own son might hint at her free status. She was nevertheless forced into servitude once more when she transitioned between clans. Regardless of their legal standing in these two communities, it is clear that their long period of concubinage or marriage within the clan had not resulted in their full integration on equal footing with other clan members. Their wellbeing was a function of their owner's presence, and in their owner's absence they faced alienation, or worse, despite the fact that they had each grown up almost entirely within the clan community. Their slave status left permanent traces.

60 TsGAKaz 4.1.198 ff. 36b–37a.

It is conceivable that these women exaggerated the alleged abuses they suffered in order to play on the sympathies of border officials, but this would hardly have been necessary: There is no evidence that the treatment of enslaved people by their owners had any bearing on Russian officials' reception or treatment of them, either as a matter of policy or as a matter of record. The fact that both women came to the border only after the death of their owners suggests, at the very least, that they faced some sort of unwanted fate within their own communities in widowhood. It is likely that both were beyond the age of possible remarriage, and that the clan was unable or unwilling to support them in lieu of their spouses.[61]

As the following Russian border report shows, however, it was not only women who could face an undesirable future in the steppe after the death of a spouse. Manas Sadykov, said to be a Kalmyk,[62] was seventy years old when he was received by border officials on the June 19, 1800. He was originally from a village near the border with China, and was taken captive in his early youth by Middle Horde Kazakhs of the Atagay clan. They changed his name to N___ Sakay, and when he came of age he was married to a Kazakh woman named Janalia. They had a son and a daughter together, whose names are recorded as Kunabay and Jaima; the latter was given in marriage to a Kalmyk former slave who lived with the clan. When Manas' wife died, however, he no longer wished to live with the clan, and he arrived at the Russian border along with his Kalmyk son-in-law, though his own son, Kunabay, remained in the *orda*. He requested to be baptized, after which he was evidently settled in Stavropol. It is possible that his advanced age made it difficult for him to do any manual labor for the clan. But ultimately there is not much reason to doubt his own explanation of his motivations: When he lost his wife, he lost his will to stay with the clan.[63]

Even the slave-concubines of a khan could face an uncertain future after their royal owner's death. G. N. Zelenin, in his remembrances of the Russian mission to Khiva in 1842, as recorded by I. N. Zakhar'in, indicates as much in a lurid tale concerning the sexual services that had been offered to Russian officers during the embassy. We may justifiably cast suspicion

[61] More personal factors might also have played a part, of course: In the case of the first woman, for example, it is possible that her owner's first wife's jealousy over their relationship could have had some impact on the way she was treated after his death.

[62] If in fact this slave was a Kalmyk, Manas was certainly not the name he was born with: Manas is, after all, the legendary Kyrgyz hero (identified as a "Noghai" in earlier versions) who, according to the epic of the same name, battled Kalmyks and slaughtered in great numbers. It is possible that his Kazakh owners renamed him ironically.

[63] TsGAKaz 4.1.198 f. 54a.

upon Zelenin's story, given its resemblance to the popular Orientalist erotica of the same period, but it is nevertheless a unique account, not altogether impossible, and it is worth reproducing here. The story begins with a Tatar that Zelenin met in Khiva:

It turned out that he was a runaway soldier of ours, a Tatar and a native of Orenburg. Serving in the Orenburg garrison, he had often met with Zelenin on the streets of the city and remembered his face, being that of an officer to whom he had needed to doff his cap. He now had his own house in Khiva, and he already had a family there. Inviting his 'countrymen' over [to his house], he treated them to tea and asked that they come back often. But Zelenin was afraid to visit him again, as the neighboring Khivans cast very unfriendly glares upon this 'Russian,' and the Tatar's home was on the outskirts of the city, along the ravine. This [runaway] soldier was later [seen] in the residence of the embassy, and he offered its occupants – all of them young and single people – quite intimate services. But such a provider's place was already occupied. The garden, in which a reserve 'palace' of the Khan was situated (and where our embassy was housed), was overseen by a special gardener from among the Persian captives, a man who knows his trade well. And here, his wife, also a Persian captive, offered the officers [of the embassy] her confidential services, costing only a *poluimperial*: in the Khan's garden, at night, accompanying this lady gardener, a female figure would appear in a veil, a silk robe, and *shalvar* [loose-fitting pants], wrapped in muslin and in a Persian scarf. Upon demand, several such figures could appear in the garden at once. In strict secrecy the Persian lady [gardener] would make assurances that the mysterious strangers were the former wives of the dead Khan, whose material circumstances under the new Khan were nothing to envy ... It is quite possible that the lady gardener exaggerated the qualities and circumstances by which she came to recommend her ladies, and that they may have been simply Persian slave-girls, maidservants from the former Khan's harem; but their costumes were always very luxurious, and simple slave-girls could not have owned such things.[64]

Whether we choose to believe the claims of the Iranian gardener (or, for that matter, of Zelenin himself), the tale offers another possible answer to the question of what happened to enslaved wives and concubines once their owners died. It seems intuitive to presume that enslaved women, even once manumitted, did not share the same potential for social mobility as their male counterparts, and indeed evidence of their mobility – beyond their place in an individual household – is largely lacking. There are few reports of enslaved women taking up crafts or trades, and if the lack of reportage is at all indicative of real social circumstances, then it is possible

[64] Zakhar'in, "Posol'stvu v Khivu v 1842 godu," *Istoricheskii vestnik* 11 (1894), 442.

that enslaved women were also less likely to secure the earnings necessary to buy their own freedom.[65]

In this light, it is not surprising that, of the several Russian slaves interviewed by Witkiewicz in Bukhara, the individual in the saddest circumstances was the lone woman among them. She was "some major's daughter," then fifty years old, who had been captured when she was fifteen. She had been manumitted at some point, but her present occupation when Witkiewicz met her was, according to him, nothing more than "following after and imposing herself on all [Russian] newcomers."[66] Murav'ev too reports on the fate of enslaved women after their owner's death, though he seems to conflate the fate of enslaved women with that of women generally. "No one, not even the nearest relation," he writes, "is permitted to enter the female apartments, and the women are condemned to a life of the strictest solitude and most dreadful ennui. They are slaves, and on a man's death, the son has a right to sell them at pleasure."[67] According to Witkiewicz, at least some manumitted Iranian women in Bukhara were able to remarry, presumably of their own volition: "Most of the captives in Bukhara are Persian, and a significant portion of the current population of Bukhara is descended from the mixing of Tajiks and Uzbeks with freed Persians. One must, however, note that the Uzbeks will take for themselves the daughter of a Tajik or even a Persian, but they will not give their own daughters [in marriage] to them."[68]

The death of an elite personage could leave a great many enslaved women in a precarious position. One khan of Khwarazm, writes the American journalist Januarius Aloysius MacGahan, had four wives and "about a hundred slave women; he seems to have some from each of the races that are found in his dominions. The exact number I did not ascertain; the Khan himself one could not ask, as it is considered extremely unpolite, in Central Asia, to make any mention to a man of his wife, or wives."[69] Vambery reports the same number of "legitimate" wives for

[65] There is some evidence, however, that in rare cases women were able to purchase themselves from their owners. One such case is confirmed by a manumission contract preserved in V. L. Viatkin's collection of sixteenth-century legal documents from Samarkand, in which an Afghan woman bought her own freedom at the age of twenty-five (*Kaziiskie dokumenty XVI veka* [Tashkent, 1937], doc. no. 16, p. 49).

[66] Vitkevich, *Zapiski o Bukharskom khanstve*, 117.

[67] Murav'ev, *Muraviev's Journey to Khiva through the Turcoman Country*, 160.

[68] Vitkevich, *Zapiski o Bukharskom khanstve*, 115.

[69] MacGahan, *Campaigning on the Oxus, and the Fall of Khiva* (London: Sampson Low, Marston, Low, and Searle, 1874), 279. According to Joseph Wolff, the Bukharan Amīr Nasrullah likewise had four wives – "but," Wolff writes, "it is said that his wives hate him,

Muzaffar al-Dīn, Amīr of Bokhara, who, he writes, "has (for it is a custom of his religion) four legitimate wives and about twenty others, the former natives of Bokhara, the latter slaves, and, as I was told seriously, only employed to tend upon the children, of whom there are sixteen, ten girls (but I beg pardon, princesses), and six boys (Tore)."[70]

As little as we know about the fate of manumitted women, it is no clearer from our sources what sort of work women tended to do while still in slavery. While we know they bore children for their owners, it is not even entirely clear that enslaved women would have been primarily responsible for raising these children. The lack of exposés from inside the harem should not surprise us, despite the comparatively vast literature on slave-women – or "odalisques" – from elsewhere in the Muslim world (particularly the Ottoman Empire). It must be remembered that most of our literature on the subject is entirely fictional, little more than the product of European fantasies, and consists of speculation rather than eyewitness reportage. Precious few foreign men ever gained admittance to the female quarters of an elite Ottoman residence, and the same may be assumed of male travelers in Central Asia. Among the few travelers who purported to describe the functioning of a Central Asian harem, we may at least note the report of Vambery, who offers the dubious claim that most Uzbeks had little taste for Iranian slaves as concubines because they did not find Iranian women sufficiently beautiful; he likewise notes, more plausibly, that relative poverty prevented most Uzbeks from indulging extensively in polygamy with slave-women:

> As for the female slaves, they do not by any means enjoy the position which is occupied by the daughters of Circassia and Georgia in the harems of Turkey and Persia. On the contrary, their position is rather to be compared with that of the negresses in those countries. It is very easy to explain why. In the first place, the daughters of Turkestan correspond better to the ideas of beauty entertained by Oezbegs and Tadjiks than the Iranian women, who with their olive complexions and large noses, would never bear off the apple of Paris from the fair, full-cheeked Oezbeg women. In the second place, in consequence of their poverty the

and that they are Persian slaves" (Wolff, *Narrative of a Mission to Bukhara in the Years 1843–1845, to Ascertain the Fate of Colonel Stoddart and Captain Conolly*, Vol. 1 [London: John W. Parker, 1845], 327).

70 Vambery, *Travels in Central Asia* (New York: Harper & Brothers, 1865), 226. Elsewhere, Vambery complicates the notion that slave-wives were not "legitimate," writing that "in Bokhara, where the Oezbeg aristocratic is of little moment by the side of the predominant Persian element, the sovereigns often take slaves for their lawful wives. Such was the mother of the present Emir, such is one of his wives, both of them of Iranian origin" (*Sketches of Central Asia* [London: W.H. Allen & Co., 1868], 221).

inhabitants of Central Asia do not indulge in polygamy to such an extent as the Mohammedans of the West. Besides this, the Oezbeg has generally too much aristocratic pride to share his bed and board with a slave, whom he has bought for money. In Bokhara it is true that we find instances to the contrary, but that is only among the high functionaries of state, and even they only take such women as have been brought as children into the country. In the middle classes such mis-alliances are very rare phenomena. Besides, marriage is much easier here than in other Mohammedan countries. Hence female slaves are kept only as articles of luxury in the harems of the great, or as domestic servants.[71]

Vambery's claims about the rarity of Iranian wives and concubines contrasts with most other accounts, but it cannot be dismissed out-of-hand: there is simply too little information on the labors of Central Asian slave-women to decisively confirm what sort of domestic roles they played and what place they tended to have in the household. It is plausible, at least, that many enslaved women served as maidservants, as Vambery suggests. Concerning Khwarazm, Zelenin recounts that "with [slave] girls, their dealings were much simpler: the beautiful ones among them filled the harems of Khivan nobles and wealthy merchants, and the ugly occupied [the same place, but] as slave-girls and servants."[72]

A still smaller body of evidence is available concerning the role of enslaved women among the Turkmens. Eyewitness and secondhand reportage on the subject is, moreover, sometimes contradictory, and it is thoroughly permeated with the tone of contempt and derision common to nearly all nineteenth-century writings on the Turkmens, whether it be English, Russian, or Iranian. General agreement exists, at least, that slave women often became concubines among the Turkmens, as Grodekov claims for the Teke: "The women are the chief prize, becoming, on their arrival at the aoul, the concubines of their captors; their children being brought up in slavery."[73] Rzhevuskii commented on these arrangements in the larger context of Turkmen marriage and social organization:

Turkmens can have several wives, and, if they have sufficient funds, they set out several tents, one for each wife, arranged near one-another. In conditions of poverty, they all live under the same roof. Divorce is completely dependent on the husband['s will]. Aside from their wives, Turkmens often associate with their female slaves, as a consequence of which all the Yomuds are divided into the *kul* and

71 Vambery, *Sketches of Central Asia*, 218–219.
72 Zakhar'in, "Posol'stvu v Khivu v 1842 godu," 445.
73 Grodekoff, *Colonel Grodekoff's Ride from Samarcand to Herat* (London: W.H. Allen & Co., 1880), 134.

the *iz*. To the first category belong all who are born of slave women; to the second, of Yomud mothers. The *kul*'s inheritance is half that of the *iz*.[74]

Whether Turkmens could actually marry their enslaved women remained a matter of debate, however. Some claimed that this practice was strictly forbidden, as in the following – highly suspect – report on the Teke:

Custom prohibits the Teke from marrying slave-women, and this is one of the most prominent motifs of Teke poetry. The beautiful, delicate Persians strongly tempt them, but their law does not permit the Tekes to enrich their tribe with cross-breeds, and for that reason, in those cases where a love-struck gentleman exercises the right of the victor by impregnating his captive and she gives birth, the baby is either killed or sold into slavery. Generally speaking, the family environment in Akhal-Teke is fairly wholesome, although (or perhaps because?) husbands often beat their wives.[75]

Suffice to say this is the only extant source that claims the Turkmens killed their own children, and I believe we may dismiss the notion as a silly fantasy. At the opposite extreme is the British traveler John Wood, who claimed not only that Turkmens could marry their slaves, but even that their free-born wives became slaves upon marriage. "The custom of man-stealing," Wood writes, "appears to have smothered every better feeling, and the practice of trafficking in human beings extends even into their domestic arrangements; for their wives are as much articles of property as their slaves, and are bought and sold with the same callous indifference."[76] Suffice to say that efforts to better understand the predicament of enslaved women among the Turkmens must await the revelation of better sources than these, if such sources exist.

The relative lack of eyewitness information on enslaved women mostly indicates an imbalance of access, and perhaps an imbalance of interest on the part of witnesses, and should not be thought to suggest a scarcity of women among the ranks of the enslaved. Among the Kazakhs, Semeniuk alleges that women and children formed the predominant enslaved demographic, and that slaves were therefore predominantly found occupying women's and children's roles in the household.[77] This makes some intuitive sense given that women and children were less likely to attack their own captors (a constant danger) or to successfully flee from them, and also

[74] Rzhevuskii, "Ot Tiflisa do Dengil'-tepe," 292.
[75] "Zavoevanie Akhal-Tekinskogo oazisa," *Istoricheskii vestnik* 7 (1881), 823.
[76] Wood, *Journey to the Source of the River Oxus*, 133.
[77] Semeniuk, "Likvidatsiia rabstva v Kazakhstane," 175. Stremoukhov made a similar claim concerning the traffic in women in Bukhara ("Poezdka v Bukharu," 690).

because slave-women could carry a price similar to that of men on the open market: they were, in other words, easier to obtain and no less valuable than men.[78] But there are few eyewitness reports by observers who actually witnessed enslaved women and children at work in Kazakh households and communities, and few of the formerly enslaved women interviewed at the Russian border described the sort of work they did. Moreover, as far as I have seen, women are in the minority among those who escaped captivity in the steppe. There are a few possible reasons for this. First, women may have been less inclined to attempt the dangerous and arduous journey to the nearest Russian fortification. Second, given that many – perhaps even most – enslaved women in the steppe bore children by their owners or by others, their children may have served as an additional incentive not to flee the clan.

MARRIAGE AMONG SLAVES

Oftentimes these children were the product of marriages that were arranged between enslaved men and women. Integrating slaves into the social fabric of the community, however temporarily, was, according to some eyewitnesses, the main reason why male slaves were permitted to marry at all. "Desiring as much as possible to tie the slaves to their new fatherland," writes Zalesov of Khwarazm, "the Uzbeks usually try to marry them off, finding them brides who, for the most part, are also Persian captives from their master's harem, or else dilapidated beauties from the Khan's harem."[79] Because the children of male slaves were likewise slaves, the owners also benefited from their slaves' marriages, as these unions could serve to produce more human property for them. It is likely for this reason – rather than pure generosity – that we find reports of some owners purchasing women specifically for the purposes of marrying them to their male slaves. Burnes, for example, interviewed an Iranian slave from Mashhad who, he writes, "gave us a favourable account of his treatment by his master, who intended to purchase a wife for him; but he had no hope of his liberty."[80] In Khwarazm and Bukhara, it seems that the purchased wives were generally Iranian, though they could be married to male slaves

[78] Some reports on Persian–Turkmen conflicts exist in which it appears that *only* women and children were taken captive – this seems especially to have been a common strategy inflicted by Persian troops on the Turkmens. See, for example, *Russko-Turkmenskie otnosheniia v XVIII–XIX vv.* (Ashgabat, 1963): doc. no. 299 (419–423); doc. no. 373 (453–454); doc. no. 373 (505–506).

[79] Zalesov, "Pis'mo iz Khivy," 286. [80] Burnes, *Travels into Bokhara*, Vol. 1, 256.

of any background. Meyendorff, among others, observed that enslaved Iranian women were used for the purposes of increasing the general labor pool: "[W]e find among the slaves in Bokhara Hezurehs, Chitrars, Siapuchs, and even Georgians; their number never diminishes, for they are given Persian women in marriage, it being the interest of their masters to keep them up."[81]

Among the Kazakhs, there is evidence of a remarkably different dynamic: while I have found no indication of slaves in Khwarazm and Bukhara marrying free, non-Iranian women (free Uzbeks, for example), it was apparently not unusual for slaves in the steppe to take free Kazakh brides. Particular customs governed this phenomenon. In at least some parts of the steppe, if a free female member of the *orda* married a slave, their children would remain technically free, but they would likewise serve the family that their enslaved father served.[82] Different customs applied to enslaved women who married free Kazakh men: These women would evidently convert and be manumitted as part of the terms of their marriage, but their original owner (if this person was not the woman's new husband) could decide even then whether to send the woman to her husband or, rejecting the marriage, keep her in servitude.[83]

Among the Kazakhs, it seems that marriage could be a very effective means of integrating male slaves into the community. The most vivid indication of this fact is the high incidence of married slaves who, having been surrendered by their owners and manumitted by decree at the Russian border, chose to return to their homes among the Kazakhs rather than opting to be repatriated elsewhere. A few exemplary individuals, all of whom were interviewed in September of 1852 and all of whom are referred to as "Afghans" in records of border officials, will serve to illustrate this and other common features of slave marriages among the Kazakhs:

(1) An Afghan, forty-five years old, was surrendered to the Russian authorities by his owner and interviewed by Russian border officials. He did not know the details of how he had been taken captive, only that he had initially been sold by Turkmens to a Kazakh named Khuday-Berdi for sixty *ṭilla*s, and that, when he was four years old, he was sold to his present owner at the same price. He lived with his present owner from that time on. During this period he received his own tent (*otdel'naia kibitka*),

[81] Meyendorff, *Journey of the Russian Mission from Orenbourg to Bokhara*, 61–62.
[82] S. Zimanov, *Obshchestvennyi stroi kazakhov pervoi poloviny XIX veka i Bukeevskoe khanstvo* (Almaty: Arys, 2009), 281.
[83] Zimanov, *Obshchestvennyi stroi kazakhov pervoi poloviny XIX veka*, 281.

married a Kazakh woman, and raised three sons and two daughters with her. Upon receiving his Russian-decreed freedom at Orenburg, he evidently returned home again to his family among the Kazakhs.[84]

(2) An Afghan, thirty-four years old and originally from Herat, told the Russian authorities that he had been captured by Turkmens nineteen years previously while he was out watching after cattle. These Turkmens carried him along with them for the next two years before finally trading him to a Kazakh for some quantity of sheep. He lived with this Kazakh from that time on. He married a Kazakh woman, though he does not report having any children with her. Upon being surrendered by his owner and receiving his Russian-ordained manumission, he too seems to have simply returned home again to his wife among the Kazakhs, choosing not to return to Herat.[85]

(3) An Afghan, forty years old, whose name was recorded as Baydullah, was also originally from Herat. He was taken captive by Turkmens at ten years old, and he remained among the Turkmens for the next five years, after which they sold him to his present Kazakh owner, with whom he lived for more than two decades before being surrendered to the Russian authorities. He had a Kazakh wife and a daughter, and opted not to be returned to his original home in Herat.[86]

(4) An Afghan whose name is recorded as Tursun[87] was twenty-two years old when he was surrendered by his Kazakh owner to the Russian authorities. He reports that he came from among the Afghans (*iz afgantsev*), but does not specify a town or village. This is likely because he was captured early in his youth, since he claimed not to know the details of his original captivity or who sold him to his present owner. He was married to a Kazakh woman, with whom he had a son. He too reported possessing his own tent, and he did not wish for border officials to return him to his original home (of which he seems to have had no knowledge in any case).[88]

According to the Soviet historian Zimanov, slaves among the Kazakhs who gained the confidence of their owners were sometimes given not only their own tents but even their own livestock. Those who attained this level of autonomy were generally withdrawn from the pool of slaves who were sold and resold as commodities, though their owners retained this right at all times.[89] It is not clear whether this custom had strong parallels among

[84] TsGAKaz 4.1.3646 ff. 47b–48a. [85] TsGAKaz 4.1.3646 ff. 48a–b.
[86] TsGAKaz 4.1.3646 ff. 48b–49a.
[87] He was most likely given this name by the Kazakhs. [88] TsGAKaz 4.1.3646 f. 49b.
[89] Zimanov, *Obshchestvennyi stroi kazakhov pervoi poloviny XIX veka*, 278.

the slaves of Khwarazm and Bukhara, though Alexander Burnes reports having met an enslaved Russian in Bukhara who had not only a wife and child, but even his own slaves.[90] In the context of the khanates too there can be little doubt about the effectiveness of marriage in developing a male slave's local loyalties – if not to his owner, then at least to his new family. When Joseph Wolff, the missionary and adventurer, met with a Bukharan official concerning, among other things, the release of Russian and Persian slaves, the official was eager to show him a selection of those Russians who had no desire to return to Russia; their disinclination was couched in terms that should not surprise us: some claimed to be deserters, but others replied, "We are married here, and have wives and children."[91]

LIMITED SPACES FOR SLAVES' AUTONOMY

Evidence of autonomy and independent initiatives among the enslaved are not abundant in our sources, which generally lack the depth of detail we find in Mīrzā Maḥmūd's narrative. Nevertheless, the evidence that exists – slaves entrusted with their own households in the steppe, for example, as well as some of the examples I will offer here – are helpful in reconstructing the possible range of slaves' experiences. On the more dramatic end of the spectrum, we have at least one account, offered by Murav'ev, of a woman who – like Mīrzā Maḥmūd – was able to convince her master to re-sell her in order to enhance her living conditions. Despite her master's eventual consent, the circumstances reported by Murav'ev, who traveled with the woman and her owner in a caravan, are tragic:

> On the leading camel sat Fatima, by birth a Kurd, and formerly Said's father's concubine. She had been 12 years his slave, and now, wishing to improve her lot, begged her master to sell her in Khiva. On his refusal to part with her, she threatened to commit suicide; so he gave in. It is incredible what this woman endured on the road. Clothed only in rags, she led the caravan day and night, hardly slept or ate, and, when we halted, attended to the camels, cooked her master's food, &c ... Said himself became disrespectful, as the following incident will show: He had taken his female slave Fatima to all the villages and bazars about, but could nowhere get his price for her. This poor woman lived in the same room with all the rest of the party, but when they went out she used to be so ill-treated by the other people in the fortress, that I had frequently to send Petrovitch to drive them off. On one of these occasions the ruffians behaved so badly to her, that

[90] Burnes, *Travels into Bokhara*, Vol. 1, 294.
[91] Wolff, *Narrative of a Mission to Bokhara*, Vol. 2, 42.

Fatima fled, and declared that she would certainly take her own life if she were not sold soon. When Said returned I represented the state of things to him, and begged him to have it altered, and to sell Fatima, whose presence was a scandal to us all. He listened to me quietly, then rose up and said, "Farewell Murad Beg! My service is at an end, for since this is to be your treatment of me, I leave you. Fatima is my slave, and I shall sell her whenever and to whomsoever I please." With those words he went away, but I called him back, and he came, probably supposing I would ask his pardon for my interference . . . I made the matter up with him, and next day he sold Fatima.[92]

Vambery offers another memorable (but, like all of his reportage, potentially fictional) story concerning the influence enslaved women could have over their owners. He claims that two of the traveling-companions who accompanied him for a short while on the road to Khiva were a Turkmen and his wife, the latter having convinced her husband to travel there. She had been captured some time previously in a surprise raid, during which her husband had been badly wounded. She undertook the journey, Vambery tells us, to ascertain whether her former husband was still alive, what person or persons had bought her children, and what had become of her 12-year-old daughter. "The poor woman," Vambery writes, "by extraordinary fidelity and laboriousness, had so enchained her new master, that he consented to accompany her on her sorrowful journey of enquiry. I was always asking him what he would do if her former husband were forthcoming, but his mind on that point was made up – the law guaranteed him his possession."[93]

Such rare anecdotes aside, there can be no doubt that the most common and widely documented means by which both enslaved men and women demonstrated their autonomy was by fleeing from their owners. Along with evidence from the many slaves who fled to the Russian border (the subject of the following chapter), stories concerning escaped slaves also appear in many travelers' reports, such as the narrative which emerged in a colonial court case witnessed by J. A. MacGahan. A Russian colonel presided over the court, into which an elderly Khivan woman entered, "leading a lubberly-looking young man about fourteen, and bowing almost to the earth at every step, and [she] addressed the Colonel, whom she took for General Kaufmann, as the 'Yarim-Padshah,' or half-emperor, which title the Colonel accepted with grave composure." She wore a tall white turban and a "dirty-looking tunic," and she presented the colonel with an

[92] Murav'ev, *Muraviev's Journey to Khiva through the Turcoman Country*, 31n; 56.
[93] Vambery, *Travels in Central Asia*, 76.

offering of bread and apricots before making her case. She claimed that her son, the "gawky boy" next to her, had been robbed of his wife by "a vile thieving dog of a Persian slave," who had also stolen her donkey and used it to carry the boy's wife away. "So he is three times a thief," the colonel replied. "He stole the donkey, the girl, and himself." The colonel then asked the woman about the identity of the stolen bride. "She is a Persian girl," the woman replied. "I bought her from a Turcoman who had just brought her from Astrabad, and I paid fifty tillahs for her. The dog of a slave must have bewitched her, for as soon as she saw him she flew into his arms, weeping and crying, and said, 'he was her old playmate.' That was nonsense, and I beat her for it soundly. The marriage was to be celebrated in a few days; but as soon as the Russians came, the vile hussy persuaded the slave to run away with her, and I believe they are as good as married." In the end, MacGahan writes, the escaped slaves were never returned to the woman and her son, and neither was the donkey.[94] Collusion among slaves was a common means of escape both in settled lands and in the steppe, with many of those who came to the Russian border arriving in the company of others.

Beyond fleeing from their owners, there were other, less drastic – albeit also less well-evidenced – means by which the enslaved endeavored to shape their own experiences. For example, those up for sale or newly purchased could try to influence their appeal to certain buyers by modulating their behavior.[95] Some documents suggest that a slave showing defects that became obvious only after his or her sale could be returned in exchange for a refund, or for a new, more satisfactory slave. A terse Bukharan document in Persian, published in facsimile by S. K. Ismailova, reveals this sort of exchange; its author writes: "[To] Muḥammadshah Bay: a female slave given by us to Qarategin has turned out to be insane [*divāna buda ast*]. On receiving her, you should punish her and keep her for yourself. In her place send a female slave [*chūrī*] brought from Nurāt."[96] That such a "refund" could be imposed through legal means is evidenced by another Bukharan document, published in facsimile by Faiziev, in which the buyer of a female slave realized only too late that his purchase had a serious skin-disease and took his complaint before the court in hopes of getting his money back.[97] It is easy to imagine slaves

[94] MacGahan, *Campaigning on the Oxus*, 199–201.

[95] See, for example, Zakhar'in, "Posol'stvu v Khivu v 1842 godu," 285.

[96] Ismailova, "Dokumenty o rabstva v bukharskom khanstve v XIX– nachale XX v." *Izvestiia Akademii nauk Tadzhikskoi SSR, otdelenie obshchestvennykh nauk* 2/72 (1973), 27.

[97] Faiziev, *Buxoro feodal jamiyatida qullardan foidalanishga doir hujjatlar (XIX asr)*, doc. no. 7, 102–103; 25.

making use of such legal processes to change owners, perhaps by faking insanity or incompetence, or otherwise by altering their behavior and managing their own conduct.

Mīrzā Maḥmūd's narrative, meanwhile, points toward the different ways in which slaves could modulate their own skills and talents in the presence of their owners in order to resist – or change the nature of – certain types of work or work-regimes. Abilities that might be put to uncomfortable use were likely hidden; skilled artisans may have been apt to conceal their craft if they feared it would increase their owners' demand for their labor without any further benefit to themselves. Women faced with concubinage could endeavor to make themselves less desirable to their owners, or to make themselves more desirable if it might result in better treatment.

In this chapter, we have seen something of the diversity of slave labor, slaves' roles, and slaves' family life in Central Asia. Slaves worked the land; they processed the land's produce; they worked as blacksmiths, artillerymen, guardsmen, herdsmen, maidservants, harem attendants, court attendants, shrine attendants, concubines, well-diggers, entertainers, carpenters, leather-workers, textile-workers, teachers, soldiers, officers, and administrators. They could be appointed as their owners' agents in commerce. They were wives and mothers. Even if an individual owned no slaves, he or she would have been immersed in a world partially made and thoroughly inhabited by slaves.

Unlike slaves who were specifically acquired to tend to a monoculture, such as slaves on colonial-era Caribbean sugar plantations, each individual Central Asian slave would likely have been put to work in a variety of tasks, occupying multiple social spheres and spaces throughout his or her lifetime. Enslaved men had a particularly broad range of mobility, as they were able to work more extensively outside the home and in a greater variety of trades. The work a slave performed could be defined by his or her capabilities, be it metalworking or leading a military regiment. Generally speaking, though, greater mobility should not be mistaken for greater autonomy: Work was delegated to slaves by their owners, and slaves' abilities to earn their own autonomous revenue or define their own labor regimen depended entirely upon their masters' will.

Having observed in this chapter some of the many roles and spheres of action occupied by Central Asian slaves, the next chapter will provide a closer look at one of the most dramatic means by which slaves asserted their autonomy: by fleeing from their masters.

5

From Slaves to Serfs

Manumission along the Kazakh Frontier

Throughout the eighteenth and nineteenth centuries, thousands of slaves, predominantly Iranians and Kalmyks, issued from the steppe and arrived at the Russian border. At first, these slaves were exclusively refugees who had escaped their owners. Later on, following the imperial decree that all steppe peoples must give up their slaves to Russian officials, those slaves who arrived at the border usually came with their owners in tow. Two difficult decisions faced the officials during this period: they had to decide who was really a slave, a process which involved defining slavery itself, and they had to decide what was to be done with those slaves who, having been freed either by escape or by decree, were now at the disposal of the Russian Empire. The results of these negotiations were often surprising, and the border authorities' internal records preserve the story of how some slaves became serfs, and how some slave-owners became foster parents. This chapter considers such decisions as these and the logic behind them, while challenging the longstanding consensus among historians that the Russian project of manumitting slaves from the steppe was motivated by ideals of abolitionism.

By the mid-eighteenth century, a steady stream of escaped slaves and captives from among the Kazakhs were arriving at Russian garrisons along the steppe frontier. What these escapees expected from the Russians is not clear; perhaps some expected safe passage to settle within the Russian Empire, or help in returning to their original homes elsewhere in the region. Others may have had no preconceptions at all, simply preferring to take their chances with the Russians rather than remain in captivity. Having taken the risk of fleeing into the steppe, either alone or in small groups, many of these escapees would have been profoundly disappointed by their fate upon arriving at the Russian border: Throughout the eighteenth century, and even well into the nineteenth, the Russian *modus operandi* was generally to return escaped slaves to their Kazakh owners. This was inspired in part by a desire to maintain good relations with local Kazakh rulers and elites, but it may also have been the legacy of a sinister Russian policy in the steppe: During the Bashkir Uprising of 1704–1711, the Tsarist authorities had evidently encouraged their Kazakh allies to plunder and enslave Bashkirs.[1] Having provided for the perpetuation and even the increase of slavery among the Kazakhs, the Russians were certainly not inclined to give quarter to those lucky enough to escape it, while offending their allies in the process. There was one exception, however, and the exception was made law by a decree issued from the Bureau of Foreign Affairs in February of 1752: escaped slaves who agreed to be baptized would thereafter be officially welcomed into the Russian Empire.[2] Three decades later, in October of 1781, an imperial edict established that all captives fleeing Kazakh lands would be free to settle in Russia or to be returned to their homelands if they so desired.[3]

By the mid-nineteenth century, the Orenburg Border Commission had decreed the end of slavery in the steppe, and even began employing Kazakh "native informants" to help free the region's slave population (a subject to which we will return in the following chapter). As border authorities would discover throughout this period, however, it was not always an easy matter to negotiate the terrain of manumission. Internal documents produced by the Orenburg Border Commission and affiliated offices provide remarkably intimate reportage in this respect. We find in these documents that Russian notions of slavery and abolition did not always map cleanly onto the Kazakh context, and that official manumission policies were not always well-understood even by the border officials tasked with enforcing them. Abolishing Kazakh slavery would entail defining Kazakh slavery, first of all – and then there was still the matter of what should be done with all the newly manumitted men, women and children who were now at the tsar's disposal.

Among those escaping slavery in the steppe, it seems that many – and especially Kalmyks – chose to convert to Christianity at the prompting of

1 Zimanov, *Obshchestvennyi stroi kazakhov pervoi poloviny XIX veka*, 283.

2 Zimanov, *Obshchestvennyi stroi kazakhov pervoi poloviny XIX veka*, 283. Evidence indicates that some – especially those professing the hardship of their prior circumstances – were allowed to remain in Russia even without being baptized, though these allowances were not evidently supported by official policy. TsGAKaz 4.1.198 ff. 36a–b.

3 TsGAKaz 4.1.198 f. 38a.

border officials in order to be resettled within the Russian Empire. These new Russians were typically resettled in communities of other refugees and immigrants, such as those that could be found in the towns of Stavropol, Sarapul, and Karakul.[4] Those choosing to be baptized sometimes reported suffering bad treatment under their Kazakh owners, as did the escaped slave whose name was recorded as Muḥammad Akhmetov. A Persian from Sabzavar, Akhmetov had been captured by Turkmens while on a trading mission to Astarabad. He had been sold to a Kazakh for 100 sheep, and he remained with this owner for the next five years. Akhmetov reports that his owner inflicted various tortures upon him and kept him in a state of starvation. For this reason, he fled to the Lower Ural'sk line "with the intention of becoming a Christian" and making his home in the town of Ural'sk.[5]

Others who chose to be baptized claimed to be attempting to join relatives who had immigrated previously. One such refugee reported having been captured some twenty years prior along with his mother and brother, both of whom had fled to Russia almost immediately. He had been too young to join them in their flight, and so he remained in service to a Kazakh woman for another two decades before making his escape. Seizing an opportune moment, he stole a horse and fled to where he hoped to make contact with his brother, who, he had learned, was serving in an Ural Cossack army regiment based in Kazan. He was unable to find his brother, but wished to be resettled in Stavropol nevertheless.[6]

In another document, we find the report that seven Iranian slaves who had fled the steppe all shared an inclination to be baptized and repatriated as citizens of the Russian Empire. These Iranians hailed from various cities – Astarabad, Mashhad, and Sabzavar among them – and were evidently unrelated. But all claimed to have relatives in Ural'sk, a coincidence we may justifiably regard as suspect. In any event, they were duly baptized, and their names were "Christianized": Muḥammad Khan became Konstantin; Muḥammad ʿAlī became Aleksei. They were then permitted to reside in Ural'sk "or some other place" under Russian dominion.[7]

Escaped slaves typically arrived at the border with no resources of their own, and with no safe, practical means of getting where they were going, whether it be to somewhere within the Russian Empire or to their original homeland of Iran or Afghanistan. Border authorities often absorbed the expenses – or, in later periods, charged Kazakh elites who had failed to

[4] TsGAKaz 4.1.198 ff. 54a–b; 137a; 173a–b. [5] TsGAKaz 4.1.198 f. 19a.
[6] TsGAKaz 4.1.198 f. 104a. [7] TsGAKaz 4.1.198 f. 15a.

ensure that the slaves were turned over – and also made arrangements for necessary lodging and transport.[8] The authorities could not allow just anyone to take advantage of these accommodations, however, and Russian officials were well aware of the possibility that an individual arriving fresh from the wilds, with an exotic tale to tell, might not be who he or she claimed to be. In cases of doubt, examinations were administered. One escapee, who arrived at the border in the Spring of 1862 and whose name was recorded as Nādir Sagarkulin, claimed to be an Iranian from Tehran, where he had lived with his mother, three brothers, his wife, and two children (all of whose names were recorded by border officials). Two years previously, he had been appointed to a military detachment tasked with raiding a Turkmen encampment, but he was taken captive in the campaign and sold to a Bukharan, with whom he lived for no more than half a year. This Bukharan sold him to a Kokandian merchant, and he went to live with that owner in Tashkent and in Turkestan. This Kokandian treated him cruelly, and he fled to Fort Perovskii in order to ask the Russian officials to send him back home, via Astrakhan, as he had no other means of making the journey. Before agreeing to this, however, the border authorities had him examined by a titular medical counselor of the Syr Darya Line, who reported that Sagarkulin appeared to be the age he claimed to be. He also offered his opinion on the matter that probably inspired this and other examinations: that there "were no signs of corporal punishment on his body by which one could suspect him of being a criminal fleeing Russia[n authorities]."[9] Another test was also deemed necessary: Sagarkulin was brought before some Bukharan merchants, who traded at the Fort Perovskii bazaar, in order to confirm that he was indeed an Iranian.[10] Having confirmed to the modest extent possible that Nādir Sagarkulin was more likely an Iranian escaped slave than a disguised fugitive from Russia, the border officials consented to transport him back home to Iran via Astrakhan.

The next step for Sagarkulin, and for any other refugee who was to be conveyed back home, was the arrangement of transport. For this, border officials relied on the region's caravans, and in some cases the safety of the passengers was ensured by the appointment of a police escort or

[8] TsGAKaz 4.1.3641 ff. 137a–b; TsGAKaz 4.1.3573 ff. 41a–b; TsGAKaz 4.1.195 f. 10b; TsGAKaz 4.1.3573 f. 68a.

[9] TsGAKaz 4.1.195 ff. 10a–11a.

[10] TsGAKaz 4.1.195 f. 11a. These same merchants also verified the origins of at least one other escaped Persian slave, whose name is recorded as Fayzullah Muhammad Kasymov (TsGAKaz 4.1.195 f. 5a).

others who might watch over them.[11] Iranian slaves headed back to Iran would sometimes be added to the ranks of caravans bound for Bukhara, and the caravan drivers themselves were made to sign a document confirming that they would guarantee the delivery of these temporary wards of the state.

One Bukharan caravan driver – Raḥīmbay Atambaev – was employed repeatedly for these purposes.[12] In the course of one of his missions, Atambaev became involved in a curious episode that reveals the lengths to which the Commission would go in order to ensure the safe repatriation of former slaves. Having been tasked with delivering an Uzbek refugee whose name is recorded as Muslimberdi, Raḥīmbay informed this Uzbek that his caravan, which was set to depart from the Orenburg trading grounds, would be traveling through the territory of the Kazakh clan among which Muslimberdi had been kept as a slave. Because his former master still lived among them, it was resolved that Muslimberdi should instead leave on another caravan that would bypass this dangerous territory. The Uzbek could rest assured that a suitable caravan would be available to him, since another Bukharan caravan was being driven by Kazakhs from a clan hostile to that of his former owner. They would most certainly avoid their rival clan's territory. The officials of the Orenburg Customs House agreed to put Muslimberdi on this caravan.

The caravan was not imminently scheduled to depart, however, and Muslimberdi had no choice but to wait in Orenburg. The problem was that Muslimberdi had no resources of any kind, and no way to care for himself in the meantime. A Customs House official named Burtsov agreed to put him to work, offering him clothing, lodgings, and the promise that he would send him off with some money when the time came. Muslimberdi ended up remaining in Burtsov's employ for the next six months, evidently opting to remain in Orenburg rather than to return home on a caravan. Nevertheless, he turned up at the border authorities' offices again sometime later, claiming that Burtsov had refused to give him the clothing and money that he had been promised. Burtsov responded with the claim that he was in no way obligated to pay him, and, moreover, that Muslimberdi had since moved on to work for an Afghan prince living in Orenburg who paid him only in food, but who ultimately turned him away. It was only, Burtsov alleged, because of his present unemployment that Muslimberdi had come to the border authorities seeking money in "reparation." At this

[11] TsGAKaz 4.1.206 f. 34a; 4.1.198 f. 15a.
[12] TsGAKaz 4.1.3573 f. 67a; TsGAKaz 4.1.1490 ff. 17a–18a.

point it appears to be Burtsov who requested that Muslimberdi be put on a Bukharan caravan and sent back home.[13]

Notwithstanding complications such as these, repatriating former slaves to their original homelands appears usually to have been a relatively straightforward matter. Those who chose to be baptized and resettled in the Russian Empire, however, occasioned a more intricate protocol. Details on the fate that awaited these refugees are preserved in a work by Nikolai Blinov,[14] and what Blinov reveals is quite astonishing. Having escaped slavery in the steppe and having placed themselves at the mercy of the Russian Empire, these former slaves were converted not only into Christians, but also into serfs. For those historians who consider serfdom a type of slavery, it could be argued that these refugees were thus promptly re-enslaved by the very state that purported to free them.

Blinov's discussion concerns just one of the many towns in which escapees were often resettled: Sarapul, a settlement on the right bank of the Kama River. He writes that Sarapul served as a point of resettlement for Persians, Khivans, Afghans, Bukharans, and "white Arabs" (*belye arapy*), and that these immigrants had, by the late nineteenth century, integrated with the population such that one often met with burghers and peasants "with hair and beards as black as pitch" – hallmarks of "Asian" descent – among the light-haired Russian population. These, Blinov tells us, are escaped slaves who had converted to Christianity and had found safe passage into the Russian Empire thanks to the government's concern for the fate of foreign migrants.[15]

Blinov dates the Russian Empire's decision to receive converted refugees to the early 1760s, the dawn of Catherine the Great's reign, citing a decree that specified that "people of the various Asian nations" who were received at the border should be asked whether they wished to settle in the Empire and, if so, where they wished to settle. Some would then enter into the employ of private individuals (as Muslimberdi had done); the rest were conveyed to Moscow, where they would receive new clothing and provisions while awaiting resettlement. The ultimate goal was for these individuals to adopt "Russian customs" and to acquire basic proficiency in the Russian language so that they would be well-adapted to their new homeland. The first group of such refugees to arrive in Moscow consisted of seventy-two men and women, none of whom spoke enough Russian to

[13] TsGAKaz 4.1.1490 ff. 17a–18a.

[14] Blinov, *Sarapul': istoricheskii ocherk'* (Sarapul, 1887).

[15] Blinov, *Sarapul'*, 13.

express precisely where in the Russian Empire they wished to settle. It was thus decided that they should be sent eastward again, to the vicinity of Kazan and Orenburg. Here they would find settlements, surrounded by suitable farmland, in which they could meet "the local peasants who, through proximity to the Bashkirs and Tatars, might know their language." The Kalmyk refugees would be separated from the Persians. Accordingly, fifty-four Kalmyks were sent to Sarapul, and eighteen Persians were sent to Karakul.[16]

The refugees were sent off in a convoy of twenty carts. They were overseen by two Russian officers, one of whom served as a translator, along with three soldiers tasked with ensuring that no harm came to them. They were ordered to travel as quickly as possible, no less than fifty versts per day, and a stipend of five kopeks per day was allotted to each refugee for food. If any among them became ill and died during the journey, they were to be buried in the nearest churchyard. Upon their arrival at Sarapul and Karakul, they would be received by local officials who were appointed as their stewards. These stewards were tasked with dividing them into groups of two, three, or four individuals – or however the steward saw fit – and arranging for them to receive training in the Russian language. These small groups would be given over to reliable local peasants who would train them in all things customary for a Russian peasant, including the mechanics of tilling and plowing, as well as Christian observances. The refugees were to attend church on Sundays and on holidays, though no abuse or injury should be inflicted upon them if they neglected to do so. During their first year of residence, each individual would continue to receive an allowance of five kopeks per day.[17]

After one year, those refugees who had proven themselves capable would receive an allotment of land, along with two horses, one cow, three sheep, three shirts, a coat, a hat, and a pair of gloves. The amount of land they were to receive was commensurate with that worked by other peasants in the area, adjusted on a case-by-case basis according to the needs of each family. They would also be given three rubles each from the treasury for the purchase of any necessary instruments, along with a monthly allotment of rye and bread until such time when they were able to produce their own bread. In all their possessions they were to be made satisfied *vis-à-vis* the other peasants in the area. If any of these new settlers should wish to marry a local, or vice versa, the marriage was not to be prevented. If anyone, moreover, was to impress any kind of unfreedom

[16] Blinov, *Sarapul'*, 14–15. [17] Blinov, *Sarapul'*, 15.

upon these new residents, the "firm gaze" of local officials would fall upon the offender. Provided with these rights and amenities, the refugees would be able to enter the "condition of peasanthood" (*krest'ianskoe sostoianie*). After six years' residence, these new inhabitants would begin to pay the notorious dues (*obrok*) demanded of all Russian peasants.[18]

According to Blinov, the system outlined here had not been developed specifically to accommodate escaped slaves from the steppe. In fact, the protocol for converting these new citizens into peasants had been adapted from an identical system that had been developed for Polish immigrants and outlined in a royal manifest from May of 1763. Evidently, the system was deemed effective for steppe refugees as well, as their numbers steadily increased in the decades to come: by 1777, 184 men and 124 women, 308 people in all, had been resettled in Sarapul alone.

Their religious conversion, meanwhile, may or may not have been considered effective, judging by the experiences of a Russian official who passed through Sarapul in 1778. This official found himself petitioned to *re-baptize* the local settlers. While many of these ones had presumably been baptized already prior to their resettlement, they had "forgotten the Christian faith" (*zabyli khrest'ianskuiu veru*) and had been eating carrion and other impermissible foods. The consistory obligingly cleansed one such offender through prayer and baptized another, teaching the latter how to pray.[19]

While Blinov characterizes the conversion of former slaves into peasants as an example of the Russian state's "concern" for migrants, it is clear that there were less charitable motives involved. Above all, these new peasants were being enlisted in the ongoing effort to colonize the Russian frontier, as the Russian Empire was engaged in bringing the borderlands under cultivation and populating them with Russian subjects. The process of resettling converted Central Asians had, moreover, been going on for decades. In 1738, for example, the head of Russia's Kalmyk Commission had resettled over 2,000 "Kalmyk new Christians" to the fort of Stavropol, north of Samara. Here, as in Sarapul, the settlers were trained in "the plow and the Russian way" and encouraged to engage with the local churches.[20] Between 1719 and 1744, the peasant population nearly tripled

[18] Blinov, *Sarapul'*, 16–17. [19] Blinov, *Sarapul'*, 17.
[20] Willard Sunderland, *Taming the Wild Field: Colonization and Empire on the Russian Steppe* (Ithaca, NY: Cornell University Press, 2004), 49.

in Saratov province, swelled by the influx of migrants resettled there by the state.[21]

The resettlement of escaped slaves was a novel development in this effort, directly linking colonization with manumission. It would not be until well into the nineteenth century, however, that Russian-sponsored manumission would be strongly linked to antislavery and abolitionism. For proof of this, we need only consider the fact that, until 1825, Russian citizens and officials were permitted – and even encouraged – to purchase Kazakh children themselves, just as long as they agreed to free them when they reached twenty-five years of age.[22]

In the early 1850s, in concert with the rising tide of antislavery sentiment throughout the Empire, orders were given that all steppe peoples under Russian rule must surrender their slaves to the nearest officials to be manumitted. These laws would greatly increase the volume of slaves turning up at Russian border offices. As we shall see, however, these notionally abolitionist orders did not often result in functionally abolitionist policies. As the border officials would soon discover, it was not always clear what should be done with these newly surrendered slaves – or even if they should be defined as slaves.

In the 1850s and 1860s, slaves surrendered by their owners to Russian officials would have had three options: returning to their original homeland; settling in the Russian Empire; or, if the slave was over twenty-two years of age, he or she could choose to return to life among the Kazakhs. In all cases, slaves were transferred only after being formally manumitted by border officials. Since many of the slaves in question had been taken captive or purchased at a young age, their owner's home was often the only home they had ever known. This helps to explain the high proportion of slaves who, once manumitted, simply chose to return to the steppe. In such cases, border officials usually interviewed both the owners who had surrendered their slaves and the slaves themselves, presumably to observe the level of correspondence between their respective tales. In these interviews, we often find claims that the slave did not really live as a slave (*ne v vide raba*), even though he or she had been purchased with money or with livestock.

Such was the case with one Kazakh slave-owner of the Altyn clan, whose name is recorded as Batygul, and who admitted that she had purchased two "Asian" slaves, whose names are recorded as Gamadan (Hamadan) and

[21] Blinov, *Sarapul'*, 19.
[22] Zimanov, *Obshchestvennyi stroi kazakhov pervoi poloviny XIX veka*, 283.

Ak-Dzhulay. She owned these children for fourteen and sixteen years, respectively. She had purchased Gamadan for thirty Bukharan coins, and Ak-Dzhulay for twenty-five. Batygul avowed that they lived with her under humane conditions (*po chelovechestvu*), without any shame and in no kind of slavery. As evidence of this, she adds that she even arranged their marriages. She placed them at the disposal of the authorities, as was demanded of her, claiming that neither of them wished to be returned to their original homeland, and implying that they would both prefer to remain with her.[23]

An interview with Gamadan appears in this document immediately following his owner's statement. He declares his age as twenty-six, and mentions that he does not know his patronymic. He is illiterate, a Muslim, originally from among the Hazara. He had been taken captive at a young age by unknown assailants (*khishniki*) and sold to Bukhara. Some fourteen years previously, he was purchased by Batygul for thirty Bukharan coins, and he had since lived with her as a son (*v vide syna*). Gamadan declares that he does not wish to return to his original homeland among the Hazara, since it was "an unknown place"; he prefers to remain with Batygul.[24]

Ak-Dzhulay's statement follows this. He describes himself as twenty-one years old, illiterate, a Muslim, and likewise originally from among the Hazara, though he adds that he does not know which clan was his. He was evidently very young when he was captured and sold to Bukhara. Sixteen years previously he was purchased in Bukhara for twenty-five coins by Batygul, who took him as her adopted son (*vzial v usynovlenii*). He adds that his original homeland is unknown to him, as is his original family, since he had been alienated from them for so long, and for this reason he did not want to return to the Hazara. He expresses the wish to remain with Batygul, under whom he claims to suffer no manner of oppression, and to fulfill all his obligations among the Kazakhs.[25]

We find a similar situation in the case of an Arab slave whose name was recorded as Derbis [Darvish] Muḥammad. This slave had also been living among the Altyn clan, and his owner reports having purchased him in Bukhara for twenty-five Bukharan coins some fourteen years previously, when Derbis Muḥammad was just eight years old. The owner, whose name was recorded as Taylanbay-Dzhan Aristanov, claims to have adopted the boy as his son, and mentions that he had even arranged his marriage. He declares that Derbis Muḥammad has no desire to return to his original

[23] TsGAKaz 4.1.3641 f. 38a. [24] TsGAKaz 4.1.3641 ff. 38a–b.
[25] TsGAKaz 4.1.3641 f. 38b.

homeland, but that he agreed to turn the young man over in accordance with the will of his superiors, which had only recently been announced to him. Placing his slave at the disposal of the authorities, Aristanov adds that if Derbis Muḥammad would be permitted by the border officials to continue living with him, he would allow the young man to do so. A statement by Derbis Muḥammad has also been preserved, and in it the young man confirms every detail provided by his owner: that he is twenty-two years old, an Arab, sold in Bukhara to Aristanov at the age of eight for twenty-five Bukharan coins; that he lives with Aristanov as his adopted son; and that he has no wish to return to his original home, of which, he says, he knows nothing. He expresses his "unashamed desire to live always among the Kazakhs" and, moreover, with this same Aristanov.[26]

It appears that a great many adult slaves who had been surrendered by their owners chose to remain in the steppe. Some may have experienced moments of indecision, weighing the chance at a new but uncertain life against their familiar captivity. One slave of Iranian origin, whose name was recorded as Kulgilbay, originally agreed to convert to Christianity, but then changed his mind and renounced that intention, choosing instead to continue living with his former owner among the Kazakhs.[27] Most others chose similarly. In one group of eight slaves – seven men and one woman – that arrived at the border, only the woman, whose name is recorded as Summanaz, expressed a wish to be returned to her original homeland. Summanaz was duly taken away from her Kazakh owner and placed in the care of the border office. Meanwhile, the others became the subject of a fatigued request by the border official tasked with processing them. This official penned an inquiry to his superiors, asking if, in order to save time and avoid "burdensome correspondence," he might simply provide those "Asians" who wished to remain among the Kazakhs with their freedom and forego the process of submitting any more "complicated reports" about them – promising, however, to submit full reports for those who wished to be sent back to their original homes.[28]

Other border officials seemed to take the process more seriously. In October of 1851, another group of Iranian slaves was divided according to their wishes: one wished to return home to Iran, and the rest to return among the Kazakhs. The official receiving this group wrote to his superior asking how he should proceed, as the process for repatriating surrendered slaves was, at that time, still in its infancy. The superior officer

[26] TsGAKaz 4.1.3641 f. 37a. [27] TsGAKaz 4.1.198 f. 49a.
[28] TsGAKaz 4.1.198 ff.56a–b.

unhesitatingly sent the slave who wished to return home back to Iran via Astrakhan, arranging for border offices to absorb any costs of transport. Regarding the rest, however, the official implored his comrades to certify that returning among the Kazakhs "was indeed their true and proper desire," and he took the opportunity to "remind the [Border] Commission of its responsibility" to ensure that former slaves returning to their former owners be treated equitably from then on in terms of their "personal rights" (*lichnaia prava*) and responsibilities among the Kazakhs. He asked to be appraised of the results once these Persians had returned to the steppe.[29]

In the case of adult former slaves who chose to return to their former owners, it must be asked: what had Russian-sponsored manumission really accomplished for them? First of all, we have no way of knowing whether manumission at the hands of the Russians was considered to be a valid form of manumission among Kazakhs. We also have no way of knowing whether this type of manumission really prevented the "freedmen" from being sold off or traded in the future. Nor do we know if the process had any real impact on the social standing, treatment, and obligations of these former slaves once they returned to the steppe. Finally, and perhaps most significantly, we do not know if most Russian officials considered these ambiguities at all significant to what they were ultimately trying to accomplish – a point to which we will soon return.

It may be tempting to presume that the widespread desire among slaves to return to their owners indicates that they were generally well-treated, but we have reason to hesitate here: Russian officials could offer these slaves transportation elsewhere, but they could not offer any alternative livelihoods beyond the unfamiliar – and quite possibly unappealing – existence of the newly minted Russian peasant. Since many of these manumitted slaves had been taken from their relatives in childhood, the communities in which they had been enslaved formed the closest thing they had to a family network. Moreover, those enslaved men who had married free women among the Kazakhs may not have been able or willing to ask their wives to abandon their homes and join them in their bid for a more total freedom. The prospect of freedom and a new beginning may, in other words, have struck many of these individuals as a profoundly lonely option. In this light, their "manumission" and return to the steppe may serve only to emphasize the fundamental tragedy of their circumstances.

[29] TsGAKaz 4.1.3573 f. 68a.

Such were the options presented to adult slaves, but border policy recognized minors – those under twenty-two – as a different case that called for different protocols. Many children were brought before border officials, and most often their owners, claimed to have "adopted them," noting also that these child slaves knew nothing of their original homelands. Three examples will suffice to give a sense of these interviews, which resemble the depositions concerning adult slaves in all but the age of the slaves in question.

In one document, a woman whose name was recorded as Sar Kulova, the wife of one Churtegen Khalimakov, reports that her husband had purchased a seven-year-old boy named Azat in Bukhara the previous winter, paying twenty-five Bukharan coins for him. Kulova avows that the boy is their adopted son, and that Azat has no desire to return to his homeland, "all the more so since [that place] is completely alien to him," given his young age. She presents Azat to the border authorities with the request that they not simply return him to his homeland, where no one knows anything of him, and where there is no one to be a mother to him to the extent that she herself is.[30]

In the same month, we find a Kazakh of the Altyn clan whose name is recorded as Mamirbay surrendering to the Commission two boys, Pivan and Khudaybergan, whom he had purchased in Bukhara earlier that year, the former for twenty-five Bukharan coins and the latter for nineteen. Hearing only now, he says, that the authorities were no longer permitting them to be kept, he surrendered them to the Kazakh Sultan who was working as an agent of the border authorities. He notes, however, that they are quite young – Pivan being no more than 14, Khudaybergan no more than 15 – and have expressed a "persistent desire" to live with him. A statement from Pivan follows in the document, and the boy confirms that he is fourteen years old. He says that he is a Muslim, from among the Arabs, and that he was taken to Bukhara two years previously by Turkmens. In the present year he had been purchased by Mamirbay. Following this we find a more concise interview with Khudaybergan, who reveals only that he is fifteen years old and was purchased by Mamirbay for nineteen Bukharan coins in Bukhara, where he was born, though he does not remember his mother and father. Both boys express that they do not wish to be returned to their original homeland, "as we do not know our parents or any relations there."[31] In Pivan's case, we may wonder if this last claim is true: in his own telling he was twelve years old

[30] TsGAKaz 4.1.3641 f. 36b. [31] TsGAKaz 4.1.3641 f. 36a.

when he was taken to Bukhara by Turkmens. It is possible that these Turkmens were his original captors and, if so, he would likely have known his biological family. We do not know these details, of course, but neither can we rule out the possibility that some child slaves expressed a desire to remain with their owners only under duress. Their owners may even have been in the room while these children were being interviewed.

In the case of an enslaved boy named Amanzhul, it appears more likely that he was truly unfamiliar with his biological family, though at least one detail in his story remains suspicious. His owner, whose name is recorded as Sansizbay, reports in his interview that he had bought Amanzhul four years previously, in Bukhara, for just fourteen Bukharan coins. The boy was at that time "no more than six years old," and Sansizbay claims to keep him as an adopted son, and not as a slave (*ne v vide raba*). He says that Amanzhul has no knowledge of his original homeland and prefers to stay with him. A brief statement from Amanzhul follows, in which the boy declares that he is ten years old, a Muslim, and illiterate; and that he is of "Central Asian" origins, though he cannot specify more than this (*prikhozhu iz sredneaziatskikh vladenii, no iz kakogo imenno ne znaiu*). He does not know how he ended up in Bukhara or whom he lived with there, though he knows that he was eventually purchased by Sansizbay for fourteen Bukharan coins. He adds that he does not wish to be sent back to his original homeland, as he knows nothing of that place, nor is he able learn anything more about it. One detail may call his narrative into question, however. The Kazakh name "Amanzhul" was apparently given to him by his present owner, as the boy claims that he does not even know what name he had gone by previously.[32] It was common for a slave to receive a new name from his or her owner, but the idea that a ten-year-old boy would not know what name he had gone by at four years old ought to make us wonder to what extent the boy chose to exaggerate the obscurity of his origins – and why he might have been inclined to do so.

What was to be done with children such as these, who had been "adopted" by the men who had purchased them? Were they really slaves? It was clear to the Border Commission, first of all, that a child's profession of loyalty to his or her owner should be regarded differently from that of an adult slave. For one thing, their prospects in the absence of any sort of guardianship were significantly worse than those of adult slaves – a fact that would not have been lost on the children themselves. Children,

[32] TsGAKaz 4.1.3641 ff. 37b–38a.

moreover, would be more vulnerable to the influence of threats, lies, or other forms of manipulation on the part of their owners. This is not to suggest that their owners were being dishonest in characterizing these boys and girls as their own adopted children. In fact, since they faced no punishment for voluntarily turning these children over to the Russians, and since – as we shall soon see – border officials' decision on what to do with these children did not rest entirely on whether or not their owners considered them to be slaves, it is most likely that we are witnessing a cultural disconnect in which Russian definitions of slavery were lost in translation for those Kazakhs drawn into the new system of enforced manumission.

In fact, Russian manumission policies – as well as official definitions of who should be considered a slave – were sometimes unclear even to border officials themselves. They were likewise unclear to some native informants tasked with rounding up and exposing the slave-owners. One internal document concerning a local Kazakh *biy* preserves an unusual ethnographic preamble, in which an official evidently felt compelled to explain to his superiors the ambiguity of notions of "slavery" in the Kazakh context. In the old days, the official explains, some Kazakhs would freely send their children into others' care. Other Kazakhs – in times of famine, for example – would sell their children. This was, the official observes, forbidden by Islamic law, but in such instances they were not being purchased as slaves, but rather in place of biological children, since their purchasers typically had no children of their own. Still others bought maidens (*devits*) to marry, and this transaction was carried out not against anyone's will, but by agreement from both sides (*ne chrez* [sic] *nevol'no a po soglasno oboikh storon*). Both Kazakhs and Karakalpaks engaged in this custom, according to the officer, who then offers his inquiry: Would those Kazakhs and Karakalpaks still be subject to the new manumission laws if, having been purchased before the passing of these laws, they currently lived as wives and children according to common consent?[33]

The officer's inquiry was not an abstract consideration; he needed an answer immediately, as he had just received a report from a Kazakh *biy*, operating as a native informant, concerning a young man who was in precisely the ambiguous position outlined here: perhaps a slave, perhaps not. Roughly fourteen years previously, in 1847, "at the time of the hunger" (*vo vremia goloda*), a Kazakh whose name is recorded as Batyrbay Baydelov purchased the young man from a Karakalpak for one

[33] TsGAKaz 383.1.89 f. 14a.

camel and one horse. The young man, named Dawlat, was at that time just two years old. He was the Karakalpak's own son. Dawlat confirmed under the *biy*'s questioning that he had been sold in early childhood, and he declared that he had no desire to return among the Karakalpaks. He was, moreover, satisfied with his present owner because, he told the *biy*, "Batyrbay Baydelov does not have children of his own and considers me his son, and he does not use me for labor" (*ne upotrebliaet na raboty*).[34]

As it turns out, the border offices already had a policy concerning cases such as these – though it is revealing that the policy was apparently not known or understood by all of the officers tasked with implementing it. The policy had been established by a pronouncement of the Orenburg Governor General on December 1, 1860, which reinforced, first of all, the fact that those immigrants who had freed themselves from slavery under Kazakhs subject to Orenburg's authority could choose to swear allegiance to Russia, or to the Kazakhs, or to be returned to their original homeland elsewhere.[35] As for slaves under twenty-two years old, however, their fate was not entirely their own to decide. Instead, border officials would have them turned over to "trustworthy hands" (*blagonadezhnye ruki*) until they reached the age of full maturity (*sovershennyi vozrast*). At that point they would achieve "full freedom" (*pol'naia svoboda*), and they would be able to make their own decision about where to go next.[36] These children would, in other words, be placed in foster care.

Regardless of age, an individual turned over to border officials was granted his or her freedom as a standard matter of bureaucratic process. When adult slaves chose to return among the Kazakhs, the documentation of their manumission would often include the detail that their former owners were henceforth forbidden from enslaving them. Children who had allegedly been "adopted" by their owners were likewise officially manumitted by the Russians. Women who had been purchased as brides were likely also manumitted, though I have yet to see a manumission document pertaining to such a woman.

Combining the above information on official policies with the nature of the information collected from slaves at the border allows us to ascertain something of the Orenburg Border Commission's working definition of slavery. First, it is useful to observe what was absent from slaves' interviews. It is clear, for example, that border officials appear remarkably unconcerned with labor as a condition of slavery; it seems that slaves

[34] TsGAKaz 383.1.89 ff. 14a–b. [35] TsGAKaz 383.1.184 ff. 11b–12a.
[36] TsGAKaz 383.1.184 f. 12a.

were only rarely asked about the nature of the labor that had been expected of them, or about the nature of their upkeep and compensation, if any. Likewise, their owners, having surrendered them, were rarely asked how they had used them and what kind of work they had assigned to them. If such questions came up over the course of these interviews, neither the questions nor the answers were typically documented.

By contrast, all surrendered slaves were asked when and where they had been purchased; from whom they had been purchased; who had purchased them; and at what price they had been sold. The fact of having been bought and sold emerges in these documents as the central defining feature of their slavery. Their owners were made to supply precisely the same information concerning purchase and sale: when, where, from whom, and at what price. This may be explained in part as both a means of checking a slave's autobiography against the testimony of his or her owner and, more simply, as a way to add a key validating detail to their categorization as slaves. Above all, the contours of these slaves' biographies are defined by periods of ownership.

A slave, then, was an individual who had been bought and sold. Purchase and sale are the two ever-present factors in these interviews, which served also as documentation of manumission. Purchasing an individual marked one, in the eyes of the border authorities, as being subject to punishment unless the purchased individual was surrendered to the state. This fact remained constant regardless of the circumstances of sale. It also remained constant regardless of what relationship the owner claimed to have with their purchase. Owners who "adopted" their purchases, arranged their marriages, and so on, were still made to surrender them to border offices.

But where did border officials find "trustworthy hands" to receive those manumitted slaves who were not yet of age? The fate of a child slave named Ashirbay reveals the surprising details of this process. Ashirbay was ten years old when he was brought to the border along with three other child slaves: Nasir, nine years old, Mazhik [?], fifteen, and Azim, eighteen. They were inspected by the Bukharan merchants at Fort Perovskii to verify their origins, and none showed any signs of abuse at the hands of his owner. The official charged with processing them logged a request that the two youngest boys – Ashirbay and Nasir – be given over into fosterage until they had reached the age of maturity.[37] A third boy, Mazhik, was eventually processed into fosterage as well.[38] Azim appears to

[37] TsGAKaz 381.1.184 ff. 18a–b. [38] TsGAKaz 381.1.184 f. 29a.

have been allowed to remain with his Kazakh owner under the conditions that the latter not attempt to re-enslave the boy, despite the fact that, at eighteen, Azim would technically have been eligible for fosterage.[39]

In the case of Ashirbay, we find that the "trustworthy hands" chosen for his fosterage were those of his former owner, the Kazakh who had purchased him as a slave. The child had expressed a wish to remain in the steppe, and while Russian border policy dictated that he be placed somewhere to receive his "education" until he came of age, there was nothing in the policy that stipulated where, precisely, a child was to be sent or who qualified as a "trustworthy" foster parent. We may assume that the Russian state lacked adequate foster homes in the region to receive the influx of freed slaves. Otherwise, the decision to send Ashirbay back to his owner seems difficult to comprehend in light of policies that seem designed specifically to prevent such a circumstance. The official in charge specified for the record that the former owner to whom Ashirbay would be returned was not to receive him as a slave. Ashirbay had, at least on paper, been manumitted. Thanks to the Russian state, his owner had become his foster father.

Here, we may find some explanation for a seeming lapse of logic in border officials' usual interview regimen. Why, after all, had officials bothered documenting so often whether or not a slave lived with his or her owner as an "adopted" child, only to manumit the child anyway? On first glance, the claim of adoption seems like a desperate and vain effort on the part of the owners to keep their slaves or avoid punishment, and on the part of the slaves to placate their owners or to avoid an uncertain fate. Even in those cases where the bond between owner and slave may truly have been close, such as that between parent and child, the owner was still made to surrender any child he or she had purchased. So why would border officials bother reporting these supposed "familial" bonds? As we see in the case of Ashirbay, it was likely these professed bonds – along with the medical examination that uncovered no evidence of his abuse – that allowed his former owner to foster him after his manumission.

We have now observed three possible outcomes in Russia's border-manumission system. Some slaves – a small number, probably – were given access back to their homelands; a larger number were resettled and turned into serfs; and perhaps a still larger number were sent back to the steppe. Should we think of these as "abolitionist" policies? Was Russia an "abolitionist" empire in the steppe?

[39] TsGAKaz 381.1.184 ff. 27a–b.

In the case of those slaves who made it back home, we can perhaps answer in the affirmative. In the case of those who were turned into serfs, the answer depends on whether one considers serfdom to be freedom. The third case, though – the case of slaves sent back to the steppe – is especially revealing. If so many slaves who had been surrendered to Russian border authorities were simply returned to the care of their former owners, then what was the purpose of manumitting these ones in the first place? Why did the Russian state bother establishing a network of native informants, for example, only to remit "freed" slaves back into the steppe?

Along with providing new agricultural laborers for the settling of the borderlands, the purpose of this system of manumission was not to ensure the freedom of the enslaved – and in most cases it did no such thing – but to impress upon the slave-owner that he was now visible to the Russian state. It was about jurisdiction. Equally, Russian-enforced manumission was the tool of an expanding bureaucracy: The information provided in border authorities' interviews served to document and make legible individuals – both slaves and their owners – who may otherwise have been practically invisible to the Empire; it served, in other words, as a sort of census.

Finally, this process served to make Russian power more visible to all the people of the steppe. It spread a powerful message: The reach of Russian colonial power could now extend into their homes and divest them of their property. It could turn their slaves into Russian serfs and – at least on Russian paper – it could turn slave-owners into foster fathers. It could even send slaves back to Iran, "legally" dismantling what many Kazakhs may have considered to be a relationship between parent and child.

6

The Khan as Russian Agent

Native Informants and Abolition

In matters of intelligence-gathering as well as enforcement, the Russian Empire came to rely extensively on informants drawn from local Kazakh and Turkmen populations along the steppe and Iranian frontiers. These informants became instrumental in Russian efforts to militate against slave-raiding when Russian victims were involved. However, while Russian authorities tried to suppress the seizure of Russians throughout the early and mid-nineteenth century, they simultaneously encouraged the Turkmens' ongoing slave raids into northern Iran. As often as not, in any case, whether along the Iranian frontier or in the Kazakh steppe, the informants did not play the roles intended for them: acutely aware of their importance to Russian officials, many Kazakh and Turkmen "agents" took advantage of their positions by manipulating their Russian patrons for their own benefit or for the benefit of their communities. Far from being mere colonial puppets, many of these informants came to use their newfound status not only for personal interests, but also as a form of resistance against their own colonial patrons. Meanwhile, the impact of the informant system on captive-taking in the region was, as we shall see, decidedly mixed.

KAZAKH INFORMANTS ALONG THE STEPPE FRONTIER

From its inception at the end of the eighteenth century, the Orenburg Border Commission involved itself in the resolution of disputes among neighboring Kazakhs, providing both an alternative source of legal authority and an alternative framework of legal enforcement for many in the steppe. A diverse range of disputes came before the Commission, concerning everything from the theft of livestock to cases of assault. In some cases, the Commission served as merely one of several Russian-officiated courts of appeal available to complainants. In one fairly typical case from the turn of the nineteenth century, for example, a Kazakh named Akutin, who claimed to have been assaulted, first brought his case before the Ural military chancery and then before the Border Commission; a record of his complaint is preserved both in Arabic-script Turkic and in Russian translation. According to the records of the case, Akutin crossed the Ural River into the steppe along with his wife in order to trade in fish. He did so without permission from the chief (*nachal'nik*) of his settlement (*krepost'*) at Topolinsk. A Kazakh demanded payment of debts from him while he was across the river, and he refused to pay. The Kazakh in question then pursued him back to Topolinsk, where they quarreled and the Kazakh made two wounds in Akutin's head and took two of his horses. The Ural military chancery evidently sent Akutin onward to Orenburg in order to seek the return of his confiscated property.[1]

Given its dual role in enforcement and adjudication, it is natural that border authorities also involved themselves early on in cases of kidnapping and enslavement. As early as 1822, a decree was issued prohibiting slaveholding among the Elder Horde, with a penalty of 150 rubles extracted from offenders.[2] Lacking a comprehensive network for patrol and surveillance across the steppe, the Commission relied from the beginning on the agency and cooperation of locals and steppe peoples to define and report crises as well as to bring forward information leading to the capture of suspected offenders. Modest and *ad hoc* in its origins, this novel system of delegating and receiving native informants in the steppe would become increasingly systematic and complex over the course of the nineteenth century. Similar strategies would be implemented to the south, along the Khurasan frontier. By the middle of the century, native informants would form the backbone of the Russian Empire's accelerating efforts toward pacifying the steppe and eliminating the phenomenon of captive-taking – at least insofar as it impacted Russian citizens.

As early as 1800, Kazakh informants were already submitting formal reports to the military governor of Orenburg in order to alert him to the presence of captives among the Kazakhs. The primary concern appears to have been the release of Russian subjects, but some Kazakh and Kalmyk captives were also freed by these means. One report from January, 1800,

[1] TsGAKaz 4.1.195 f. 48a. [2] Semeniuk, "Likvidatsiia rabstva v Kazakhstane," 236.

recognizes the "diligence and laudable deeds" of a Kazakh sultan who delivered to the Commission a number of captives who had previously been taken by Kazakh "thieves," including two Saratov "peasants" and nine officials from the Ural Office. "Along with these," the document adds (leaving little ambiguity as to the captives' relative order of priority) that twenty-one Kazakhs of both genders were also delivered. One Kazakh, named Imangul, was held "under guard" at Ural'sk, and the sultan asked that he be released. In recognition of the sultan's service, the border authorities honored the request and set Imangul free.[3] It is not clear how the sultan managed to secure more than two dozen captives for the border authorities, and we cannot rule out the likelihood that they were taken in a raid, perhaps accomplished specifically for the purposes of securing a reward.

Other missions were undertaken with a higher level of cooperation from the Russian side. On one occasion, a Kazakh khan of the Junior Horde contacted the Commission in order to alert officials that he knew the whereabouts of some Kazakhs who had been implicated in the kidnapping of a young Russian boy. The alleged kidnappers, the khan claimed, had taken refuge in a dense expanse of reeds on the seashore, and he offered the Russians his services: "I, for my part," the khan testified, "will not fail to point out which reeds the nomads are hiding in." The Russian officials, with the khan's assistance, evidently undertook the delicate operation of seizing the kidnappers and freeing the boy.[4]

The use of Russian funds rather than troops or favors was often necessary to affect the release of captives. In one case recorded by border officials in 1799–1800, some Kazakhs took the son of a merchant named Poliakov, along with fifty rubles in plunder. Somehow, a Kazakh sultan ended up in possession of the boy (named Vasilii) and pledged to the Russians that he held him in safekeeping. He promised to turn the boy over, but, evidently, only in exchange for payment.[5] While the documentary record of the exchange does not explicitly accuse the sultan of complicity or participation in the boy's capture, it is clear that the payment is tantamount to ransom. In such a case, the informant was clearly a beneficiary of the crime itself.

Engaging with Kazakh informants to secure captives could sometimes be a relatively straightforward affair, as in the previous examples, but other cases suggest a world of possible complications, and point toward the

[3] TsGAKaz 4.1.195 f. 34a. [4] TsGAKaz 4.1.195 ff. 151a–152a.
[5] TsGAKaz 4.1.195 f. 204a.

innumerable avenues by which Russian colonial forces could find themselves manipulated by their would-be colonial subjects. One of the most detailed narratives along these lines is provided by Witkiewicz, who was personally involved in the freeing of a Russian captive during his mission to the Bukhara in the mid-1830s. After twenty-five horses were stolen from a caravan in which Witkiewicz was traveling, patrols were sent forth from the caravan to search alongside the Syr Darya, and this search turned up a "famous" thief named Kuldzhan Karakchi of the Diurtkara clan. When the alleged thief was brought back to the caravan, he gave assurances that he had only made himself vulnerable to capture in order to alert the Russians that a Cossack captive named Ivan Stepanov was in residence with his clan. Stepanov had been captured along with his wife while making hay, and the captors were said to be Dzhegalbay fugitives who had been living among the Diurtkara. The stolen horses were also among the Diurtkara, and Kuldzhan Karakchi promised to return all of them along with Stepanov. The merchants of the caravan wanted to detain Karakchi and deliver him to Khwarazm for punishment, but Witkiewicz forbade it, since the suspect was technically a Russian subject.[6]

Witkiewicz ordered Karakchi's release and demanded that he bring forth the captive and the stolen horses. Karakchi returned to his clan along with a caravan guide, a Kazakh from among the Chumekey, who would be tasked with transporting the captive and the horses back to the caravan. Once back at the alleged thief's aul, Witkiewicz writes, "a comedy played out": the people of the aul tied Karakchi up, acting as if they suspected him of giving false testimony, and insisted that the stolen horses were not among them. Those responsible for the theft, they claimed, could be found at some headland or peninsula on the Aral Sea. There, at Aran, north of the mouth of the Syr Darya, lived some 500 tents of alleged "robbers" known as the Karkru-Aranchi, consisting of forty clans who subsisted through trapping saiga and goats, growing grain, and thieving.[7]

Stepanov, however, unlike the stolen horses, was found among the Diurtkara. A sultan-governor from Orsk sent a Cossack agent to collaborate with Witkiewicz in order to secure his release. The man had refused to travel to the aul with Kuldzhan Karakchi, fearing the latter would kill him, but he wished to make an attempt at buying Stepanov's freedom. Witkiewicz forbade it, but the agent insisted on being given the necessary

[6] Vitkevich, *Zapiski o Bukharskom khanstve*, 118.
[7] Vitkevich, *Zapiski o Bukharskom khanstve*, 118.

funds. These funds were promptly divided among the Diurtkara, who declined to release Stepanov. In the meantime, they had sold his wife – who had given birth in the steppe – to some Khivans. In all, the initial efforts by Witkiewicz and his fellow-travelers to free Stepanov while on their way to Bukhara were a disaster.[8]

Later, on the way back from Bukhara, he would have another opportunity to rescue Stepanov. When the caravan was passing roughly 100 versts from where the Diurtkara were residing, Witkiewicz sent them a guide as an envoy. The guide returned with a Kazakh named Bulush Bay, who was identified as the son-in-law of the man with whom Stepanov was living, a Diurtkara Kazakh named Kulbay. Witkiewicz "informed him of his obligation to render service" to the Russian Empire, promising him also a reward if he brought forth the captive. Bulush Bay returned among the Diurtkara, but came back to the caravan empty-handed seven days later, requesting an official document which pledged that he would not be prosecuted after bringing the captive. Witkiewicz provided him with the requested papers along with some gifts and sent him back to the Diurtkara. Four days later, Bulush Bay returned empty-handed once again – this time, badly beaten and bloody. He returned the gifts Witkiewicz had given him, not wanting to receive payment for an unfulfilled mission. He had, it turned out, quarreled with his father-in-law, who resented the prospect of giving up the captive with no visible ransom on the table, especially in light of the ransom that had been brought earlier by the Cossack agent. In the midst of their heated discussions, a man named Bek Mirza, who had sold Stepanov's wife to Khiva, managed to convince many others in the clan not to give up their captive. Kuldzhan Karakchi argued likewise, even offering to buy the captive himself, with the aim of re-selling him to some Khivans.[9]

On the verge of losing hope, Witkiewicz sent Bulush Bay back to the clan once again, this time accompanied by two others. These three returned to the caravan twelve days later, reporting that they had met with a man named Tlyaulii, of the Diurtkara. Tlyaulii, identified as a "robber," had previously fought with Bek Mirza and was presently on the run from some Khivans. It was, therefore, not difficult to convince him to serve the Russian Empire. Tlyaulii sent Kuldzhan Karakchi (who had evidently changed his tune) along with the caravan envoys and some others to Kulbay to negotiate the release of Stepanov. This group managed to

[8] Vitkevich, *Zapiski o Bukharskom khanstve*, 118.
[9] Vitkevich, *Zapiski o Bukharskom khanstve*, 118–119.

intimidate Kulbay into giving up the captive, and Stepanov was promptly sent to join the caravan.[10]

Along with the captive came a letter from Tlyaulii. In it, Tlyaulii evidently blamed the oppressive tactics of the Russian Empire for discord in the steppe. He requested that Witkiewicz address Russian commanders in order to mediate and enact a peaceful settlement between the clans of the Diurtkara, Dzhagalbay, Tamyn, and Tabyn. The ultimate goal would be to enact a separation between the Russians and these clans, in order to ensure a relationship "free of harassment" between Russians and nomads. As a gesture of goodwill, Tlyaulii also offered to facilitate the capture of Bek Mirza's band of robbers.[11]

As for the liberated man, Stepanov, it seems that the hardships of his captivity and the loss of his wife had taken a tragic toll on him. He was, Witkiewicz writes, "a sick man, weak and foolish. It was impossible to learn anything from him."[12]

In Witkiewicz's story, as well as in previous examples, the initiative of local, non-Russian actors guides all efforts and determines the outcome in securing the release of captives. The relationship between Russian colonial forces and steppe natives was hardly one in which the "Great Power" was able to simply delegate mercenaries to do its bidding. Until the mid-nineteenth century, at least, captors or slave-owners were free to negotiate ransom settlements with Russian officials, and agents in the employ of the Russians could negotiate the terms of their own remuneration. As we see in the case of Stepanov, captors could boldly decline to free a captive after receiving ransom, though such a betrayal would have been counterproductive for those hoping to make a steady business out of Russian ransom payments. Go-betweens, meanwhile, could decline to deliver the freedmen, choosing instead to pocket their pay and sell off their new cargo. These agents could – and did – conspire together with captors to extract larger sums in ransom;[13] perhaps they were sometimes paid off or

[10] Vitkevich, *Zapiski o Bukharskom khanstve*, 119. [11] Ibid.

[12] "*Kazak Stepanov—chelovek bol'noi, slabyi i glupyi; iz nego nel'zia bylo vyvedat' nichego.*" Vitkevich, *Zapiski o Bukharskom khanstve*, 119.

[13] Vambery writes of meeting in his travels "one of two sailors from the new station at Ashourada; the other had died in captivity about a year before. They had fallen into the hands of the Karatchis some years previously, in one of their night expeditions. Their government offered to ransom them, but the Turkomans demanded an exorbitant sum (five hundred ducats for one); and as during the negotiation Tcherkes Bay, the brother of Kotshak Khan was sent by the Russians to Siberia, where he died, the liberation of the unfortunate Christians became matter of still greater difficulty; and now the survivor will soon succumb under the hardships of his captivity, as his comrade has done before him."

otherwise encouraged by their contacts to deliver false information to Russian officials. In short, those residents of the steppe who served as points of contact between Russian officials and captors or slave-owners had a practically unlimited ability to guide negotiations by controlling the nature of the information passed between the two camps. Witkiewicz, for one, reports only what was related to him by his interlocutors; he had to choose whether to believe them.

The initiative of these interlocutors – whether they be khans-turned-informants or caravan guides-turned-emissaries – could also serve ends beyond mere personal gain. With Russian influence becoming ever more visible in the steppe, go-betweens could use their privileged positions for the purposes of resistance. This could be accomplished both by foiling Russian ambitions on a case-by-case basis or, as in the case of Tlyaulii, by positioning oneself to submit a request. Though there is no evidence that Tlyaulii's request was taken seriously by Russian officials, the nature of his appeal is striking in itself. It shows a keen awareness that the incursions of Russian influence had interfered with relations among steppe clans. Witkiewicz makes no mention of Tlyaulii being offered any form of compensation other than the chance to submit his appeal.

By the mid-nineteenth century, the *ad hoc* process by which Russian officials endeavored to free captives and slaves from the steppe was replaced with a more rigorous, deliberate, and wide-ranging system. By 1851–1852, the Orenburg Border Commission had begun circulating, among Kazakhs in the western reaches of the steppe, decrees in Arabic-script Turkic ordering the release of slaves and captives. Some of the earliest decrees that I have seen specify that Iranian Shiʿites – called simply "Qizilbash" in these documents, which doubtless indicated Iranian slaves – were living in the area (*shu örinda qizilbāsh vilāyatlik yasarlar bar*), and that it is these particular slaves that must be surrendered.[14] One decree from December of 1851 mentions "Persian [captives] and other captives" bought from Khiva or from "Khivan subjects," with the captives in question being "transferred from one owner to another" or given as dowries. The decree calls upon all Kazakhs under Orenburg's authority, without

He adds, in a note: "When I afterwards drew the attention of the Russians to the occurrence, they laboured to excuse themselves, saying that they did not desire to accustom the Turkomans to such large ransoms, for that with any encouragement these bold robbers would devote themselves night and day to their profitable depredations" (Vambery, *Travels in Central Asia*, 79).

[14] TsGAKaz 4.1.3573, unnumbered folio.

exception, to turn over these captives promptly. Henceforth, the decree explains, if any slaves or captives were to be found living with any Kazakhs, regardless of rank, that individual would be exposed and brought to justice, and they would be subject to "a monetary penalty of 150 silver rubles for each captive and 6 months' imprisonment or, depending on the gravity of the circumstances surrounding the acquisition of the captive, deprivation of property rights, corporal punishment, and banishment to Siberia."[15]

The Border Commission evidently printed and circulated at least 1,000 copies of this decree by January of 1852.[16] Further copies of this or similar decrees – in groups of 100 and of 230 pressings – were issued in the months to come.[17] No information is available on the reception of these documents in the steppe. Since the majority of Kazakhs were illiterate at the time, we may assume that the decrees were meant to be read aloud. We know, at least, that two or three issuances of the general emancipation order were not considered sufficient: The Border Commission would issue still more decrees of a very similar nature over the course of the next two decades. We also know that the Kazakh informants who chose to cooperate early on in the process of liberating slaves in the steppe included powerful figures like Sultan Arslan. The Sultan received reports from his own informants on slaveholders under his authority, ensured the release of captives, and then delivered them to the Border Commission along with testimony that often included a chain-of-transmission revealing how he learned of the captive's presence among his subjects.[18]

In general we can only speculate about the various individual motivations that would have inspired Kazakh elites to cooperate with the Russians in enforcing manumission decrees. The contents of one Russian-authored decree in Turkic, however, dating from 1860, can help to clarify at least one motivation: Here, Russian officials threaten punishment not only for those Kazakhs who held slaves and captives, but also for those leaders who claimed the offenders as subjects. Bearing the signatures and seals of five Kazakh *bays* (elites), this decree, like the others, declares that "if any Kazakh is in possession of a slave, he must turn this slave over to the governor, and after this he must not buy any [other] slave" (*gar kim birär qazaqning qolinda qul bolsa, ul qulni ḥākim husurina täbshurur wa mundan song qul sätub älmas*). It concludes with the announcement that if any

[15] TsGAKaz 4.1.3573 ff. 112a–113a. See also Semeniuk, 237.
[16] TsGAKaz 4.1.3573 f. 132a. [17] TsGAKaz 4.1.3573 ff. 147a; 188a.
[18] TsGAKaz 3573 f. 193a.

Kazakh is to "open his hand" (*qol ächilsa*), i.e. to release his or her slave, then this Kazakh *as well as* the bay overseeing him or her (*ul qazaq ham aning ustidan qarab turguvchi bay*) would not be "subject to merciless inquiry" (*hich bir raḥimsiz tekshirdilar*).[19] Elites, in other words, could be held accountable for the slaveholding of their subjects.

Another document, dating from June of 1852, hints at more direct threats against noncompliant steppe elites. Having been informed of the captivity of an Iranian whose name is recorded as Asan Yakubov, Russian officials informed the sultan of Asan's owner's *orda* that the captive was henceforth to live and work where he pleased, and that no others should take him into slavery. The sultan was tasked with the execution of these orders, which were evidently passed to him in secret by way of one of his retainers. (This individual was referred to as a "clerk" in the document; the official who drafted it noted that he disapproved of the instructions, all the more so since the "clerk" was merely a dependent of the sultan and therefore provided no additional influence over the outcome). The secret orders included an explicit warning: If anything transpired that was inconsistent with the above demands, Russian officials would be informed of it.[20]

In reality, slaveholding Kazakhs whom other Kazakhs brought before Russian officials were not always dealt the punishments specified in these dramatic Russian decrees. One group of offenders, who were charged with owning four slaves among them, was evidently pardoned entirely; according to the official report, it was not thought necessary to hold them to any liability for failing to surrender their slaves, since they simply "did not know of the prohibitive order" (*o zapretitel'nom rasporiazhenii*) against slave-owning.[21]

Captors and slave-owners, meanwhile, could stand to benefit from surrendering their contraband at border offices, at least after 1852. In January of that year, a Russian border official proposed that offenders who surrendered their captives should receive compensation (*voznograzhdeniia*) for their loss.[22] It appears that this policy was implemented in at least some cases; one slave owner, for example, was issued one ruble and fifty kopeks in compensation for each of the thirty-six sheep he had formerly paid to a fellow Kazakh for the Iranian slave he surrendered at the border.[23] This kind of compensatory system may hint at the disappointing impact of previous emancipation decrees. Compensating slave-owners for

[19] TsGAKaz 383.1.89, unnumbered folio. [20] TsGAKaz 4.1.3641 f. 22a.
[21] TsGAKaz 383.1.184 f. 19a. [22] TsGAKaz 4.1.3641 f. 140a.
[23] TsGAKaz 4.1.3573 f. 133a.

their loss, moreover, is not altogether different from paying ransom, and the new system surely risked offering a further incentive for captive-taking. Nevertheless, authorization was given for systematized compensation, to be implemented in June of 1852.[24] It is not clear that the system was fully implemented, however, and may have been stalled by officials' misgivings: By September of 1852, the official who had recommended the compensation system eight months earlier submitted a report noting that he still had not received a decision from his superiors on the question of compensating compliant slaveholders. He reiterated his recommendation, urging them to come to a final decision on the matter.[25]

Slaveholders and informants were not the only parties who sometimes stood to gain compensation during the manumission process. The testimony of an Iranian slave whose name was recorded as Yul-Muhammad Asanov indicates that the freedmen themselves could sometimes earn reparations for their suffering. Asanov relates in his interview with Russian officials that he was first taken captive at the age of seven by Turkmens who soon sold him to a Kazakh of the Alchin clan. He spent eight years with this owner before being sold to a Kazakh of the Dzhagalbay clan. He fled this owner, but he was captured and then sold to a Kazakh of the Chagatay clan whose name is recorded as Bay Murzabek Yamanbaev. He lived as Yamanbaev's slave for the next twenty-three years until, in 1854, he was freed. "Upon being freed from 24 years of slavery," Asanov testifies, "Murzabek Yamanbaev, instead of giving me any remuneration, cut my head with a knife and hit me in the face with a whip, knocking out one of my teeth. Hoping for nothing more than what is my share, I have repeatedly appealed to the Russian officials. But for their part, down to the present time, I have received neither my recompense nor any information [concerning my case]." Upon being freed, Asanov reports having been given only "meager rags" to wear, and he could not find a way to provide for himself "even by the most strenuous effort." In these dire circumstances, he turned to Russian officials to seek compensation from his former master and, as he phrased it in his interview, to "dispense gracious satisfaction to me for my years of slavery."[26] Following his testimony, the wheels of justice turned at a leisurely pace. Asanov first came before officials on August 2, 1857. By April of 1858, his former owner had evidently died, and it was his heirs who were at that time ordered to "render compensation" (*okazat' posobie*) to Asanov for his

[24] TsGAKaz 4.1.3573 f. 187a. [25] TsGAKaz 4.1.3641 f. 140a.
[26] TsGAKaz 4.1.3730 ff. 16a–18a.

twenty-three years of service. Finally, in November of that same year, it was confirmed that he had received some compensation from these heirs.[27]

Taken altogether, the influx of slaves and slaveholders arriving at the border in the 1850s and 1860s demonstrates that Russian abolition decrees and the policies and practices that came with them had at least some impact on the steppe's slave population. Even at mid-century, however, progress was decidedly gradual: Further abolition decrees were disseminated in 1860 and again in 1861; the last known decree was circulated in the steppe as late as 1869.[28] By that time, the influx of Iranian slaves from Khurasan had slowed considerably. While the conquest of the Khwarazmian domains in 1873 did not, as we have seen, end the slave trade, a major waystation and market for slaves was thrown into turmoil. The resale market in Khwarazm that had long been available to Kazakh captors and dealers surely contracted. Meanwhile, with the strengthening of Russian border defenses and the weakening and increasing dependency of neighboring Kazakh clans, fewer Russian subjects were falling into Kazakh hands. It was in this context that Russian-sponsored emancipation, however modest in its impacts, further depleted the steppe slave population from within. The final quarter of the nineteenth century was tantamount to dusk for the slave trade in the Kazakh steppe.

The sun would not set on slavery itself, however. As I have shown in previous chapters, many slaves who were "manumitted" at the Russian border were simply returned to their former owners, either as "foster children" or as laborers. Some slaves had free Kazakh wives and had integrated into free society to a degree unimaginable for slaves in other regions of the world. Many others were not so lucky.

The success of Russian emancipation efforts relied entirely on Kazakh informants. The Empire was at the mercy of these informants simply to identify slaveholders and slaves amid the general population. Other agents were often needed to transport offenders to the border along with their slaves. The pool of local go-betweens willing to take on these roles was remarkably diverse: Khans and sultans, fugitives and thieves all played a part. Each had his or her own motives, and each was seemingly able to negotiate individual terms of compensation. Rich opportunities for manipulating these negotiations must have presented themselves to many an agent. In the end, however, whatever the costs, it appears that the Russian Empire, by engaging informant networks, achieved certain

[27] TsGAKaz 4.1.3730 f. 28a. [28] Semeniuk, 238.

substantial aims: it reduced the threat of captivity for Russian subjects in or near the steppe; it engaged in a novel means of extending Russian governance over subjects and neighboring populations; and it initiated new forms of dependency and service among the Kazakhs.

INFORMANTS AND LOCAL AGENTS AMONG THE TURKMENS

Meanwhile, a parallel strategy was being enacted to the south, along the shores of the Caspian. In 1828, the Treaty of Turkmenchay stipulated that Iranian ships would cede the right to navigate the Caspian and its coasts freely; henceforth, no Iranian military vessels would patrol the Sea. These rights were transferred exclusively to the Russian Empire. Russia's newfound supremacy on the sea came with certain responsibilities for the benefit of Iran, however: The Russian military would take over the task of policing the Caspian shore, along which Turkmen raiding parties had long engaged in systematic attacks on Iranian villages for the purpose of taking captives for ransom or sale. In this effort, the Turkmens had been aided by the challenges of patrolling the terrain: The thick reed-beds offered them excellent cover; their narrow, flat-bottomed boats presented a low profile as they cruised along the coastline; and, if caught on their way to launching an attack, empty-handed Turkmens could always claim that they were merely fishing.[29]

For more than a decade before the 1828 treaty, the Russian Empire had been using the Turkmens as a "proxy" weapon against Iran. Yomut Turkmens who supported an 1813 rebellion against the shah in Astarabad are believed to have been acting as Russian agents. Kiyat Khan, leader of the Jafarbay clan of Turkmens, likewise enjoyed Russian support even as the governor of Mazandaran led military expeditions against him in 1826.[30] British officials stationed in Tehran, observing the Turkmens' continual borderland raids, were well aware of Russia's strategy; in 1837, the minister Sir John McNeil wrote that the Yomut Turkmens "in all probability will not submit to Iran so long as the connection they have formed with Russia will afford them sufficient protection."[31] That same year, Kiyat Khan, who had been leading kidnapping raids along the

[29] Cf. C. A. Gunaropulo, "V Turkmenskoi stepi. (Iz zapisok chernomorskogo ofitsera)," *Istoricheskii vestnik* 12 (1900), 1037.

[30] Mohammad Ali Kazembeyki, *Society, Politics, and Economics in Māzandarān, Iran, 1848–1914* (London: Routledge, 2003), 45.

[31] Kazembeyki, *Society, Politics, and Economics in Māzandarān, Iran, 1848–1914*, 45.

Caspian coast, was able to escape an Iranian punitive expedition by taking cover with the Russian military, which spirited him to safety and even sent navy forces to head off the Iranian mission. Mohammad Ali Kazembeyki sums up the situation: "Those of [the Turkmens] who navigated with a Russian passport, remained out of Iranian judicial jurisdiction, and even when they committed piracy, Russian protection prevented the local authorities in Māzandarān and Astarābād prosecuting them."[32] Meanwhile, the Russian military monopoly over the Caspian Sea made it impossible for Iranian forces to pursue Turkmens beyond the beaches.

The basics of this dynamic – Turkmens raiding northern Iran and then taking cover in Russian-patrolled territory – persisted for decades, such that, in 1860, the British consul C. F. MacKenzie was reporting much the same news as had been reported by McNeil over twenty years prior: "No point of the coast up to Ashraf," he wrote, "is free from [Turkmen] attacks ... The Russians are perfectly aware of this and laugh at the insufficient efforts, supineness, and apathy of the Persian chiefs."[33]

By the late 1850s, however, a problem had emerged for Russian military personnel stationed in the region. It seems that the same Turkmens who captured Iranians sometimes also captured Russian soldiers and officers.

The services of informants – agents who might tip off the Russians to coming raids, or identify chief raiders – were thus badly needed, and the Russians sought them among Turkmen elites. As they had done with the Kazakhs of the steppe, Russian military officials attempted to build new patronage networks among the Turkmens. Backed by the ever-present threat of military force, some Turkmen groups along the Caspian surrendered to a system by which their khans would have to be confirmed in their status by Russian officials at the seaside military station. According to the officer C. A. Gunaropulo, the khans who consented to working with the Empire could receive considerable benefits: They drew a salary and received gifts along with it. But their position could be precarious. In those cases in which perpetrators of raids and robberies were not caught in the act, and their captives were not returned, the responsibility would fall on the nearest *aul* and its headmen. The community would have either to extradite the criminals, if they were known to them, or to make every effort to find them. Otherwise, the chief elder of the *aul* would be faced with stern punishment. According to Gunaropulo, the man regarded as the chief of the community could carry exclusive responsibility in these cases.

32 Kazembeyki, *Society, Politics, and Economics in Māzandarān, Iran, 1848–1914*, 46–47.
33 Kazembeyki, *Society, Politics, and Economics in Māzandarān, Iran, 1848–1914*, 49.

Aware of the benefits of cultivating good relations with the Russian military station, they would sometimes make an effort to stop raids and robbers themselves.[34]

The story of the notorious slave-raider Ergeld Khan serves as a remarkable case study in Russian patronage along the Caspian shore. After years of Russian military patrols and interventions had interfered in his main line of work, Ergeld Khan was in a desperate situation. Nevertheless, after his long tenure as the chief raider in his community ("bravely serving his tribe," as Gunaropulo phrases it), he maintained considerable influence over his comrades and high esteem among them. The elders of his *aul*, observing the benefits of maintaining peaceful relations with the Russian military station, resolved to propose Ergeld as khan – pending Russian approval, of course.[35] It was a highly intelligent maneuver on the part of the elders: With this gesture, they could relieve themselves of the accusation that their community was harboring a felon "at large"; they could alleviate the destabilizing pressure that the presence of a destitute and dissatisfied warrior and his followers could have on the *aul*; they could maintain good relations with the station and reap its rewards; and they could ensure all of this by offering the Russians something of immense value: an ally in the fight against slave-raiding who knew the business very intimately indeed.

The benefits of working with Ergeld Khan were not lost on the Russians, or on Ergeld himself. Lengthy negotiations followed, during which it was resolved that Ergeld Khan would be well-compensated for his cooperation. Gunaropulo had the opportunity to meet him during the khan's visit to the station, and the Russian officer barely conceals his admiration in describing him: "He was quite a remarkable individual, both in his outward appearance and in the details of his life, which was full of sundry adventures. He was a tall man of majestic bearing, expressive features, and a penetrating gaze. He was covered in [old] wounds. This man, with his appealing appearance, did not give the impression of being a robber. He was no more than 40 years old, and his name inspired terror in the Persian coastal dwellings, but he rarely resorted to the dagger – only [doing so] to save his own life."[36] In the end, Ergeld took the title of "khan-intermediary" (*khan-posrednik*).

It was not long before Ergeld Khan would have a chance to demonstrate his usefulness to his new patrons. An Iranian captive was taken by

[34] Gunaropulo, "V Turkmenskoi stepi. (Iz zapisok chernomorskogo ofitsera)," 1039–1040.
[35] Ibid.
[36] Gunaropulo, "V Turkmenskoi stepi. (Iz zapisok chernomorskogo ofitsera)," 1040.

Turkmens, and Ergeld Khan informed station officers that the captive was presently located in an *aul* far from the coast, but that the relatives of his captors could be found in the *aul* of Gasan-Guli (*sic*). Russian station officers had previously shown relatively little interest in freeing Iranian captives, but they made an exception in order to enlist Ergeld Khan's services. Gunaropulo joined Ergeld in the efforts to secure the captive's release, and he provides a detailed narrative of his adventure with the Khan. As with Witkiewicz's narrations of the effort to free a captive from the steppe, Gunaropulo's account offers a rich view of the politics of manumission on the "frontlines."

The proximity of the captors' relatives was considered a useful lead: "Among the Turkmens," Gunaropulo writes, "there is the custom of avenging any insult to their relatives, but also of answering for their actions."[37] Gunaropulo set off in a schooner along with the station chief, Ergeld Khan, an interpreter, and some others. They were accompanied by ten armed sailors divided between two Turkmen boats – brought, Gunaropulo writes, for the sake of "presentation." They anchored the schooner about four miles from shore, and continued onward in the two Turkmen boats, entering the mouth of the Gasan Guli River. On either side of the river there were "countless tents," and the arrival of the boats evidently inspired "great wonder and surprise" among the Turkmens. "It seemed as if the entire population of the aul poured forth to meet us," writes Gunaropulo, "and the banks of the river resembled two colorful, rippling ribbons, from which could be heard a vague hum [of voices], which accompanied us the whole time as we moved along the river."[38]

To avoid the throngs of people, they sailed onward and made landing slightly downriver. A few minutes later, elders from the village came to find out the reason for their arrival. Gunaropulo suggested to the khan that he should take charge in the negotiations. A servant of the khan brought out a samovar, a chest, some carpets, some dried fruit, and other items, and the Turkmen elders sat in a circle and had tea. The khan invited Gunaropulo to join them, ordering his servant to provide the officer with a pillow, of the kind provided to esteemed guests at Turkmen gatherings. Gunaropulo asked the interpreter to convey to him the precise contents of the ensuing discussions. After some pleasantries, the khan explained to the elders that the Russian station chief was very unhappy with them because they knew the location of the Iranian captive but had made no efforts to secure his

[37] Ibid. [38] Ibid.

release. In light of the privileges available to them and the good relations they had thus far maintained with the Russians, the khan asked that they not rupture that "friendship" by impeding the common effort to free the captive.[39]

The elders swore that they had taken no part in what had befallen the Iranian captive, and that they did not know if he was really located in the *aul* mentioned by the khan. They insisted on the veracity of their testimony as Ergeld reiterated his suspicions. Gunaropulo allows that the elders may well have spoken honestly, but the khan had been provided with "overwhelming evidence" by his trustworthy scouts (*lazutchiki*), and he felt certain of the captive's whereabouts. Ergeld was unwavering in the matter; indicating to Gunaropulo and the interpreter that they should follow him, he stepped away from the gathering and proposed that it was necessary to invite the elders onto the schooner, and to hold one of them in captivity as collateral for the return of the Iranian captive. When Gunaropulo invited the elders to join him onboard the schooner, where they should receive a personal audience from the station chief, they bowed deeply and indicated their consent.[40]

Their distance from the village had not, in the meantime, provided much relief from the throngs of onlookers. "We were surrounded by a dense, colorful ring," Gunaropulo writes, "which, gradually closing in, would have crushed us had the requests and admonitions of the khan and the elders not mitigated the crowd's intensity."[41] The elders' march toward the boats provoked alarm among the crowd, and several Turkmens with "fearful, questioning eyes" ran over and grabbed Gunaropulo by his sleeves and the tails of his coat, crying out "Sibir! Sibir!" ("Siberia, Siberia!") – they evidently recognized the possibility that their elders could be imprisoned, and feared that they would be sent to the notorious prison camps of Siberia. A dangerous moment followed:

> At this time, a sailor who was overzealous in the performance of his duty . . . shoved a Turkmen woman off of me so violently that she fell. Words cannot express the brutal expressions which then appeared on the faces of most of these Turkmens, of both sexes. Fearing a formidable demonstration on their part of the deep indignation which, although somewhat weakened, evidently still gripped them, I made a show in that same moment of striking the sailor, though really I merely knocked his cap from his head. A single moment, and there was a metamorphosis: the grim, embittered faces brightened, and we [managed to] enter the boat, albeit not

[39] Gunaropulo, "V Turkmenskoi stepi. (Iz zapisok chernomorskogo ofitsera)," 1040–1041.
[40] Gunaropulo, "V Turkmenskoi stepi. (Iz zapisok chernomorskogo ofitsera)," 1041.
[41] Ibid.

without some effort in delicately reducing, as much as possible, the impediments presented to us by the Turkmens who were holding onto the elders, while assuring them that the elders would return to the village that same day.[42]

As they sailed downriver with the elders, "angry Turkmens dotted the shoreline" shouting at the boats, running after them, shaking their fists, and spitting in their direction. Arriving at the schooner, the station chief greeted the elders and they made their introductions. After this, the Russian official pointed to one of the elders who had been recommended to him by Ergeld as a relative of the captors who were sought, and he announced that he was to be placed under arrest until the return of the Iranian captive. The elders – unlike the others from their *aul* – evidently did not expect this outcome. They expressed their displeasure, but had no choice other than to submit. The schooner weighed anchor with its hostage onboard.[43]

As the schooner approached the military station, the Turkmen elder caught sight of something which filled him with palpable dread: a three-masted transport vessel, decommissioned from service and standing on dead anchors. The primary purpose of the vessel was to store gunpowder, but it served also as a dungeon for the "lower sorts and guilty Turkmens" (*dlia nizhnikh chinov i provinivshikhsia turkmen*). This fact, Gunaropulo writes, was well-known among Turkmens. It is not clear whether this dungeon is where they detained the elder, who was innocent of all but being related to a suspected slave-raider. A few days later, his fellow elders from the *aul* came to plead with the station chief to release their associate, vowing to see the Iranian captive returned.

The Russians' tactics here were inarguably brutish, inhumane, and quite possibly counterproductive in the long term: It is unlikely that they could, in the future, expect anything but the harshest welcome from the *aul* whose elders they had offended. It seems that the people of that community already knew very well the dangers involved in negotiating with the Russians. Their outrage upon seeing their elders heading downriver was well-founded, and it hardly seemed to surprise Gunaropulo. The presence of Ergeld Khan may or may not have impressed the elders, but it certainly did not serve to ease the minds of the general populace. Which is not to say that Ergeld's participation had no value: From the beginning, the entire operation appears to have been under his direction. His own network of informants identified the likely whereabouts of the Iranian captive; he

42 Gunaropulo, "V Turkmenskoi stepi. (Iz zapisok chernomorskogo ofitsera)," 1041–1042.
43 Gunaropulo, "V Turkmenskoi stepi. (Iz zapisok chernomorskogo ofitsera)," 1042.

pointed out their relatives' community; he undertook negotiations with the elders entirely on his own; and he suggested the hostage trick. He was no mere informant for the Russians in this enterprise; he was the mission's commander.

The mission, moreover, was a success: Promptly after pleading with Russian officials to free their compatriot, the elders managed to deliver the Iranian captive to the station.

Such complicated missions for the freeing of hostages were not always necessary. Most often, it appears that the Russians of the Caspian station simply engaged in the ransom economy, paying a redemption fee for Russian captives. According to Gunaropulo, the station had a special fund for ransom payments, formed out of the voluntary contributions of officers serving there. Each officer contributed three "Dutch coins" (*gollandskii chervonets*) per year.[44] The informal nature of this arrangement – and the fact that the ransom fund was not subsidized by higher authorities – suggests that ransoming captives was not part of the mission that the Empire had intended for the Caspian station. Most likely, the "ransom collection" arose as a practical response to the complexities involved in the more general mission of "pacifying" the Turkmens. Suffice to say, however, it is not clear how perpetuating the ransom economy might have aided in reducing the deprivations wrought by Turkmens. Instead, it proves the bargaining power of the Turkmens and the relative weakness of the Russians, their powerful station and equipment notwithstanding.

Sometimes ransom exchanges went terribly wrong for the Russians. In early 1860, two Russian sailors, named Potakeev and Ivanov, were captured by Turkmens along the Iranian coastline. These two captives became the joint property of three families of Turkmens, and these families were jointly involved in negotiating the terms of his release. Several times, Gunaropulo tells us, the negotiations were concluded to the satisfaction of all parties, and the agreed-upon ransom money was brought to the families, only to be rejected: Each time, the families would dramatically raise the ransom price. The process, overall, was incredibly dilatory: The captives remained with their Turkmen captors for *seven years*, "performing the most burdensome of labors," before another strategy was attempted. Once again, it was a Turkmen "khan-intermediary" who led the way. Ana-San Khan [sic] proposed a novel approach: The khan suggested that a trustworthy Turkmen should be sent to the *aul* where the captives were residing with the ostensible mission of purchasing an

[44] Gunaropulo, "V Turkmenskoi stepi. (Iz zapisok chernomorskogo ofitsera)," 1043.

arghumak horse – a Central Asian breed famous for its speed and hardiness. Once in possession of the horse, the Turkmen agent would seize an opportune moment to give it over to the Russian captives, so that they might ride it to freedom. Incredibly, the plan was a success: The sailors were freed, and the horse on which they escaped became joint property of the station guards.[45]

The "khan-intermediaries" in the employ of the Russian Empire could, no doubt, serve as very effective agents. It is clear that they served the Russians as a survival strategy, both for themselves and for their communities. Threatened with the loss of proceeds from raiding and ransoming, and naturally alarmed by the proximity of the Russian navy, these intermediaries did what was necessary to maintain a measure of independence as well as to secure some revenue. In the short term, these aims appear to have been met: Compensations were offered, and "indirect rule" remained the order of the day for communities led by "intermediary" khans. But in the long term, some Turkmen leaders found their aims tragically frustrated by their Russian patrons.

In a letter dating from no later than 1839, Kiyat Khan, the Turkmen ruler who had enjoyed the protection of the Empire for decades as he led raids in Iranian territory, related his sorrow and disappointment to a top Russian official in the Caucasus. In 1812, the khan writes, a Russian general sent an envoy to the Teke, Yomut, and Gökleng Turkmens, and members of these tribes chose Kiyat Khan by common agreement to conduct necessary political errands in Russia. "Now," he writes, "I am fading and nearing the end of my life; it is a pity that not one of my desires has been fulfilled." He made "repeated requests" to leading Russian officials concerning various subjects, but never received any satisfaction. Even so, the khan pledges that he has not lost his zeal for diligently serving the Russian state. The greatest disappointment had come quite recently: He had received the news that a Russian plenary minister had indicated to the Iranian court that the khan's territories along the Atrek and Gurgen Rivers would be the rightful territory of Iran. The minister evidently paid the khan a visit thereafter: "Yesterday the minister came to our post, and he very easily learned the business of centuries! We entreat Your Excellency to ask [him] what graves are in the aforesaid domains: [are they] Turkmen or Persian? Your Excellency will likely not agree with the perspective according to which we should be deprived of land left to us by our forefathers." The Khan concludes his complaint with a request that he himself may have known to be outlandish:

45 Gunaropulo, "V Turkmenskoi stepi. (Iz zapisok chernomorskogo ofitsera)," 1043.

> I have an abiding desire which, to my misfortune, has not hitherto been achieved, though I disclosed all to the chief superintendent [Rtishchev]; I disclose it now to Your Excellency, so that the weight of it shall not lie upon my chest. Here it is: I have wished that His Majesty the Emperor should give me an army for the conquest of Astarabad and the subjugation of its local inhabitants to my will. But, to my boundless regret, this goal has not been reached. Nearing the end of my life, it is a pity to die without having achieved my desire.[46]

As disappointed as the khan may have been that he never had a chance to conquer Astarabad, his bold appeal should not overshadow the deeper tragedy in his letter. Caught, like his fellow Turkmen elites, between Russia, Khwarazm, and Iran, the khan worked with the Russians for some three decades only to find, at the end of his life, thanks to Russian negotiations, that his Turkmen forefathers' graves were on Iranian soil.

[46] *Russko-turkmenskie otnosheniia v XVII–XIX v.* (Ashgabat, 1963), doc. no. 244.

7

The Conquest of Khiva and the Myth of Russian Abolitionism in Central Asia

The Russian conquest of Khiva in the spring of 1873 came with high expectations among the abolitionists of rival empires. "The first steps have already been taken," the British officer Herbert Wood would soon afterwards write, "for the diffusion of light in these dark places of the earth, for Humanity owes to Russia the cessation of brigandage and slavery, which from the earliest historical times have been the scourges of the Oxus countries."[1] When the expected emancipation was accomplished, in the form of a decree drafted by the khan at General Kaufman's behest, few were likely surprised. But perhaps they should have been. In this chapter, I will argue that the Russian-sponsored emancipation of Khwarazm's slaves was far from inevitable; that it had not been planned in advance by Kaufman or his superiors; that abolitionism, contrary to popular belief, played no significant part in motivating the Russian conquest of the region; and that credit for the slaves' mass emancipation – one of the most revolutionary acts in the history of Central Asia – should rightfully go to the slaves themselves.

Throughout the 1860s and early 1870s, right down to the eve of Khiva's conquest, a declining but significant trade in Iranian slaves had continued, notwithstanding the near-total cessation in raids among steppe Kazakhs and the concurrent Russian and Qajar efforts to subjugate Turkmens to the south. In fact, imperial efforts in Khurasan sometimes served only to provide more captives for Central Asian markets. In 1860, for example, a Qajar campaign brought an estimated 13,000 infantry, 10,000 cavalry, and 33 cannons to Merv, only to be routed by Teke adversaries; so many

[1] Wood, *The Shores of Lake Aral*, xii.

captives were taken and sold that, according to Kuropatkin, the price of a single Iranian slave in the markets of Bukhara and Khiva fell to seven rubles and fifty kopeks.[2] M. Alikhanov-Avarskii ventured to propose the scope of the disaster: "a Persian detachment of Prince Sultan Murad, on its way to Merv, left *no less than 20,000* of their soldiers in the hands of local Teke, and the majority of those were sold to Khiva."[3]

Miserable conditions in northern Iran in the early 1870s may also have contributed to the trade: Grodekov observes that the "terrible famine that raged throughout Persia" in 1871 resulted in the Iranians being "so weakened by want of food that they offered the Tekes no resistance whatever." He met with a man who had been held captive by Tekes for many years, and the man related to him the ease with which these weakened victims could be taken: "[he] told me that the poorer nomads used to ride on donkeys to Serakhs, armed only with cudgels, and drive back the villagers in droves to slavery at Merv. He himself was captured in this manner during one of the Alamans."[4]

As we have seen in a previous chapter, the subjugation of Bukhara by June of 1868 had not brought about the end of the slave trade in those quarters either – nor did such a goal appear to be a matter of urgency for its Russian conquerors. It was not until 1873, some five years later, that the Russians would write abolition into a treaty with the Bukharan Amīr, and even then the ruler was allowed a deferment of *ten years* before full emancipation would have to take effect. In the eighteen-point treaty in question, in which ten of the points related to commercial relations between Russia and Bukhara, the abolition of the slave trade occupied the seventeenth point:[5]

In deference to the Emperor of all the Russias, and for the greater glory of His Imperial Majesty, His Eminence the Amir Sayed Muzaffar has resolved that henceforth and for ever the shameful trade in men which is so contrary to the laws of humanity, shall be abolished within the limits of Bukhara. In conformity with this resolution, Sayed Muzaffar shall immediately send to all his beks the strictest orders to that effect. Besides the order abolishing the slave trade, commands shall be sent to all the frontier towns of Bukhara to which slaves are brought for sale

[2] A. N. Kuropatkin, *Zavoevanie turkmenii: pokhod v akhal-teke v 1880–81 gg.*, 96. A. Maslov offers a similar summary of the ill-fated campaign, estimating the Qajar forces at 20,000 and the resulting price of a slave at an even more shocking 1.5 rubles each: See Maslov, *Rossiia v srednei azii*, 386.

[3] M. Alikhanov-Avarskii, *Pokhod v khivu (Kavkazkikh otriadov) 1873*, 280. Emphasis added.

[4] Grodekoff, 129.

[5] Demetrius Charles Boulger, *England and Russia in Central Asia*, Vol. 1 (London: W.H. Allen, 1879), 337.

from neighbouring countries, to the effect that in case slaves should be brought to such places, notwithstanding the orders of the Amir, the same should be taken from their owners and immediately liberated.

The ambitious language of the treaty was surely undermined by the ten-year grace period permitted, and indeed the slave trade in Bukhara continued. Nevertheless, the rumor had evidently spread both among Central Asian slaves and among foreign journalists that the era of slavery was drawing to a close and that Russian troops were consummate liberators, breaking slaves' shackles wherever they went. So it was that the slaves of Khwarazm began to revolt against their masters and free themselves before the Tsar's invading armies had even arrived at the capital.[6] The closer the Russian detachments came to the city, the greater the number of slaves seizing the occasion to liberate themselves in the "conviction and the hope ... that the fall of Khiva would also bring them their freedom ... [A]t first they appeared in small parties, but the bands steadily increased as the [Russians] advanced."[7] Many joined the Russians, marching beside them.

The possibility of slaves fleeing or rebelling at the approach of the Russian forces had been anticipated by many slave-owners well in advance of the Khivan campaign.[8] Alikhanov-Avarskii witnessed that Iranians, freeing themselves, "flee from their masters and appear at our camp in masses, despite the fact that the Khivans, as a precaution, have in recent times been keeping them chained and under close supervision."[9] By all accounts, slaves met their presumed liberators with dramatic displays of ecstatic joy and relief. Grodekov described how "[t]he people loudly greeted the troops, and especially boisterous were the noisy greetings of the Persian slaves. They had begun to free themselves immediately upon the troops' entry into the capital of the Khanate, and in the crowd one could see many slaves jostling forward, showing the troops arms and legs bloodied from tight shackles."[10] MacGahan would later witness a similar spectacle, writing how he and the group of Russian soldiers he accompanied "came upon a crowd of Persian slaves, who received us with shouts,

[6] E. Zheliabuzhskii, *Ocherki i zavoevanie khivy* (Moscow, 1875), 116.

[7] Schmidt, 121. See also V. N. Trotskii, *Opisanie khivinskago pokhoda 1873 goda* (St Pb, 1898), 229.

[8] While traveling to Khiva, David Ker interviewed a Russian citizen who predicted that "as soon as our brothers get within cannon shot of the place, the Persians will up and chop the Khivans to bits" (Ker, *On the Road to Khiva* [London: Henry S. King and Co.], 101).

[9] Alikhanov-Avarskii, 217.

[10] Grodekov, *Khivinskii pokhod 1873 goda deistviia kavkazskikh otriadov*, 314.

cries, and tears of joy. They were wild with excitement. They had heard that wherever the Russians went slavery disappeared, and they did not doubt that it would be the case here. Some had already liberated themselves; and I saw several engaged in cutting the chains of three or four miserable beings, shouting the while, and laughing and crying all at once in the wildest manner."[11]

Foreign observers, too, would have had good reason for suspecting that abolition was on the Tsar's list of priorities. After all, the Tsar's public announcement and explanation for the campaign, which appeared in the newspaper *Russkii invalid* and was translated for the *New York Times*, makes no fewer than four references to slavery and captivity in describing its incentives. For example, the circular alleges that the khan had previously been prompted to "immediately set at liberty all Russian prisoners," but that he had declined to do so, and so they remained "slaves in the possession of the Khan and his high functionaries."[12] It also notes "several merchants and others" who were killed or "dragged into slavery" on the road between Orsk and Kazalinsk.[13] Slavery was a topic of concern and an incentive for the campaign at the highest levels – or so it was made to seem.

It is perhaps for this reason that the khan's final, desperate effort to stave off invasion came in the form of selective manumission. The khan ordered twenty-one Russian slaves gathered together and sent off to General Kaufman along with a petition (*ʿarznāma*) asking for peace, all to be delivered by a high-ranking emissary (identified in a Khivan source as Murtażа Biy Khwāja, *ḥākīm* of Khwāja Eli). Kaufman neither accepted the petition nor permitted the emissary to return home, keeping Murtażа Biy with his retinue on the way to Khiva. The twenty-one former slaves were duly received, but their manumission did nothing to slow Kaufman's advance.[14] These freedmen, of whom eleven were Cossacks, had all been captured in 1869 and 1870 by Kazakhs and sold to Khiva; it was evidently claimed by the khan that they were the only Russian subjects still held as slaves there, "with the exception," MacGahan writes, "of one old man taken in Perovsky's disastrous expedition" of 1839–40, who had converted to Islam, married, and preferred not to leave.[15] It is unlikely that

[11] MacGahan, 233; see also Alikhanov-Avarskii, 217.
[12] "Russia and Khiva: The Empire's Manifesto Prefatory to the Expedition," *New York Times*, April 13, 1873.
[13] Ibid.
[14] MS IVAN Uz No. 12581, ff. 21b–22a. See also MacGahan, *Campaigning on the Oxus*, 20.
[15] MacGahan, 20. More Russian slaves were to be freed during the ensuing conquest.

the khan believed these concessions alone would be sufficient to convince Kaufman to turn his troops back. He probably hoped the gesture might show his willingness to negotiate given the opportunity. Indeed, the previous year he had sent two envoys – one to the Grand Duke Mikhail in the Caucasus and another to Orenburg – in an apparent effort to arrive at a diplomatic resolution.[16] But the opportunity was not to come.

As Kaufman entered the capital on March 28, 1873, a large-scale slave uprising had begun in earnest. Emboldened by rumors of the city's imminent downfall, slaves broke from their owners, plundered them, and in some cases, according to a later Khivan source called the *Āzādnāma*, began tormenting them.[17] Scenes like this could be witnessed not only in the capital but also in towns and villages throughout Khwarazm, and it was reported that both owners and their (now former) slaves seized the occasion to engage in acts of cruelty against one another.[18] Before long, groups of Khivans began approaching Kaufman, pleading that he do something to help put down the uprising. In what may have been the first act of governance on the part of the Russian Empire in Khwarazm, Kaufman ordered an inquiry into the crimes of rebelling former slaves, in the course of which two were found guilty and hung from the gallows.[19]

MacGahan witnessed the aftermath. "I saw their dead bodies hanging from the beams in one of the bazaars," he writes, "where they remained for several days. I may mention that many of Kaufmann's officers strongly condemned this act, thinking that the Persians had too much reason for taking some vengeance on the masters, to be thus severely treated. The punishment, however, had the double effect of cowing the Persians and of encouraging the masters to punish them severely for the use they had made of their liberty. Several poor fellows came into our camp and showed us gashes in the soles of their feet or in the calves of their legs, in which was strewed cut horsehair."[20] This evidently quelled the uprising for a time, but it was not long before the unrest was resumed with renewed ferocity.[21]

[16] I am grateful to Alexander Morrison for this observation.

[17] MS IVAN Uz No. 12581, f. 24a. Ḥassan Muḥammad Amīn Oghlï claims that the leader of the slave uprising was a man who was called Ibrahīm Basmachi, known as the first lithographic publisher (using stone plates: *tash maṭb'aachilik*) in Khwarazm. For his efforts in the uprising, he was allegedly dubbed "Ibrahīm Sulṭān").

[18] Zheliabuzhskii, *Ocherki i zavoevanie khivy*, 116; Schmidt, *The Russian Expedition to Khiva in 1873*, 121; MacGahan, *Campaigning on the Oxus*, 310.

[19] MS IVAN Uz No. 12581, ff. 24a–25b.

[20] MacGahan, *Campaigning on the Oxus*, 311.

[21] MS IVAN Uz No. 12581, ff. 24b–25a.

Kaufman's decision to demand the liberation of the slaves was directly inspired by the uprising undertaken by the slaves themselves. Granted, some Russian officers had supported individual acts of manumission on an *ad hoc* basis during the campaign: those slaves who had escaped and joined themselves to General Verevkin's ranks, for example, were welcomed by that officer, who declared them to be free. In early June, Verevkin corresponded both with officials in Astrakhan and with Kaufman concerning the liberation of slaves, and the latter replied that he would propose the subject of general abolition to the new council that he had formed among Khivan elites to negotiate the surrender and future governance of Khwarazm. As Schuyler notes, however, echoing the sentiments of both Central Asian and foreign commentators, "the most impelling reason for the emancipation was, that slaves who had run away from their masters had begun to rob, pillage, and murder; and the masters, fearing to be deprived of their slaves, were imprisoning and torturing those who remained to prevent them from running away."[22] So it was that, shortly after Muḥammad Raḥim Khan returned to the conquered capital from his temporary hiding place among the Yomuts, he was compelled by Kaufman to draft an edict of abolition and general manumission, to be circulated throughout the Khanate.[23] Khwarazm's emancipation proclamation read:[24]

22 Schuyler, *Turkistan*, 353; see also MS IVAN Uz No. 12581, f. 25a; MacGahan, *Campaigning on the Oxus*, 311.

23 Kaufman, reflecting on these events in an interview with MacGahan, offered a mocking appraisal of the Khan's political abilities and intelligence, which, ironically, may actually reveal the naiveté of the general himself: "Having decided to emancipate the slaves, [Kaufman] wrote the Khan a letter one day, informing him of his decision, and requesting him to issue a proclamation to that effect. The last part of the letter contained advice and counsel as to the best means of carrying out the measure, and among other things, requested the Khan to make arrangements with the governors of the different provinces to have the proclamation read all over the Khanate the same day, in order not to give the Uzbegs an opportunity for maltreating the Persians. The Khan, however, having read the first part of the letter, immediately, without stopping to finish it, wrote out a proclamation, and ordered it to be proclaimed through the streets next day by a herald, and then went to Kaufmann, with childish eagerness, to tell him what he had done, and show him how prompt he was to obey his wishes. 'But,' said Kaufmann, 'did you not read the last part of my letter ?' 'No,' said the Khan, 'I did not know it was necessary.' 'Why, yes,' said Kaufmann, 'with us the last part of a letter is often the best. In it I advised you not to issue your proclamation for a few days yet'" (ibid., 278–279). It is much more likely that the Khan's "mistake" was a deliberate and none-too-subtle attempt at resistance, intended to undermine Kaufman's efforts.

24 Zheliabuzhskii, *Ocherki i zavoevanie khivy*, 117; see also Trotskii, *Opisanie khivinskago pokhoda 1873 goda*, 246.

I, Sayyid Muhammad Rahim Bahadur Khan, out of deep respect for the Russian Emperor, command all of my subjects promptly to provide total freedom [*pol'naia svoboda*] to all the slaves of my Khanate. Henceforth slavery is to be abolished in my Khanate for all time. May this humanitarian act [*chelovekoliubivoe delo*] serve as a pledge of eternal friendship between all of my glorious people and the great Russian people.

I command that my will be carried out precisely, under threat of strict punishment. All former slaves, henceforth free, must be considered to have rights equal to those of my other subjects, and subject to the same penalties as they are, and tried for disturbing the peace in the country and for disorderliness – thus I urge all of them to maintain order.

All former slaves are granted the right to live anywhere in my Khanate, or to leave it for wherever they desire. For those who wish to leave the Khanate, special measures will be taken. Female slaves [*zhenshini-rabyni*] are freed on equal footing with men. Disputes between married women and their husbands will be sorted out according to sharia law [*po sharigatu*].

This edict was to be followed, several weeks later, in mid-August, by a treaty between the Khan and the Russian Empire which included the provision that all slaves were officially freed, and that reducing people to slavery and trading in human beings were absolutely prohibited.[25]

The June decree was announced publicly in towns and villages throughout Khwarazm.[26] Soon, slaves could be seen celebrating all across the Khanate, shouting out joyfully in the streets. Freedmen were witnessed affixing Russian imperial emblems and colors to their clothing in a show of gratitude.[27] In the weeks to come, these freedmen – whose numbers have been estimated at anywhere between 27,000 and 58,500 – would have to choose whether to remain in Khwarazm or to attempt to return to their original homeland. For nearly all of them, that homeland was Iran, and the journey there would involve crossing dangerous ground. There was no guarantee that homecoming parties venturing south would be safe from Turkmen raids. Indeed, those who were most eager to return home in the days that followed the news of their liberation met a miserable end: "[F]ollowing the announcement of freedom," Alikhanov-Avarskii writes,

[25] MS IVAN Uz No. 12581, ff. 26a–b; see also MacGahan, *Campaigning on the Oxus*, 419; S. V. Zhukovskii, *Snosheniia Rossii s Bukharoi i Khivoi za poslednee trekhsotletie* (Petrograd, 1915), 179–83; *Das Staatsarchiv: Sammlung der officiellen Actenstücke zur Geschichte der Gegenwart* (Leipzig: von Duncker & Humbolt), 134–137. The Russian text of the decree has *rabstvo i torg liud'mi* for "slavery and trading in human beings."

[26] MS IVAN Uz No. 12581, f. 25b; MacGahan, *Campaigning on the Oxus*, 311.

[27] MS IVAN Uz No. 12581, f. 25b. Ḥassan Muḥammad Amīn Oghlï writes that even some famous Khivan personages – among whom he lists Murād ʿAlī Mahram and Muḥammad ʿAlī Mahram – did the same.

"Persians began to gather into large parties for the return to their homeland. Two such parties, of 700–800 souls each, have already left the oasis and moved into the desert where, they say, they were slaughtered without exception by Turkmens fleeing Khiva ... In light of such rumors, the unfortunate Persians no longer hurry home, but instead collect near our detachment – their numbers already adding to some 1,500 men, women, and children – in order to follow along the Caspian shore during the return march of the Caucasians ... "[28]

Although those who wished to remain in Khwarazm rather than risking a journey elsewhere were guaranteed equal rights with other freedmen under the provisions of the liberation decree, Emil Schmidt claims that, at first, few showed any desire to stay where they were.[29] The author of the *Āzādnāma*, Ḥassan Muḥammad Amīn Oghlï, provides quite a different assessment, however, estimating that a substantial proportion of the freedmen, totaling no less than 22,500 Iranians and "Azeri Turks," wished to become Khwarazmian citizens. By this author's estimation, that left some 36,000 who were prepared to journey to Iran and elsewhere.

Grodekov recalled seeing the fourth group of freedmen to leave Khwarazm following behind Russian troops on the way to the Mangyshlaq. Each was given a daily allowance of twenty kopeks, though "it was noted that they were not making good use of the allotment given to them, and instead of stocking up on provisions for the voyage through the desert, they bought only some goodies which were made available to them in Kungrad ... Little benefit was had from the Persians in the armed forces. They were for the most part weak and sick, depleted by being overworked by masters who, for the slightest offense, laid shackles upon them and punished them cruelly. There were, of course, healthy and strong individuals among the Persians, but these too did nothing without prodding. They were sometimes caught stealing."[30] It is not clear why Grodekov would have expected military or tactical assistance from these refugees, but his remarks help to reveal something of their poor condition during the long march home. This group would suffer still more on the road. They – as well as their Russian escorts – were tormented by thirst on their journey through the desert. Grodekov recalls that "[o]n coming to a well, six Persians climbed down into it and did not

[28] Alikhanov-Avarskii, *Pokhod v khivu*, 280. Schmidt observed that "[t]hose who returned alone without availing themselves of the Russian convoy and aid have had much to suffer, and many of these unprotected helpless creatures were murdered by the Turkomans on the road." (Schmidt, *The Russian Expedition to Khiva in 1873*.)

[29] Schmidt, *The Russian Expedition to Khiva in 1873*, 122.

[30] Grodekov, *Khivinskii pokhod 1873 goda*, 326.

want to leave, even when ropes were lowered to bring them back up. One of the ropes broke while hauling a Persian up, but he survived."[31]

When they arrived at Krasnovodsk, on the Caspian Sea, these Iranians were offered provisions totaling two pounds of flour and one-eighth of a pound of butter per day for each adult, and half this amount for each child. Grodekov recalls that a number of them expressed a desire to accompany the detachment all the way back to Russia. "But," he writes, "when the first steamship arrived to take the Persians back to their homeland, all of them abandoned these intentions, some from a desire to see their fatherland and others for fear of being taken into the army as soldiers, as was claimed by a rumor someone spread among them. Although the officers tried to explain to them that the White Tsar had no need of the services of such people, dozens of whom could be sold to Khiva or Bukhara by a single Turkmen, they were thoroughly convinced by the [rumor] they had heard, and not one of them went off to Russia."[32] MacGahan confirms that this group arrived safely at their destination.[33] Another group of some 500 freedmen, however, which had set off at the same time but had opted to travel along the Atrek River, was pillaged and massacred by Teke Turkmens.[34]

Among the thousands of freedmen who had gathered in certain Khwarazmian villages and bazaars to await their journey home, there were many who could not immediately afford the expenses required for the long journey. According to Ḥassan Muḥammad Amīn Oghlï, these ones could expect aid neither from their former masters nor from Iran (nor, presumably, from the Russian military). Still, they hoped to manage the return journey eventually, and as time wore on their patience grew thin. In the villages of Katta Bāgh and Tāshḥawż, some of them began taking out their frustration by attacking their former masters, while others resorted to banditry and other forms of aggression.[35]

The *Āzādnāma* recounts the tragic events that followed. At this tense time, a man named ʿAwz Keldi Khan from among the Yomuts came to the freedmen in Katta Bāgh, telling them that he could lead them, safe and sound, through the Turkmen deserts and back to their homeland in Iran. The former slaves made a show of gratitude for his offer, and some went to

[31] Grodekov, *Khivinskii pokhod 1873 goda*, 330.
[32] Grodekov, *Khivinskii pokhod 1873 goda*, 342.
[33] MacGahan, *Campaigning on the Oxus*, 311–312.
[34] MS IVAN Uz No. 12581, f. 27b. This may be the group to which Schuyler refers on p. 354 of his *Turkistan*.
[35] MS IVAN Uz No. 12581, ff. 27b–28a.

their comrades in Tāshḥawż in order to spread the news. Many agreed to follow him. Several days were spent working out the preparations. The plans gained the favorable attention of the local headman, ʿAlī Muḥammad Khan, and on his orders a large group departed for Iran via Kohne Urgench, under the leadership of ʿAwz Keldi Khan. All the while, the *Āzādnāma* relates, this self-proclaimed guide had been surveying the freedmen's worldly possessions and, in a clandestine manner (*yashirin ravishda*), had passed along the details of his plan to his fellow Yomuts, telling them that the former slaves would have many possessions among them (*qullarning qolida māl-i dunyā köbdur*).[36]

With this information in hand, a massive host of some 17,000 armed Yomut horsemen gathered while ʿAwz Keldi Khan led a trusting cohort of several thousand former slaves into the desert. First, they stopped in Kohne Urgench, where they stocked up on supplies and provisions for the arduous road to come. For several days they traveled deeper into the desert, their water supply gradually depleting. Finally, they came upon a well and stopped to drink. It was here that, all of a sudden, they found themselves being fired upon. The 17,000 mounted Turkmens emerged and engaged them in a grueling siege, which lasted the next twelve hours. At the end of it, some 5,000 former slaves lay dead. All of their possessions were pillaged.[37]

Schmidt also reports on the misery that awaited the former slaves of Khwarazm following the departure of the Russian troops, although he gives a lower casualty estimate. "No sooner had the last Russian troops turned their back upon the Khanate," Schmidt writes, "than the news reached Petro-Alexandrovsk that the Turkomans had attacked a numerous party of former slaves (about 1,700 in number) near Kunya-Urgenj, who were on their way home; of these wretched people a considerable number had been sabred on the spot and the rest captured by the Turkomans."[38] A courier on his way from Petro-Alexandrovsk reported seeing "the bodies of hundreds of Persians who had been massacred after the Russians left the country"; another messenger, headed to Mangyshlaq, likewise reported "hundreds of corpses" of Iranian former-slaves by the roadside.[39]

These acts of cruelty on the part of the Turkmens were unprecedented: Central Asian tribes had never before been known to slaughter Iranians *en*

[36] MS IVAN Uz No. 12581, ff. 28a–29b. [37] MS IVAN Uz No. 12581, ff. 30a–31a.
[38] Schmidt, *The Russian Expedition to Khiva in 1873*, 169.
[39] Schuyler, *Turkistan*, Vol. 2, 354.

masse, a strategy that, among other things, would have undermined the business of slave-dealing. For all the reports of dehumanizing treatment inflicted upon slaves while in Turkmen captivity, reports of outright murder before 1873 are strikingly rare, and can usually be explained by rational means: Those captives who were too slow or ill to manage the journey north from Khurasan might be killed, for example, or those who fought back. But it is difficult to ascertain any practical reason for the mass murder of thousands of former slaves. Perhaps some wanted to send the message that abolition for the sake of the slaves themselves would only lead to further misery – a desperate attempt to reinforce the market for slaves that abolition undermined. Some may have hoped to send a message to the slaves themselves that nothing good would come of fleeing their masters, perhaps in the hope of "stabilizing" the slave system. But these practical-minded explanations are ultimately unconvincing.

It is more appropriate to reflect on these massacres both as acts of resistance and as expressions of collective desperation. In the weeks after the conquest of Khiva, Kaufman had wasted little time in proving his cruelty to the Turkmens. Soon after the return of the khan to the capital, Kaufman imposed upon the Yomuts a war indemnity totaling the impossible sum of 600,000 rubles, of which half was demanded to be paid by the Yomuts of Khwarazm within two weeks.[40] The Yomut elders did not resist, despite the absurdity of the demand in light of their meager assets, which mostly consisted of livestock: They agreed to pay, but asked for more time to collect the funds. Instead, Kaufman arrested twelve elders, holding seven of them as hostages. The general did not wait even the allotted two weeks before sending a detachment to the Yomuts in western Khwarazm, ordering them to "proceed to the work of slaughter" if there was no evidence that the required indemnity was forthcoming.[41] The Cossacks massacred the Yomuts, who were not expecting the assault and were not prepared to fight back. The other Turkmen tribes of Khwarazm were then ordered to pay the remaining 310,500 rubles of the fine. They could raise only 92,000 rubles among them, but Kaufman – already facing domestic criticism for the slaughter of the Yomuts – softened his approach, taking twenty-six Turkmen hostages

[40] Zheliabuzhskii, *Ocherki i zavoevanie khivy*, 119; Becker, *Russia's Protectorates in Central Asia*, 59.

[41] Gali Oda Tealakh, "The Russian Advance in Central Asia and the British Response, 1834–1884" (Ph.D. Dissertation, Durham University, 1991), 209. A witness claims to have heard the leader of this detachment, Golovachev, ordering his men to "kill all of them" (i.e. the Yomuts), without respect to sex or age (Schuyler, *Turkistan*, Vol. 2, 359).

but sparing their lives.[42] All the Turkmens of the region, whether subjects of Russia or self-independent tribes, must have been horrified by these events, which appear calculated to ensure – rather than to prevent – ongoing conflict with the Tsar's army.

After these acts of terrorism on the part of the Russian military, allowing the safe passage of the freed slaves through Turkmen country would have been a tacit admission of Turkmen weakness, or even of Turkmen subjection to Russia. Their territories had never been a safe space for Iranians before; if that should change simply because Russian officers gave Iranians permission to return home, it would be as if the Russians – or still worse, the Iranians themselves – had dictated the terms by which one could pass through the Turkmen-dominated deserts. The Turkmens could, at the very least, assert their dominion over the shrinking territory in which they could still move and act freely. Inasmuch as their massacre of the freedmen served as a desperate assertion of their independence from the forces closing in from the north, we must observe a terrible irony: The imperial drive which had freed these slaves had likewise sealed their fate.

The Turkmens now had to face an uncertain future. Raiding and slave-dealing had been a major economic force in Turkmen communities for which viable alternatives for securing a livelihood were few. Largely alienated from the agricultural lands of the oases, which were mostly owned by Uzbeks (in Khwarazm and Bukhara) and Iranians (in northern Iran), Turkmen tribes took advantage of every available means of securing food and resources, engaging in fishing, hunting, herding, and artisanship. Raiding and slave-dealing, however, not only provided for influxes of capital and trade-goods on a grander scale than these other occupations, but also served as the foundation for valued customs and social phenomena. The raids provided the supreme template for the proving of masculinity: A small-scale herder or fisherman could moonlight as a warrior. Young men, sharing the experience with their elders, could come of age in combat. The world-renowned horse culture of the Turkmens had also become closely linked to the raiding expeditions, and it was in these contexts that the horsemanship and gallantry praised in the Turkmens' vast oral literature, music, and poetry found its most vivid contemporary expression. The raids also served as a catalyst for the redistribution of goods, and the social functions that this engenders: the enactment of hierarchy, the proving of generosity, and the apportioning of prestige.

[42] Becker, *Russia's Protectorates in Central Asia*, 58.

The wealth generated by raids and slave-trading also provided for the creation of trade networks. The luxury goods and animals looted in raids, as well as the captives and the revenue generated from selling them, allowed for liaisons with neighboring Turkmens as well as with Kazakhs, Uzbeks, and others. The importance, moreover, of the goods, materials, animals, enslaved laborers, and luxury wares gained by raiding can hardly be overstated in light of the poverty and chronic instability that characterized tribal life in the deserts in Central Asia. In an environment where herdsmen could lose the majority of their livelihood in a single season of brutal weather, the small measure of stability provided by supplemental revenue must have been precious indeed.

In light of all this, one can begin to comprehend the desperation and outrage that must have gripped many Turkmen communities as they realized that the markets and infrastructure for their trade in slaves was collapsing with the Russian advance. What's more, they could see the very cargo they had gone to such lengths to secure literally walking back to freedom before their eyes. And for those who believed that slavery among Sunnis was a charitable fate for Shiʿites, as it often brought about the auspicious occasion of conversion, the slaves' return to Iran must have been all the more galling. The Turkmens' work was undone, and their own futures were uncertain. At the very least, they could endeavor to steal what little goods the freedmen carried with them on the way back home. Having dehumanized their Iranian victims for decades already, it is no great surprise that the Turkmens' anger should have found its outlet in astonishing acts of inhumanity.

THE RUSSIAN CONQUEST OF THE TURKMEN DESERTS

The conquest of Khiva is sometimes portrayed as the campaign that ended the slave trade in Central Asia. It was nothing of the sort. The slave trade continued, as we have seen, bolstered mostly by the ongoing tensions to the south between Turkmen tribes and the Iranians. Nor was it intended to be anything of the sort: Russian operations against the Turkmens in the 1850s and 1860s, more often than not, were justified as a means of ensuring the safety only of *Russian* citizens and soldiers; and the establishment of Russian military outposts on the Caspian Sea must be understood in light of the larger imperial project of establishing a permanent presence south of Khwarazm. Before the 1870s and 1880s, however, this presence was peripheral. As we have seen, the activities of the Russians' Caspian bases, in consultation with its Astarabad consulate, had some impact in reducing the incidence of raids on Iranian towns and villages in the region, and the establishment of patronage networks and alliances between the Russian military and Turkmen elites was a profound and novel development. But the slave trade was also reduced by many factors that had little or nothing to do with Russian interventions.

In the eighteenth and nineteenth centuries, the geography of slave-raiding among the Turkmens was generally distinguished by several spheres: The Salar Turkmens raided from their base at Sarakhs and took captives in their campaigns for the control of that town and its environs; the Sarïqs did the same in vicinity of Marv; the Ersaris took captives in and around Herat; the Chawdurs conducted raids along the Russian frontier; the Yomuts raided the Caspian coast and the villages in the vicinity of Astarabad; and the Tekes, based at Akhal, likewise raided the Iranian frontier, though some authors claim that their raiding activities were less frequent than those of other tribes before the 1860s.[43] By the time Khiva fell in 1873, all of these vectors in the slave trade had been interrupted to some extent, or even erased entirely. The Salars suffered a massive defeat in ʿAbbās Mīrzā's Sarakhs campaign of 1833, and would never again regain their former notoriety for taking captives in battle or raiding local settlements. The Chawdurs were reported by a Caspian flotilla commander to have ceased their raids on Russian subjects completely after the construction of the Novo-Petrovsk fort on the Mangyshlaq peninsula in 1846.[44] Relatively little is known about the Ersaris in the mid- and late nineteenth century, but there is no evidence that they conducted significant raids in the vicinity of Herat after the city fell decisively into the hands of the Afghans after 1863.

As for the Sarïqs, their ascendancy – as well as their ability to take captives – eroded along with their hold on the oasis of Merv. In 1855, Khwarazmian forces suffered a major defeat near Sarakhs at the hands of the Tekes, who proceeded to drive the Sarïqs from the vicinity of Merv as they migrated into the region. The Khwarazmians, who had long employed Turkmens of various tribes in their struggle for Merv, would never retake the oasis, nor would they have any further need of hiring Turkmens as mercenaries (in which capacity they were also often captive-takers); the Sarïqs, who during their troubled residency there had allegedly become one of the

[43] Marvin, *Marv, the Queen of the World*, 179.

[44] *Russko-turkmenskie otnosheniia v XVIII–XIX vv.*, 469, doc. no. 341; see also Vambery, *Sketches of Central Asia*, 212.

principal Turkmen tribes engaged in slave-raiding,[45] abandoned Merv entirely by 1858. "Thus," William Wood writes, "both of the major players at Merv in the first half of the nineteenth century suddenly found themselves on the outside looking in."[46] Meanwhile, from 1855 to 1867, Khwarazm was rocked by uprisings among Yomuts and other Turkmen groups within the Khanate, undermining whatever slave trade might have persisted between those groups and Khwarazmian markets.[47]

The Tekes consolidated their control over Merv and held their ground against Qajar campaigns; they would maintain that control until 1884, when the Russians occupied the city. In the intervening years, they took advantage of the persistent demand for slaves in the markets to the north to become the preeminent slave dealers of the region. In 1859, they formed an alliance with the Salars and Sarïqs, and dominated a considerable expanse of territory under two simultaneous rulers (Kushīd Khan in Merv and Nūr Verdi Khan in Akhal). But the market for their slave trading was curtailed by the fall of Khiva. "The march to Khiva," writes Grodekov, "and its results – the suppression of slavery in Khiva and Bokhara – struck a heavy blow at the ascendency of the Tekes. It became useless for them to steal the Persians for slaves, since they had no market for the disposal of them. For two years after the fall of Khiva the Alamans entirely ceased; and although they recommenced again in 1876, they have never yet reached the proportions they attained before the closing of the slave markets."[48]

In the cases concerning the decline of slave-raiding among Turkmen groups, Russian influence was either nonexistent, as in the fall of the Salars at Sarakhs, the Sarïqs at Merv, and the ascendancy of the Afghans in Herat, or indirect, as in the interruption of markets (i.e. in Khwarazm) or access to victims (i.e. along the Russian frontier). In the case of the Yomuts along the shores of the Caspian, however, we find a more direct engagement, involving – as we have seen – skirmishes, intelligence-gathering operations, the hiring of native informants, and other tactics of war. (It is, naturally, for this reason that the decline of raiding among the Yomuts is better-documented than among any other Central Asian population except perhaps the Kazakhs.) While some Yomut elites chose to serve – or at least manipulate – the Russians as informants and ostensible allies, a great many others responded to Russian encroachments with energetic and sustained

[45] Marvin, *Marv, the Queen of the World*, 179.
[46] Wood, "The Sariq Turkmens of Merv and the Khanate of Khiva in the Early Nineteenth Century," 253.
[47] See Bregel, *Khorezmskie turkmeny*, 197–228. [48] Grodekov, 132–133.

resistance. Caught between the forces of the tsar and those of the shah, many directed their opposition toward both, and submitted to neither.

The violence was generally reciprocal. In 1850, in response to increasing Russian influence and control in their territory, a group of Yomuts launched an abortive campaign against the tsar's Ashur Ada sea-station. They arrived on Easter night in forty large boats. "Leaping ashore," Gunaropulo writes, "the Turkmens rushed to the brightly-lit church, being the only place clearly visible against the background of dark night. The people, praying in the garden adjacent to the church, saw the armed Turkmens approaching and, with a desperate cry, rushed into the church. At that moment the Turkmens heard gunfire, as the guard team had quickly assembled, and they fled, leaving four of their own dead but still taking three women with them."[49] According to Gunaropulo, the next few years saw a decline of Russian influence over the Yomuts. In 1854, however, station officials resolved upon a violent reassertion of Russian force: They made a landing assault on the Yomut village of Hassan-Quli, burning twenty-eight boats and taking several prominent men as captives ("for whom the Turkmens paid dearly in ransom").[50]

Yomut relations with the Qajars were still more combustible. In 1858, after the Qajar governor of Astarabad, Jaʿfar Qulī Khan Ilkhan, forcibly expelled Turkmens from the vicinity of Kara Kala with a force of some 10,000 men, taking some back to Astarabad as captives, the Turkmens began plundering the countryside and taking captives of their own in reprisal.[51] The raids continued for the next three years, undoubtedly both as a means for the Yomuts to generate revenue as well as a means of asserting that they could not be evicted from their homes without repercussions. In September, 1863, while likely still reeling from their disastrous defeat by the Tekes at Merv two years earlier, the Qajars led an ambitious series of attacks against the Yomuts of Astarabad and the Atrek. This campaign too came with significant losses: At first their advance was beaten back, and one Qajar detachment had to retreat from Astarabad after being stricken with a typhoid outbreak that killed up to twenty soldiers per day. But the military governor of Bujnurd, Ḥaydar Qulī Khan, led a successful raid on the upper Atrek. Sixty-three Yomut captives were taken, along with 3,000 camels and 20,000 sheep. Fifteen Turkmens who were killed during the attack were beheaded, and their severed heads

49 Gunaropulo, "V Turkmenskoi stepi," 1043.
50 ibid. "Since that time," Gunaropulo writes, "the pirates have been subdued, and have never since dared to attack the station."
51 *Russko-turkmenskie otnosheniia v XVIII–XIX vv.*, 453–54, doc. no. 328.

sent to Ḥaydar Qulī Khan's camp. This "success" inspired the Qajar minister of war to demand that the coastal Turkmens return all of the Iranian captives they had taken in recent years. Turkmen elders readily agreed to this, though naturally many of these captives would already have been sold into slavery in Khwarazm or Bukhara.[52] By the next year, the Yomuts had evidently given up just thirty captives, and in November of 1864 they suffered another attack at the hands of the Qajars. An Iranian detachment ventured along the Atrek River, capturing fifteen elderly Turkmen women, as well as some 1,000 camels and 12,000 sheep. According to Russian internal documents, the Qajars were demanding not only the surrender of captives, but also that the Turkmens submit to becoming Iranian citizens.[53] In fact, given the clear impossibility of meeting the Qajar government's demands – that is, of surrendering captives who had already been sold and, in some cases, may already have been dwelling as far away as the Kazakh steppe – we may conclude that these demands were little more than a pretext for the ongoing efforts to subjugate the Turkmens.

A Turkmen uprising against the brutal Astarabad governor came in 1867, followed by a Qajar counter-assault, which pushed many Yomuts north of the Atrek. Turkmens who were left behind – including women and children – suffered torture at the hands of the Iranians and were massacred. Some who had fled returned home to become Qajar subjects.[54] While north of the Atrek, the fleeing Yomuts seem to have been careful not to draw the Russians into the conflict. But it was during this same period, in the mid-1860s, that we find a distinct shift in Russia's diplomatic conception of the Turkmens: We find in Tsarist political discourse a heightened preoccupation with putting a stop to their "predatory practices." These "practices" among the Turkmens, sporadic and ongoing as they were, had not substantially increased in the mid-1860s. So what had changed? As Mehmet Saray observes, the shift in diplomatic language corresponded precisely with the dawn of Russia's conquest of the region; it served as a rationale and provided an ideological basis for the conquests of Turkmen country that would follow in the coming two decades.[55]

With Russia's recognition in 1869 of the Atrek River as the northern boundary of Iran, the Turkmens occupying the borderlands found themselves facing both new challenges and new possibilities for resistance.

[52] *Russko-turkmenskie otnosheniia v XVIII–XIX vv.*, 503–504, doc. no. 373.
[53] *Russko-turkmenskie otnosheniia v XVIII–XIX vv.*, 505–506, doc. no. 374.
[54] Saray, "Russo-Turkmen Relations up to 1874," 26. [55] ibid., 27.

V. I. Markozov, commander of the newly constructed Krasnovodsk garrison, recognized the inorganic nature of the new border and the curious manner in which it divided Turkmen territory:[56]

> Man's nature and way of life are completely identical on the right and left banks of the Atrek. And both here and there … live the same Yomut Turkmens, who, as mentioned, migrate now on one side of the river and now on the other, depending on the time of year … Thus, the Atrek does not constitute an ethnographic boundary. As a habitat boundary, the Atrek differs little from the Kara-Suu, and still less from the Gurgen, and in any case it has not the integrity of the Danube or anything of that sort because it is everywhere easy to ford, except, of course, in periods of flooding. Moreover, Persia never had any sort of rights to the strip of land between the Atrek and the Kara-Suu, because she never genuinely possessed it. In all that expanse, one could see Persians only in the form of slaves among the Turkmen population. There were almost no tents whose owners did not have at least one Persian, held in shackles.

The commander's chief concern, however, was not to preserve the territorial integrity of the Turkmens, but to patrol and subjugate them more easily.[57] He notes that his men had often engaged in shootouts with Turkmens who lived for part of the year on one side of the border and part of the year – beyond Russian jurisdiction – on the other. The inconvenience of policing such a population, he implies, likewise had negative consequences for the Iranians themselves, whose citizens the Russian troops sometimes had the occasion to liberate. "Consequently," he writes, "when the Krasnovodsk detachment approached the Turkmen predators' nest [*priblizilsia k gnezdu turkmenskikh khishchnikov*] and began to subdue their thieving impulses and to cross the Atrek, [the soldiers] many times liberated Persians who had been languishing in pits on iron chains, and sent them off to Astarabad through the medium of our Astarabad consulate or the Ashur Ada sea

[56] Markozov, *Krasnovodskii otriad*, 24.

[57] The appearance of the Krasnovodsk garrison on Turkmen territory (the land where it stood was called Kizil-Suu by the Turkmens) produced multiple responses among the Yomuts and Tekes. The latter opposed it unreservedly. The Yomuts, however, were internally divided. The Atabay branch of the Yomuts, living to the north and south of the Atrek, opposed Russian occupation in any form. The Jafarbay branch, who fished the Caspian and traded with the Russians, showed no opposition to it whatsoever. The new Russian incursions were certainly the inspiration for a new wave of sporadic attacks, including an abortive assault on a Russian encampment at Mikhailovsk Bay in October of 1870. Meanwhile, the Tekes reportedly cautioned Yomuts of the region to avoid any sort of partnership with the Russians. The Yomuts quickly learned, however, that resisting Russian demands could be futile: In 1872, when Markozov's exorbitant demand for 3,500 camels for his troops was rebuffed by the Yomuts, the camels were simply taken by force. See Saray, "Russo-Turkmen Relations up to 1874," 29–33.

station, which itself owes its existence to the need to protect Persia from seaward incursions by the Turkmen, for which ends it was taken over by Russia in the Turkmenchay treaty."[58] Markozov's suggestion that the sea station was created mostly to protect Iranian citizens is dishonest, even preposterous, but his evidently sincere exasperation with the challenges posed by the Atrek border is revealing.[59]

The irony of the fact that Russian and Qajar missions of "pacification" were themselves significant motivators of Turkmen violence and resistance – and thus of ongoing captive-taking – was surely lost on Markozov. An awareness of this cause-and-effect is absent among our Russian eyewitnesses in general, for whom Turkmen raids seem to have been nothing more than the reflexive and age-old "custom" of a barbarous people. In any case, Markozov was not alone in complaining that the militant subjugation of the Turkmens along the Russo-Iranian frontier had become, by the late 1860s, a disproportionately Russian endeavor. And he was surely correct in observing that this endeavor was complicated by the placement of the border itself. Regarding the Turkmens living south of the Atrek, Grodekov wondered with good reason whether they could really be considered Qajar subjects: "'How are we Persian subjects,' the Turkmens say, 'when we carry their people into captivity, and they ours?'"[60]

The Turkmens along the Atrek meanwhile found ingenious ways to take advantage of the curious division of their territory. Their continued raids on their "fellow" Qajar subjects, combined with the Qajars' inability to effectively police the territory between Astarabad and the Atrek, apparently induced a kind of agreement whereby the Qajars would cease their punitive assaults entirely if the Turkmens would restrict their raiding forays to the lands north of the river. The appeal of this alleged agreement would have rested, for the Turkmens, on the presumption that the Russians would not cross the river into Iranian territory to avenge or take back their

58 "Russo-Turkmen Relations up to 1874," 24.

59 It is worth noting that the evident incentive behind Markozov's memoir was his effort to exculpate himself for his own failure to reach Khiva with his detachment in 1873; and that one of the reasons for that failure was apparently the refusal of local Turkmens to supply his troops with camels. I am grateful to Alexander Morrison for these observations.

60 Grodekov, *Khivinskii pokhod 1873 goda*, 59. Nevertheless, the Shah had been laying claim to the Turkmens of the Atrek region and the Caspian coast for many years by this time, and by the eve of the 1869 border agreement the Qajars were still claiming dominion as far north as Krasnovodsk. A. M. Gorchakov, the Russian foreign minister and imperial chancellor, scoffed that Iran "had no better claim to the country of the Turkmens than the King of Italy to the throne of Jerusalem" (Saray, "Russo-Turkmen Relations up to 1874," 28–29).

own subjects. Indeed, protocols were in place that would make such forays inconvenient: The Russian embassy in Tehran and the consulate in Astarabad had to be informed of any Russian missions south of the Atrek, and the Qajars themselves would likely object to them.[61] Thus an appealing tactic arose for the resistant Turkmens of the borderland: They could use Iran as a safe harbor while continuing to undermine the paralyzed Russian troops to the north or, in the event that the Russians actually ventured south of the Atrek, they could potentially benefit from the resulting tensions as their two adversaries, the Qajars and Russians, squabbled over border violations and the details of who should risk their troops fighting the Turkmens. This tactic, described by both Grodekov and Markozov, could also involve an additional, incidental benefit for the Qajars: the inevitable injuries that the Russians might inflict upon the Turkmens who attacked them.

In July of 1871, Markozov read a letter from the chief of the Ashur Ada marine station giving notice of a joint attack on Russian troops by Tekes, "Khivans," and Atabays (a branch of the Yomuts). These Atabays were reportedly supported by the Qajar governor of Astarabad, who hoped to distract them from conducting raids in the Iranian provinces and, incidentally, to ensure "that they would suffer greatly by making an attack on [Russian] troops."[62] For their part, the Turkmens, from Grodekov's perspective, seemed to be attempting to incite Markozov's forces into crossing the Atrek, as Turkmen raiding parties repeatedly stole regimental camels and occasionally captured soldiers sent out into the desert to gather fuel. Meanwhile, some Turkmen elders complained to Markozov that people in their community were continually finding their camels stolen and mutilated – they suspected this was meant as punishment by other Turkmens who were understandably upset by their devotion to the Russians. The Russian consulate at Astarabad urged the town's Qajar governor to send border guards to the Atrek shores, but, unsurprisingly, the governor declined: Any loss suffered by Russians and their allies was a Russian – not Qajar – problem, and if the Russians wished to "pacify" Turkmens along the Atrek, it would henceforth be their own initiative. The Russians, led by Markozov, campaigned southward to the Atrek in February, 1872, killing several Turkmens.[63]

Notwithstanding incidents like this, the majority of Yomuts appear to have resolved upon nonviolent relations with the fervently militant

[61] Saray, "Russo-Turkmen Relations up to 1874," 59.
[62] Markozov, *Krasnovodskii otriad*, 26.
[63] Grodekov, *Khivinskii pokhod 1873 goda*, 60–62.

Russians well before the fall of Khiva. Between 1869 and 1873, hostilities on the part of the Yomuts were relatively rare, and for the most part limited to Atabay camel-stealing near the Atrek. After the failure of Khwarazmian Yomut resistance during the Khivan campaign, many Yomuts had chosen to subject themselves to the Tsar, and the wave of submissions only increased after Khwarazm's conquest. As Markozov, on Kaufman's orders, surveyed Yomut territories in the western part of the Khanate in the summer of 1873, he and his men were met with no hostility whatsoever; on the contrary, the Turkmens "not only professed their entire submission but showed it in deeds."[64]

Though peace prevailed, it was not peace that Kaufman was looking for, but a pretext for further campaigns of conquest. This is the most likely explanation for his "punitive" massacre of the noncombative Yomuts of Khwarazm in July of 1873, which doubtless had the effect of teaching Turkmens in the Khanate and beyond that making peace with the Russians was a futile exercise. The hostilities were not long in coming: Later that same month, a group of Yomuts attacked a Russian camp, only to be driven back. At least 500 – and perhaps as many as 1,300 – Turkmens died in battle.[65] Further Russian raids came in the winter, when Kaufman had Lieutenant Colonel N. A. Ivanov lead a harsh attack on two Yomut clans implicated in the slaughter of the freedmen.[66] The remaining years of the 1870s would be marked by troubled attempts to affect the staged annexation of the Turkmen country. In 1877, Kizil Arvat fell to General Lomakin, though he was soon compelled to retreat.[67] In that same year, Chikishlar on the Caspian coast was established as a base for further campaigns against the Turkmens, but soon became a beacon for their raids.[68] Further Russian campaigns also ended in failure, and the Tekes, undeterred and evidently unintimidated, showed their resistance with a successful raid on Krasnovodsk in April of 1879 and further attacks on both Chikishlar and Krasnovodsk after that. That same year, an ambitious charge by a large Russian army on the Teke stronghold of Geok Teppe was repulsed.

[64] Tealakh, "The Russian Advance in Central Asia and the British Response, 1834–1884," 207.

[65] Grodekov, *Khivinskii pokhod*, 293–300; MacGahan, *Campaigning on the Oxus*, 3385–3386; 390; Saray, "Russo-Turkmen Relations up to 1874," 40. The next day, in pursuit of the fleeing Turkmens, the Russians torched Turkmen houses and grain reserves, "and the cavalry, which was in advance, cut down every person, man, woman, and child" (Schuyler, *Turkistan*, Vol. 2, 361–362; Saray, "Russo-Turkmen Relations up to 1874," 40).

[66] Becker, *Russia's Protectorates in Central Asia*, 64.

[67] Kuropatkin, *Zavoevanie turkmenii*, 96.

[68] Teren'tev, *Istoriia zavoevaniia srednei azii*, Vol. 3, 3–4.

Russia's humiliating inability to put down the hostilities that the Tsar's generals had chosen to instigate led to the installation of a new general to lead the charge against the Turkmens. M. D. Skobelev, a veteran of the Khiva and Kokand campaigns as well as the Yomut massacre, was installed and instructed by the Tsar to make an example of the Turkmens; the Tsar demanded "no retreat from the plan once adopted, no dangerous backward step that might be taken as evidence of our weakness in the eyes of Europe and Asia, that might encourage our foe."[69] Skobelev eagerly adopted the language of punishment and vengeance when rallying his men, but his initial efforts against the Tekes in 1880 ended in failure. He nevertheless invited the Tekes to submit, making preposterous demands by way of peace terms. These demands included the payment of a 1,000,000 ruble war indemnity, the full Russian occupation of major Teke towns and villages, the surrender of many Teke elders and chieftains as Russian captives, and the release of all remaining Russian captives.[70]

The Turkmens, unsurprisingly, declined these terms of surrender, and in January of 1881 Skobelev led a siege of Geok Teppe that would be remembered as a massacre of astonishing brutality. The number of victims has been estimated at up to 20,000 Akhal Teke Turkmens.[71] Ashgabat was occupied by the Russians two months later, following which the Tekes were offered – and generally accepted – Russia's "protection" within the newly created Trans-Caspian district. The Russians then pressed onward toward Merv. When the city was surrendered without a battle in 1884, it marked the final stage in the Russian conquest of Turkmen territories. The legendary independence of the Turkmens – cherished among the tribes themselves and elegized by foreign observers – became a thing of the past.

CONCLUSION

To what extent was the eradication of slavery a factor in Russia's conquest of Central Asia? Were the Tsar's troops really the vanguard of abolitionism that many observers assumed? A closer look at the evidence suggests that they were not. Time and again, it was the liberation of *Russian* slaves, and

[69] Tealakh, "The Russian Advance in Central Asia and the British Response, 1834–1884," 220.

[70] Grodekov, *Voina v turkmenii*, Vol. 2, 70–72.

[71] Slavomír Horák, "The Battle Gökdepe in the Turkmen post-Soviet Historical Discourse," *Central Asian Survey* 34/2 (2015), 153.

not the extermination of slavery in general, that served as a rhetorical rallying point in the war effort. In the Tsar's written address to the Russian people, published on the eve of the Khivan campaign and offering a list of justifications for it, slavery is, as noted earlier, mentioned no less than four times – but no mention is made of the Iranian slaves, of which there were no fewer than 30,000. It was, rather, the Russian slaves alone that were targeted for liberation. The disastrous Perovskii campaign of 1839 had likewise been, among other things, a mission to liberate Russian slaves, and it was exclusively Russian slaves that the khan turned over as a concession at that time. Once again, on the eve of the Khivan conquest, a different khan tried the same old tactic, releasing Russian slaves in hopes of pacifying the Tsar. The release of these twenty-one slaves as a concession when the total slave population of the realm numbered anywhere from 30,000 to 60,000 would seem nearly comical, and could perhaps have been taken as a sarcastic taunt, had the liberation of *all* slaves actually been one of the Empire's demands. But, after all, there had never been any demand that the khan liberate *non-Russian* slaves in the icy diplomatic exchanges leading up to the conquest.

MacGahan's claim, moreover, that "the emancipation of the slaves has always followed the occupation of any place in Central Asia by the Russians"[72] was simply untrue. The Russian conquest of Bukhara in the late 1860s had resulted in a number of concessions rendered in ambitious treaties, but an order of general emancipation was not among them. Kaufman reportedly voiced his displeasure to the Bukharan ruler over the continuance of the trade, and claimed, in 1870, to be convinced that it had ceased; but it had not. Schuyler alleges that, two years later, a Russian official from the ministry of finance offered Kaufman an impassioned report calling his attention to the flourishing of the slave trade, but that "no notice was taken" of the information provided.[73] If in fact this report produced any effect at all, it must have been a delayed effect: It was only in the autumn of 1873 – some five years after Bukhara's conquest – that, by Russian demand, the universal emancipation of slavery became a law in the territory. But as we have seen, the enforcement of that law involved the bizarre concession that the Bukharan Amīr could take an entire decade to enact that emancipation, during which time all slaves would stay with their present masters. Attempts to escape to freedom were

[72] MacGahan, *Campaigning on the Oxus*, 233.
[73] Schuyler, *Turkistan*, Vol. 2, 310. I have been unable to find a copy of this report or its contents.

punishable by death. In 1874, Kaufman alerted the Amīr to evidence of an ongoing slave trade, but the ruler denied that any such trade existed. It did indeed, however, and one Russian agent even witnessed a slave market operating in Bukhara as late as 1878. Nevertheless, Kaufman declined to press the issue, and in 1876 he instructed an official in Zarafshan *okrug* "in the majority of cases to decline interference in the slaves' affairs."[74] These may seem like strange instructions coming from the "emancipator" of Khiva, but they make perfect sense once we abandon false notions of Russian abolitionism and realize, as Seymour Becker observes, that "slavery was, after all, an internal affair of no vital practical interest to Russia."[75]

By the time Merv fell to the Russians, moreover, captive-taking and slave-dealing had already been on the decline in the region for decades, for reasons that usually had little to do with Russian influence. In fact, Russian presence sometimes *increased* the incidence of captive-taking. The ongoing raids perpetrated by Tekes and Yomuts in the 1860s and 1870s were a direct result of the violence inflicted upon them by the Tsar's armies and the staged annexation of their territories. The Russian imperial narrative of these events, employed by officers like Markozov and Skobelev, reversed the relationship between cause and effect, creating a cyclical rationale of conquest: Russian officers deliberately provoked and inflamed Turkmen hostilities, and then observed that further punishment was necessary to "pacify" these tribes.[76]

Kaufman's agreement with the Khwarazmian khan to liberate the Iranian slaves was notable not because it was the final strike against Iranian slavery in Central Asia, but because it was the first. We must wonder why the slaves of Khwarazm were liberated by decree within weeks of the city's conquest, while the slaves of Bukhara waited nearly half a decade for an "emancipation" decree stipulating that they would be freed only after another ten years of bondage. The slave uprising of Khwarazm provides the answer. By casting off their chains and rising up against their masters, the slaves revealed the fundamental weakness of the slave-owning elites. While the slaves hailed the arrival of Russian troops and the new governance that they would bring,

[74] Becker, *Russia's Protectorates in Central Asia*, 67–68. [75] ibid., 68.

[76] Granted, the annexation of Merv likely helped to reduce the taking of Iranian captives among the Tekes and their allies: Before General Komarov agreed to meet a deputation suing for peace outside the town, he insisted that all the slaves in Merv be liberated (A. Maslov, *Rossiia v srednei azii*, 380). But there is no reason to believe that this result was a significant motivation in Merv's occupation, nor in the brutal campaigns of conquest leading up to it.

they simultaneously proved their own ability to make the region ungovernable. They forced the Russians to take sides: With newspapers around the world reporting on the events, the Tsar's men could side with the slave-owning classes, attempt to crush the uprising, and see that the slaves were shackled and chained once more, or they could take their chances by liberating the slaves.

It was not a foregone conclusion that the Russians would side with the slaves. On the contrary, the public hanging of two slaves for their participation in the uprising was, as we have seen, perhaps the first act of Russian governance in Khwarazm. The two bodies, left to rot in the heat of the summer sun, were displayed for all to see, offering a grim "official" comment on the uprising and certainly creating confusion among those slaves who had anticipated having Kaufman as their ally. If the uprising had ended with the execution of these two slaves, alleviating for Kaufman the challenges of governing a realm in chaos, perhaps – as in Bukhara – the emancipation decree would not have been issued for months or even years to come. But the uprising began again with a fresh intensity, the slaves proving that not even the threat of death could stop them. They had already defied their masters; if the Russians wished only to become their new masters, then the slaves would defy them too.

Kaufman, then, was left with no choice but to facilitate the movement of liberation that was already in progress. He had no other reasonable option: If he had turned his troops on the rioting slaves, the Russians could have found themselves facing 30–60,000 new enemies, a great many of whom had already demonstrated their boldness, their determination, and their anger. The Khwarazmian military, itself consisting largely of Iranian slaves, had just been routed and could hardly be relied upon to put down the uprising for the convenience of their new occupiers (or, for that matter, on behalf of their fallen khan). The slaves, inspired by the anticipation of Russian solidarity, acted together to make it a foregone conclusion, even if their confidence in its inevitability had been unwarranted.

The decision to abolish (however gradually) slavery in Bukhara, a step which was undertaken just a few months later, must also be credited in large part to the slaves of Khwarazm. By forcing Kaufman's hand in abolishing slavery in their territory, these slaves made it inevitable that the same privilege should be extended to the slaves of the neighboring domain. Continuing to countenance Bukharan slavery would have been supremely awkward for Russian administrators who were about to reduce Bukhara to "protectorate" status. Having gained a reputation as emancipators, Russian officials had to consolidate their position in Central Asia with the eyes of the world upon them. Still more urgently, the possibility of a slave uprising in Bukhara, patterned on events next-door, could not have escaped their attention.

However, the Russian press was all too happy to give Kaufman full credit for the emancipation, and he has been credited for it ever since. On the 25th anniversary of the conquest, the popular Russian journal *Niva* offered a typical rhapsody: "The immediate consequences of the campaign were: the liberation of 40,000 captives and slaves, the complete pacification [*polnoe umirotvorenie*] of the country, the cessation of license, looting, and brigandage in the Khivan oasis and neighboring territory . . . This achievement is inscribed in golden letters in the annals of Russian history, and the memory of it will be cherished by the Russian people forever."[77] The "golden letters" would read "Kaufman," though the General may very well have been more surprised than pleased to find himself the emancipator of 30–60,000 Muslims. This had never been his intention until his hand was forced.

Ultimately, then, visions of the conquest of Khwarazm as a Russian abolitionist enterprise are a fiction. There is no evidence that the liberation of tens of thousands of Iranian slaves played a significant role – or any role whatsoever – in inspiring the campaign, nor any good evidence that Kaufman had planned their liberation at any time before the slave uprising began. In the five previous years following the conquest of Bukhara, the Russians left no legal infrastructure or treaties in place to guarantee the manumission of even a single Bukharan slave, let alone the complete abolition of slavery, and there is little reason to believe that anything more ambitious was planned for the slaves of Khwarazm. On the contrary, it was the slaves who created the conditions for their own liberation. Their courageous uprising rendered it more convenient for the Russians to facilitate their freedom than to force them back into bondage. For Kaufman, the erstwhile executioner of rebelling slaves, emancipation became the only rational option. Despite his role in drafting the emancipation decree, then, it cannot be said that he freed the slaves; they had not waited for a Russian invitation to cast off their chains. The slaves of Khwarazm had freed themselves.

In this book, I have attempted to show that slavery was a fundamental aspect of Central Asian society down to the late nineteenth century; that the decentralized slave trade involved the circulation of slaves and their sellers throughout the region, linking the metropole and periphery as well as the

[77] "Dvadtsatipiatiletie pokoreniia Khivy," *Niva* 24 (1898), 477–478.

nomadic and the sedentary; that the slave trade was a key issue in diplomacy between Central Asia, Russia, and Iran, as well as a factor which motivated imperial invasions; that slaves could exert an influence on the nature of their captivity by using or concealing their talents, or by manipulating the Islamic legal system to their own advantage; that escaped slaves "liberated" at the Russian border were often simply transferred into another corvée labor system as part of the Russian effort to develop settler colonies in the borderlands; that there was never any coherent Russian "abolitionist" enterprise in Central Asia; that Turkmen "raiders" and "native informants" were used as proxy fighters on the Iranian frontier; and that the slaves of Khwarazm, by freeing themselves through courageous rebellion, provoked the abolition of slavery throughout the region.

This book approaches slavery in Central Asia from multiple angles, in other words, but it hardly exhausts the subject. Future research – both my own and others' – will, I hope, make use of the many documents on slavery that, no doubt, have yet to be uncovered in the region's archives. Much remains to be said, moreover, about the parallels between Central Asian slavery and forms of slavery elsewhere in Eurasia and in the wider world. (A global-comparative approach to Central Asian slavery might start by pointing out a conspicuously parallel "cotton connection": The collapse of the slave trade in the Civil War-era American South helped to crush the cotton economy there, thus providing a market for Central Asian cotton, but developing the cotton economy in Central Asia would allegedly require the collapse of its slave trade as part of the Russian "pacification" of the region.[78]) Several recent books, meanwhile, offer intriguing avenues for comparative studies focused more narrowly on Russia and Central Asia. First, while I have attempted to show the surprising degree of autonomy that was possible for "native informants" tasked with policing the slave trade for the Russian Empire, recent work by Ian Campbell[79] has shown how Russia's Kazakh "informants" demonstrated this kind of agency in other spheres as well, oftentimes carving out advantages not only for themselves, but also for their communities. A similar agency is seen in the legal sphere, and new work by Paolo Sartori[80] demonstrates the extent to which Muslim jurists were permitted to carve out and maintain spheres of influence even as other aspects of governance were being subsumed rigorously under Russian

[78] I am grateful to James Millward for this observation.

[79] Campbell, *Knowledge and the Ends of Empire: Kazak Intermediaries and Russian Rule on the Steppe, 1731–1917* (Ithaca, NY: Cornell University Press, 2017).

[80] Sartori, *Visions of Justice: Sharī'a and Cultural Change in Russian Central Asia* (Leiden: Brill, 2017).

imperial jurisdiction – a dynamic demonstrated by the extant legal documents on slavery as well, which prove that the manumission, sale, and purchase of slaves was still being supervised by Islamic court judges well into the 1880s. Recent research by Christine Nölle-Karimi and Mohammad Ali Kazembeyki, meanwhile, has shed light on the intricate political dynamics of northern Iran and Afghanistan in the nineteenth century.[81] Finally, a recent book by Erika Monahan[82] on Siberian merchants has expanded our knowledge of the trade networks crisscrossing early modern Central Asia, further illuminating the decentralized nature of Eurasian overland commerce.

When it comes to further research on Central Asian slavery, the impact of slavery's decline on the region's agricultural and mercantile economies is a particularly promising topic, which, unfortunately, I was not ready to address here. It seems likely, for one thing, that the slave trade's collapse served to make some Turkmens more dependent on labor opportunities in the industries developed under Russian imperial governance, such as cotton agriculture. A related question concerns the agricultural workforce: Who replaced the Iranian slaves as laborers in the fields, and what kinds of social changes did this transition of manpower involve?

One question haunts me above all others: What happened to Central Asia's slaves – emancipated or otherwise – after the mid-1870s?

In 1877, four years after the conquest of Khiva, a petition arrived before Muḥammad Raḥīm Khan, who was by this time reduced to the Tsar's puppet ruler, bearing a complaint from a maker of fur coats. The author of the petition was named Nūr Muḥammad Makhdūm, and his complaint was that he and his fellow furriers at a Khiva bazaar were being taxed at a rate they could no longer afford. Times had changed. "Business at our bazaar is stagnant," the furrier writes. "In times past, everyone had 5 or 10 slaves. The slaves received coats. Now the slaves are free and they have gone off, and no one will take the coats."[83] Slavery, at least in Khiva, appeared to be a thing of the past.[84]

[81] Kazembeyki, *Society, Politics, and Economics in Māzandarān, Iran, 1848–1914*; Nölle-Karimi, *The Pearl in its Midst: Herat and the Mapping of Khurasan (15th–19th Centuries)* (Austrian Academy of Sciences Press, 2014).

[82] Monahan, *The Merchants of Siberia: Trade in Early Modern Eurasia* (Ithaca, NY: Cornell University Press, 2016).

[83] "*Brunlar har kimning besh-on dāna dughma bolur érdi dughmalargha fustun alur érdilar emdi dughmalar āzād bolup ketip turur fustunni hichkim almay turur.*" MS IVAN Uz No. 12581, f. 11.

[84] According to some, slavery would persist in Bukhara even into the Soviet period: see M. A. Abduraimov, *Ocherki agrarnykh otnoshenii v bukharskom khanstve v XVI–pervoi polovine XIX veka, t.* 2. Tashkent: Fan, 1970, 236.

Or did the slave system simply take other forms, while becoming less visible to foreign observers? Large agricultural estates still needed hands to work them, and the will to secure cheap labor no doubt still existed among the owners of those estates. While the flow of captives into the khanates had been interrupted, more localized systems of corvée labor – such as debt-based servitude, indentured servitude as a means of private dispute resolution, and indenturing oneself as a last resort in circumstances of extreme poverty – would presumably have continued unabated. After all, there was nothing in the Khwarazmian or Bukharan abolition declarations that would militate against these forms of bondage. Travelers and observers in the region in the final decades of the pre-Soviet era, convinced of the success of Russian-sponsored abolition, would likely have overlooked more subtle signs of unfree servitude. Unfortunately, available sources do not provide much basis for speculation on this front.

It is clear from our sources, at least, that the centuries-long crisis of Iranian captives being channeled into Khwarazm had finally come to an end. But what became of the tens of thousands of former slaves who chose to remain in the khanate? This demographic must have constituted a very large proportion of the total number of freedmen. While reports of parties massacred on their way to Iran are many, reports and eyewitness accounts of freedmen returning home safely are scarce, scattered, and lacking in detail. The most notable instances of repatriation were those accomplished via Russian steamships that departed for Iran from Krasnovodsk, but as far as I can tell, the fortunate former slaves boarding these ships numbered no more than a few thousand at most. Others likely made their way to Russia eventually, as had some Iranian former slaves of previous generations, though there is scant information on such migrations. A lack of sources undermines efforts to reconstruct the freed slaves' fates; the tide of foreign observers that arrived with the Russian regiments dissipated long before the trajectory of all the freed slaves could be observed. Thus Schuyler writes, "[t]here were estimated to be 30,000 slaves in the Khanate, but it is supposed that not more than 5,000 of these were actually freed before the departure of the Russians."[85] By the phrase "actually freed," Schuyler is hinting at a distinction between decree and effect, which was likewise pursued by MacGahan, who wrote that "Those who remained in Khiva, though emancipated, are not, I fancy, much better off than before. Some Russian officers seemed to think that three-fourths of the Persians would remain slaves still, and were of the opinion that General Kaufmann did not act vigorously enough in this matter. However that be,

[85] Schuyler, *Turkistan*, Vol. 2, 354.

there can be little doubt that the theoretical abolition of slavery will ultimately result in its practical abolition."[86] These observations are, of course, little more than guesswork.

Fortunately, Central Asian sources offer some hints as to the fate of the freedmen who remained in Khwarazm. The evidence they provide suggests a diverse spectrum of outcomes, ranging from degrees of eventual assimilation into Khwarazmian society to the establishment of communities that were quite separate and distinctive. Many former slaves settled in the capital, where they and their descendants could be found living in their own neighborhood (*mahalla*) well into the Soviet period. Two distinctive mosques catered to this demographic in Khiva.[87] Others chose to settle in Tāshḥawż and other small towns and *qishlaq*s where they had gathered soon after the declaration of abolition. According to the *Azādnāma*, by the early Soviet period these communities had come to resemble the Uzbek communities of Khwarazm both in their language (with Uzbek predominating over Persian, which had allegedly been forgotten) and in their customs (*urf-adatlar*).[88]

Today in Uzbekistan, members of an *eroniy* ("Iranian") diaspora community can be found throughout the country. Many attend a distinctive Shiʿite mosque in Samarqand's Panjob neighborhood. Many others live in Tashkent, and overall the population of *eroniy* citizens in the country numbers in the thousands. Some are descended from Iranian merchants and others from migrant laborers. Many, however, can surely trace their histories down a darker path. As we have seen, their enslaved forebears were ubiquitous in Central Asia for a matter of centuries. In certain regions, such as Khwarazm, slaves occupied such a diverse range of jobs and roles, in such large numbers, that they can be considered a fundamental element of society. The impact of slavery on Central Asian history has gone largely unrecognized, but it can hardly be overestimated.

[86] MacGahan, *Campaigning on the Oxus*, 312. [87] MS IVAN Uz No. 12581, f. 27a.

[88] MS IVAN Uz No. 12581, ff. 31a–b. The fact of assimilation is especially striking when contrasted with the distinctiveness of a proximate Iranian diaspora community, then living in Ghazi-Abad *rayon*, consisting at that time of some 100 households of "Farsiyanlar" who had retained Persian and maintained Iranian customs. These "Farsiyanlar" had never been enslaved, having been relocated to Khwarazm from Aq-Darband in the time of Allāh Qulī Khan and offered enough land so that they eventually commanded their own mounted force of retainers (*atligh nökar*) and gained tax exemptions owing to their elite status (see MS IVAN Uz No. 12581, ff. 31b–32a). One can well imagine that the Iranian former slaves, starting their free lives in Khwarazm at the bottom of the social ladder, may have felt greater pressure to assimilate in order to find work and gain a social foothold.

Bibliography

ARCHIVAL COLLECTIONS

Tsentralnyi Gosudarstvennyi Arkhiv Respubliki Kazakhstan (TsGARKaz)/Central State Archive of the Republic of Kazakhstan. Almaty, Kazakhstan.

PUBLISHED DOCUMENT COLLECTIONS

Agadzhanov, S. G., ed. *Russko-turkmenskie otnosheniia v XVIII–XIX vv.: do prisoedineniia Turkmenii k Rossii: sbornik arkhivnykh dokumentov.* Ashkhabad: Izd-vo Akademii nauk Turkmenskoi SSR, 1963.

Faiziev, T. *Buxoro feodal jamiyatida qullardan foydalanishga doir hujjatlar (XIX asr).* Tashkent: Fan, 1990.

Fitrat, Bedil and B. S. Sergeev, eds. *Kaziiskie dokumenty XVI veka. Tekst, perevod, ukazatek' vstrechaiushchikhsia iuridicheskikh terminov i primechaniia.* Tashkent: Izd. Komiteta Nauk UzSSR, 1937.

Ismailova, S. K. "Dokumenty o rabstva v bukharskom khanstve v XIX– nachale XX v." *Izvestiia Akademii nauk Tadzhikskoi SSR, otdelenie obshchestvennykh nauk* 2/72 (1973), 20–30.

Materiali po istorii turkmen i turkmenii, t. II. XVI–XIX vv. Iranskie, bukharskie, i khivinskie istochniki. Moscow: 1938–39.

Roloff, Gustav, ed. *Das Staatsarchiv: Sammlung der officiellen Actenstücke zur Geschichte der Gegenwart.* Leipzig: von Duncker & Humbolt. 1861–71.

Serebrennikov, A. G., ed. *Sbornik Materialov dlia istorii zavoevaniia Turkestanskogo Kraia* (1839–1844), 4 vols. Tashkent: Tip. Sht. Turkestanskogo V.O., 1908–12.

PRIMARY SOURCES

Abbott, James. *Narrative of a Journey from Heraut to Khiva, Moscow, and St. Petersburgh, during the Late Russian Invasion of Khiva*, 2 vols. London: W.H. Allen and Co., 1843.

Alikhanov-Avarskii, M. *Pokhod v Khivu (Kavkazkikh otriadov) 1873*. St. Petersburg: Step' i oazis, 1899.
Amīn Oghlï, Ḥassan Muḥammad. *Āzādnāma*. MS IVAN Uz No. 12581.
Anonymous, "Iz istorii Kazakhstana XVIII v." *Krasnyi arkhiv* 2/87 (1938), 129–154.
Anonymous. "Nevol'niki v Khive," *Vestnik Evropy* 80:7 (1815), 244–247.
Anonymous. "Khiva za sto let nazad." *Syn otechestva* 1 (1842), 33–38.
Anonymous. "Dvadtsatipiatiletie pokoreniia Khivy," *Niva* 24 (1898), 477–478.
Anonymous. "Zavoevanie Akhal-Tekinskogo oazisa." *Istoricheskii vestnik* 7 (1881), 577–596.
Anonymous. "Russia and Khiva: The Empire's Manifesto Prefatory to the Expedition," *New York Times*, April 13, 1873.
Āshtīyānī, Mīrzā Maḥmūd Taqī. *'Ibratnāma: Khatirati az dawran-i pas az jangha-yi herat va merv*, ed. Husayn 'Imadī Āshtīyānī. Tehran: Nashr-i markaz, 1382/2003.
Atkinson, Lucy. *Recollections of Tartar Steppes and Their Inhabitants*. London: J. Murray, 1863.
Beisembiev, Timur. *The Life of Alimqul: A Native Chronicle of Nineteenth Century Central Asia*. New York: Routledge, 2015.
Blaramberg, *I. F. Vospominaniia*. Moscow: Glavnaia redaktsiia vostochnoi literatury; TSentral'naia Aziia istochnikakh i materialakh XIX–nachala XX veka, 1978.
Blinov, N. *Sarapul': istoricheskii ocherk'*. Sarapul, 1887.
Boulger, Demetrius Charles. *England and Russia in Central Asia*, Vol. 1. London: W.H. Allen, 1879.
Brydges, Harford Jones. *The Dynasty of the Kajars*. London: John Bohn, 1833.
Burnes, Alexander. *Travels into Bokhara*, 2 vols. London: John Murray, 1839.
Dal', V. I. "Pis'mo k druziam iz Khivinskoi Ekspeditsii." *Russkii Arkhiv* 3 & 4 (1867), 402–431, 606–639.
de Levchine, A. *Description des hordes et des steppes des Kirghiz-Kazaks ou Kirghiz-Kaissaks*. Paris: Impr. royale, 1840.
de Meyendorff, *Georges. A Journey from Orenburg to Bukhara in the Year 1820*. Calcutta: Foreign Department Press, 1870.
DuBois, W. E. B. *The Suppression of the African Slave Trade to the United States of America, 1638–1870*. New York: Longmans, Green, and Co., 1904.
Ferrier, J. P. *Caravan Journeys and Wanderings in Persia, Afghanistan, Turkistan, and Beloochistan*. London: J. Murray, 1857.
Ghafūr, Muḥammad *'Alī Khan. Rūznāma-yi safar-i Khvārazm*. Tehran: Daftar-i Muṭāla'āt-i Siyāsī va Bayn al-Milalī, Vizārat-i Umūr-i Khārijah, 1994.
Gladyshev and Muravin. *Poezdka iz Orska v Khivu i obratno, sovershennaia v 1740–41 godakh poruchikom Gladyshevym i geodezistom Muravinym*. St. Petersburg, 1851.
Gordon, Edward. *The Roof of the World: Being a Narrative of a Journey over the High Plateau of Tibet to the Russian Frontier and the Oxus Sources on the Pamir*. Edinburgh: Edmonston and Douglas, 1876.

Grodekov, Governor-General N. I. *Khivinskii pokhod 1873 goda deistviia kavkazskikh otriadov.* St. Petersburg: Tip. V.S. Balashova, 1883.

Grodekoff, N. I. *Colonel Grodekoff's ride from Samarcand to Herat, through Balkh and the Uzbek States of Afghan Turkestan.* Translated by Charles Marvin. London: W.H. Allen, 1880.

Gunaropulo, C. A. "V Turkmenskoi stepi. (Iz zapisok chernomorskogo ofitsera.)" *Istoricheskii vestnik* 11/12, 555–584, 1033–1051.

Hidāyat, Rizā Quli Khan. *Sifāratnāma-yi Khwarazm (Relation de l'Ambassade au Kharezm [Khiva] de Riza Qouly Khan. Texte Persan)*, ed. Charles Schefer. Paris: Ernest Leroux, 1876.

Iskandar Beg Munshī, *Tārīkh-i 'ālamārā-yi 'Abbāsī.* Translated by Roger Savory as *History of Shah 'Abbas the Great*, Vol. 2. Boulder, CO: Caravan Books, 1978.

Ivanin, M. *Opisanie Zimnego Pokhoda v Khivu v 1839–40 g.* St. Petersburg, 1874.

Ivanin, M. and Golosov, D. "Pokhod v Khivu v 1839 godu otriada russkikh voisk, pod nachal'stvom General-Ad'iutanta Perovskago." *Voennyi Sbornik* (1863) 1, 3–72; 2, 309–358; 3, 3–71.

Jenkinson, Anthony. *Early Voyages and Travels to Russia and Persia by Anthony Jenkinson and Other Englishmen*, Vol. 1, ed. E. Delmar Morgan and C. H. Coote. London: Hakluyt Society, 1886.

Karpiuk, S. G., ed. *Puteshestviia po Vostoku v opokhu Ekateriny II.* Moscow: Vostochnaia literatura, 1995.

Kemp, P. M., ed. and trans. *Russian Travelers to India and Persia (1624–1798): Kotov, Yefremov, Danibegov.* Delhi: Jiwan Prakashan, 1959.

Ker, David. *On the Road to Khiva.* London: Henry S. King and Co., 1874.

Khalfin, N. A., ed. *Zapiski o Bukharskom khanstve.* Moscow, 1983.

Khan, 'Abbās Qulī, *Safarnāma-yi Bukhārā*, ed. Ḥussain Zamānī. Tehran: Pizhūhishgāh-i 'Ulūm-i Insānī va Muṭāla'āt-i Farhangī vā bastah bih Vizārat-i Farhang va Āmūzish-i 'Ālī, 1373/1995.

Khanykov, Ia.V. *Poezdka iz Orska v Khivu i obratno, sovershennaia v 1740–1741 godakh Gladyshevym i Muravinym.* St. Petersburg, 1851.

Khoroshkhin, A. *Sbornik statei: Kasaiushchikhsia do Turkestanskago kraia.* St. Petersburg, 1876.

Kostenko, L. F. *Puteshestvie v Bukharu russkoi missii v 1870 godu.* St. Petersburg, 1871.

Kosyrev, E. M. "Pokhod v Khivu v 1839 godu (Iz zapisok uchastnika)." *Istoricheskii vestnik* 8 (1898), 538–545.

Kraft, I. I. "Unichtozhenie rabstva v kirgizskoi stepi." *Iz kirgizskoi stariny.* Orenburg, 1900.

Kraft, I. I. *Sudebnaia chast' v Turkestanskom krae i stepnykh oblastiakh.* Orenburg, 1898.

Kuropatkin, A. N. *Zavoevanie turkmenii: pokhod v akhal-teke v 1880–81 gg.* St. Petersburg, 1899.

Lal, Mohan. *Travels in the Panjab, Afghanistan, and Turkistan, to Balk, Bokhara, and Herat; and a Visit to Great Britain and Germany.* London: W.H. Allen, 1846.

Leskov, Nikolai. *The Enchanted Wanderer and Other Stories*, trans. Richard Pevear and Larissa Volokhonsky. New York, NY: Alfred A. Knopf, 2013.
MacGahan, J. A. *Campaigning on the Oxus, and the Fall of Khiva*. London: Sampson Low, 1874.
Major Blankenagel'. *Zamechaniia maiora Blankenagelia, vposledstvie poezdki ego iz Orenburga v Khivu v 1793–94 godakh*. St. Petersburg, 1858.
Marghīnānī, 'Alī ibn Abī Bakr. *The Hedaya*, trans. Charles Hamilton. London: Allen & Co., 1870 (second edition).
Markozov, V. *Krasnovodskii otriad. Ego zhizn' i sluzhba so dnia vysadki na vostochnyi bereg Kaspiiskogo moria po 1873 g*. St. Petersburg: 1898.
Maslov, A. "Rossiia v Srednei Azii. (Ocherk nashikh noveishikh priobretenii)." *Istoricheskii vestnik* 5 (1885).
Meyendorff, Baron Georg von. *A Journey from Orenburg to Bukhara in the Year 1820*. Calcutta, 1870.
Mīrpanja, Isma'īl Sarhang. *Khātirāt-i asārat: ruznāma-yi safar-i Khwarazm va khiva*, ed. Safā' ad-Dīn Tabarrā'iyān. Tehran: Mu'ssassa-yi Pazhuhish va Mutāla'at-i Farhangī, 1370/1991.
Munis, Shīr Muḥammad Mīrāb and Rizā Mīrāb Āgāhī, Muḥammad. *Firdaws al- iqbāl*, trans. Yuri Bregel. Leiden: Brill, 1999.
Murav'ev, N. N. *Muraviev's Journey to Khiva through the Turcoman Country, 1819–20*. Calcutta: Foreign Department Press, 1871.
Petrusevich, N. G. "Turkmeny mezhdu starym' ruslom' Amu-Daryi (Uzboem') i severnymi okrainami Persii." *Zapiski kavkazskago otdela imperatorskago russkago geograficheskago obshchestva*, Vol. 11. Tbilisi, 1880.
Rzhevuskii, A. "Ot Tiflisa do Dengil'-tepe." *Voennyi sbornik* 9 (1884).
Schmidt, Emil. *The Russian Expedition to Khiva in 1873*. Calcutta: Foreign Department Press, 1876.
Schuyler, Eugene. *Turkistan: Notes of a Journey in Russian Turkistan, Khokand, Bukhara, and Kuldja*. New York, NY: Scribner, Armstrong, 1876.
Shubinskii, P. "Ocherki bukhary," *Istoricheskii vestnik* 7 (1892).
Stremoukhov, N. P. "Poezdka v Bukharu." *Russkii vestnik* 6 (1876).
Tugan-Mirza-Baranovskii, V. A. *Russkie v Akhal-Teke*. St. Petersburg, 1881.
Vambery, Arminius. *Travels in Central Asia*. New York, NY: Harper & Bros., 1865.
Vambery, Arminius. *Sketches of Central Asia*. London: W.H. Allen & Co., 1868.
Vambery, Arminius. *History of Bokhara from the Earliest Period down to the Present*. London: Henry S. King, 1873.
Wolff, Joseph. *Narrative of a Mission to Bukhara in the Years 1843–1845*, Vol. 2. London: J.W. Parker, 1845.
Wood, Herbert. *The Shores of Lake Aral*. London: Smith, Elder & Co., 1876.
Yate, C. E. *Khurasan and Sistan*. London: Blackwood and Sons, 1900.
Zakhar'in, I. N. *Graf V. A. Perovskii i ego zimnii pokhod v Khivu*. St. Petersburg: Tip. P. P. Soikina, 1899 and 1901.
Zalesov, N. "Pis'mo iz Khivy," *Voennyi sbornik* 1 (1859).
Zalesov, N. "Posol'stvu v Khivu v 1842 godu." *Istoricheskii vestnik* 11 (1894).
Zheliabuzhskii, E. *Ocherki i zavoevanie khivy*. Moscow, 1875.

SECONDARY SOURCES

Alam, Muzaffar. "Trade, State Policy and Regional Change: Aspects of Mughal-Uzbek Commercial Relations, c. 1550–1750." *Journal of the Economic and Social History of the Orient* 37:3 (1994), 202–227.

Amanat, Abbas and Arash, Khazeni. "The Steppe Roads of Central Asia and the Persian Captivity Narrative of Mahmud Mirza Taqi Ashtiyani." In Nile Green, ed., *Writing Travel in Central Asian History*, 113–133. Bloomington, IN: Indiana University Press, 2014.

Ayalon, David. *The Mamluk Military Society: Collected Studies*. London: Varorium, 1979.

Becker, Seymour. *Russia's Protectorates in Central Asia: Bukhara and Khiva, 1865–1924*. New York, NY: Routledge, 2004 (1969).

Beckwith, Christopher I. *Empires of the Silk Road: A History of Central Eurasia from the Bronze Age to the Present*. Princeton, NJ: Princeton University Press, 2009.

Bregel, Yuri. *Khorezmskie turkmeny v XIX veke*. Moscow, 1961.

Bregel, Yuri. "The New Uzbek States: Bukhara Khiva and Qoqand: *c*. 1750–1886." In Nicola Di Cosmo, Allen J. Frank and Peter B. Golden, eds., *The Cambridge History of Inner Asia: The Chingghisid Age*, 392–393. Cambridge: Cambridge University Press, 2009.

Burton, Audrey. *The Bukharans: A Dynastic, Diplomatic, and Commercial History 1550–1702*. New York, NY: St. Martin's Press, 1997.

Campbell, Ian. *Knowledge and the Ends of Empire: Kazak Intermediaries and Russian Rule on the Steppe*, 1731–1917. Ithaca, NY: Cornell University Press, 2017.

Chatterjee, Indrani and Richard M. Eaton, eds. *Slavery & South Asian History*. Bloomington, IN: Indiana University Press, 2006.

Clarence-Smith and Gervase, William. *Islam and the Abolition of Slavery*. Oxford: Oxford University Press, 2006.

Crossley, Pamela K. "Slavery in Early-Modern China." In David Eltis and Stanley Engerman, eds., *The Cambridge World History of Slavery*, Vol. 3, 186–216. Cambridge: Cambridge University Press, 2011.

Dale, Stephen. *Indian Merchants and Eurasian Trade, 1600–1750*. Cambridge: Cambridge University Press, 1994.

Davies, Brian L. *Warfare, State and Society on the Black Sea Steppe, 1500–1700*. New York, NY: Routledge, 2007.

Drescher, Seymour. *Abolition: A History of Slavery and Anti-Slavery*. Cambridge: Cambridge University Press, 2009.

Erdem, Y. Hakan. "Slavery and Social Life in Nineteenth-Century Turco-Egyptian Khartoum." In Terence Walz and Kenneth M. Cuno, eds., *Race and Slavery in the Middle East: Histories of Trans-Saharan Africans in 19th-Century Egypt, Sudan, and the Ottoman Mediterranean*, 125–146. Cairo: American University in Cairo Press, 2010.

Farah, M. D. "Autocratic Abolitionists: Tsarist Russian Anti-Slavery Campaigns." In William Mulligan, ed., *A Global History of Anti-Slavery Politics in the Nineteenth Century*, 97–117. New York, NY: Palgrave, 2013.

Fisher, Alan W. "Muscovy and the Black Sea Slave Trade." *Canadian-American Slavic Studies* 6:4 (1972), 575–594.

Gao, Yuan. "Captivity and Empire: Russian Captivity Narratives in Fact and Fiction." M.A. thesis, Nazarbayev University, 2016.

Golden, Peter B. "The Terminology of Slavery and Servitude in Medieval Turkic." In Devin DeWeese, ed., *Studies on Central Asia in Honor of Yuri Bregel*, 27–56. Bloomington, IN: Research Institute for Inner Asian Studies, 2001).

Grant, Bruce. *The Captive and the Gift: Cultural Histories of Sovereignty in Russia and the Caucasus*. Ithaca, NY: Cornell University Press, 2009.

Gross, Jo-Ann and Asom Urunbaev, eds. *The Letters of Khwāja 'Ubayd Allāh Aḥrār and his Associates*. Leiden: Brill, 2002.

Gustafson, James M. "Qajar Ambitions in the Great Game: Notes on the Embassy of 'Abbas Qoli Khan to the Amīr of Bokhara, 1844." *Iranian Studies* 46:4 (2013), 535–552.

Hopkins, Benjamin D. "Race, Sex and Slavery: 'Forced Labour' in Central Asia and Afghanistan in the Early 19th Century." *Modern Asian Studies* 42:2 (2008), 629–671.

Hopper, Matthew S. *Slaves of One Master: Globalization and Slavery in Arabia in the Age of Empire*. New Haven, CT: Yale University Press, 2015.

Horák, Slavomír. "The Battle Gökdepe in the Turkmen post-Soviet Historical Discourse." *Central Asian Survey* 34:2 (2015), 149–161.

Kazembeyki, Mohammad Ali. *Society, Politics, and Economics in Māzandarān, Iran, 1848–1914*. London: Routledge, 2003.

Khazanov, Anatoly. *Nomads and the Outside World*. Madison: University of Wisconsin Press, 1994 (second edition).

Khazanov, Anatoly and Andre Wink, eds. *Nomads in the Sedentary World*. New York, NY: Routledge, 2001.

Khazeni, Arash. "Across the Black Sands and the Red: Travel Writing, Nature, and the Reclamation of the Eurasian Steppe circa 1850." *International Journal of Middle East Studies* 42 (2010), 591–614.

Kreiten, Irma. "A Colonial Experiment in Cleansing: the Russian Conquest of Western Caucasus, 1856–65." *Journal of Genocide Research* 11:2–3 (2009), 213-241.

Kurtynova-D'Herlugnan, Liubov. *The Tsar's Abolitionists: Languages of Rationalization and Self-Description in the Russian Empire*. Leiden: Brill, 2010.

Lee, Anthony A. "Enslaved African Women in Nineteenth-Century Iran: The Life of Fezzeh Khanom of Shiraz." *Iranian Studies* 45:3 (2012), 417–437.

Levey, Benjamin. "Jungar Refugees and the Making of Empire on Qing China's Kazakh Frontier, 1759–1773." Ph.D. dissertation, Harvard University, 2013.

Levi, Scott C. "Hindus beyond the Hindu Kush: Indians in the Central Asian Slave Trade." *Journal of the Royal Asiatic Society* 12:3 (2002), 277–288.

Levi, Scott C. *The Indian Diaspora in Central Asia and Its Trade, 1550–1900*. Leiden: Brill, 2002.

Levi, Scott C. "Early Modern Central Asia in World History." *History Compass* 10:11 (2012), 866–878.

Levi, Scott C. "India, Russia and the Eighteenth-Century Transformation of the Central Asian Caravan Trade." *Journal of the Economic and Social History of the Orient* 42:4 (1999), 519–526.

Levi, Scott C. and Muzaffar Alam, eds. *India and Central Asia: Commerce and Culture, 1500–1800*. Oxford: Oxford University Press, 2007.

Markovitz, Claude. *The Global World of Indian Merchants, 1750–1947: Traders of Sind from Bukhara to Panama*. New York, NY: Cambridge University Press, 2000.

Markovitz, Claude, Jacques Pouchepaass and Sanjay Subrahmanyam, eds. *Society and Circulation: Mobile People and Itinerant Cultures in South Asia, 1750–1950*. London: Anthem, 2003.

Marvin, Charles. *Merv, Queen of the World, and the Scourge of the Man-Stealing Turcomans*. London: W.H. Allen, 1881.

McChesney, Robert D. *Central Asia: Foundations of Change*. Princeton, NJ: Darwin Press, 1996.

Miller, Joseph C. *Slavery and Slaving in World History: A Bibliography*, 2 vols. Armonk, NY: M.E. Sharpe, 1999.

Mirzai, Behnaz A. *A History of Slavery and Emancipation in Iran*. Austin, TX: University of Texas Press, 2017.

Montana, Ismael M. *The Abolition of Slavery in Ottoman Tunisia*. Gainesville, FL: University Press of Florida, 2013.

Morier, James. *The Adventures of Hajji Baba of Ispahan*. London: MacMillan, 1902.

Morrison, Alexander. "Twin Imperial Disasters. The Invasions of Khiva and Afghanistan in the Russian and British Official Mind, 1839–1842." *Modern Asian Studies* 48:1 (2013), 253–300.

Morrison, Alexander. "Killing the Cotton Canard and Getting Rid of the Great Game: Rewriting the Russian Conquest of Central Asia, 1814–1895." *Central Asian Survey* 33:2 (2014), 131–142.

Mukminova, R. K. *Sotsial'naia differentsiatsiia naseleniia gorodov Uzbekistana v XV–XVI vv.* Tashkent, 1985.

Newby, Laura. "Bondage on Qing China 's North-Western Frontier." *Modern Asian Studies* 47:3 (2013), 968–994.

Nölle-Karimi, Christine. "'Different in All Respects': Bukhara and Khiva as Viewed by Ķāğār Envoys." In Yavuz Köse, ed., *Şehrâyîn: die Welt der Osmanen, die Osmanen in der Welt: Wahrnehmungen, Begegnungen und Abgrenzungen; Festschrift Hans Georg Majer*, 435–446. Wiesbaden: Harrassowitz, 2012.

Nölle-Karimi, Christine. *The Pearl in its Midst: Herat and the Mapping of Khurasan (15th–19th Centuries)*. Austrian Academy of Sciences Press, 2014.

Nölle-Karimi, Christine. "On the Edge: Eastern Khurasan in the Perception of Qajar Officials." *Eurasian Studies* 14 (2016), 135–177.

Petrushevsky, I. P. *Islam in Iran*. Albany, NY: State University of New York Press, 1985.

Ricks, Thomas. "Slaves and Slave-Trading in Shi'i Iran, AD 1500–1900." *Journal of Asian and African Studies* 36:4 (2001), 407–418.

Rossabi, Morris. "The 'Decline' of the Central Asian Caravan Trade." In James Tracey, ed., *The Rise of Merchant Empires*, 351–370. Cambridge: Cambridge University Press, 1990.

Saray, Mehmet. "Russo-Turkmen Relations up to 1874." *Central Asian Survey* 3:4 (1984), 15–48.

Sartori, Paolo. *Visions of Justice: Sharī'a and Cultural Change in Russian Central Asia*. Leiden: Brill, 2017.

Shepherd, Gill. "The Comorians and the East African Slave Trade." In James L. Watson, ed., *Asian and African Systems of Slavery*, 73–99. Oxford: Basil Blackwell, 1980.

Sela, Ron. *The Legendary Biographies of Tamerlane: Islam and Heroic Apocrypha in Central Asia*. Cambridge: Cambridge University Press, 2013.

Sela, Ron. "Prescribing the Boundaries of Knowledge: Seventeenth-Century Russian Diplomatic Missions to Central Asia." In Nile Green, ed., *Writing Travel in Central Asian History*, 69–88. Bloomington, IN: Indiana University Press, 2014.

Semeniuk, G. I. "Likvidatsiia rabstva v Kazakhstane." Reprinted in Zh. O. Artykbaev, ed., *Raby i tiulenguty v kazakhskoi stepi*. Astana: Altyn Kitap, 2006.

Sergeev, Evgeny. *The Great Game, 1856–1907: Russo-British Relations in Central and East Asia*. Baltimore, MD: Johns Hopkins University Press, 2013.

Smolarz, Elena. "Speaking about Freedom and Dependency: Representations and Experiences of Russian Enslaved Captives in Central Asia in the First Half of the 19th Century." *Journal of Global Slavery* 2 (2017), 44–71.

Sneath, David. *The Headless State: Aristocratic Orders, Kinship Society, & Misrepresentations of Nomadic Inner Asia*. New York, NY: Columbia University Press, 2007.

Stanziani, Alessandro. *Bondage: Labor and Rights in Eurasia from the Sixteenth to the Early Twentieth Centuries*. New York, NY: Berghahn, 2014.

Subtelny, Maria. *Timurids in Transition: Turko-Persian Politics and Acculturation in Medieval Iran*. Leiden: Brill, 2007.

Sunderland, Willard. *Taming the Wild Field: Colonization and Empire on the Russian Steppe*. Ithaca, NY: Cornell University Press, 2004.

Tealakh, Gali Oda. "The Russian Advance in Central Asia and the British Response, 1834–1884." Ph.D. Dissertation, Durham University, 1991.

Terent'ev, M. A. *Istoriia zavoevaniia Srednei Azii*, 3 vols. St. Petersburg, 1906.

Toledano, Ehud R. *As If Silent and Absent*. New Haven, CT: Yale University Press, 2007.

Toledano, Ehud R. *The Ottoman Slave Trade and its Suppression: 1840–1890*. Princeton, NJ: Princeton University Press, 1982.

Toledano, Ehud R. "Abolition and Anti-slavery in the Ottoman Empire: A Case to Answer?" Forthcoming, 2018.

Trotskii, V. N. *Opisanie khivinskago pokhoda 1873 goda*. St. Petersburg, 1898.

Troutt Powell, Eve. *Tell This in My Memory: Stories of Enslavement from Egypt, Sudan, and the Ottoman Empire*. Palo Alto, CA: Stanford University Press, 2013.

UNESCO / Ecole d'Architecture Paris Val de Seine EVCAU Research Team. *Inventory of Caravanserais in Central Asia*. 2004.

Witzenrath, Christoph, ed. *Eurasian Slavery, Ransom and Abolition in World History, 1200–1860*. Aldershot: Ashgate, 2015.

Wood, William A. "The Sariq Turkmens of Merv and the Khanate of Khiva in the Early Nineteenth Century." Ph.D. dissertation, Indiana University, 1998.
Zhukovskii, S. V. *Snosheniia Rossii s Bukharoi i Khivoi za poslednee trekhsotletie*. Petrograd, 1915.
Zimanov, S. *Obshchestvennyi stroi kazakhov pervoi poloviny XIX veka i Bukeevskoe khanstvo*. Almaty: Arys, 2009.

Index

Other titles in the series

Agricultural Innovation in the Early Islamic World: The Diffusion of Crops and Farming Techniques, 700–1100, Andrew M. Watson
Muslim Tradition: Studies in Chronology, Provenance and Authorship of Early Hadith, G. H. A. Juynboll
Social History of Timbuktu: The Role of Muslim Scholars and Notables 1400–1900, Elias N. Saad
Sex and Society in Islam: Birth Control before the Nineteenth Century, B.F. Musallam
Towns and Townsmen of Ottoman Anatolia: Trade, Crafts and Food Production in an Urban Setting 1520–1650, Suraiya Faroqhi
Unlawful Gain and Legitimate Profit in Islamic Law: Riba, Gharar and Islamic Banking, Nabil A. Saleh
Men of Modest Substance: House Owners and House Property in Seventeenth-Century Ankara and Kayseri, Suraiya Faroqhi
Roman, Provincial and Islamic Law: The Origins of the Islamic Patronate, Patricia Crone
Economic Life in Ottoman Jerusalem, Amnon Cohen
Mannerism in Arabic Poetry: A Structural Analysis of Selected Texts (3rd Century AH/9th Century AD–5th Century AH/11th Century AD), Stefan Sperl
The Rise and Rule of Tamerlane, Beatrice Forbes Manz
Popular Culture in Medieval Cairo, Boaz Shoshan
Early Philosophical Shiism: The Ismaili Neoplatonism of Abu Ya'qub Al-Sijistani, Paul E. Walker
Indian Merchants and Eurasian Trade, 1600–1750, Stephen Frederic Dale
Palestinian Peasants and Ottoman Officials: Rural Administration around Sixteenth-Century Jerusalem, Amy Singer
Arabic Historical Thought in the Classical Period, Tarif Khalidi
Mongols and Mamluks: The Mamluk-Ilkhanid War, 1260–1281, Reuven Amitai-Preiss
Knowledge and Social Practice in Medieval Damascus, 1190–1350, Michael Chamberlain
The Politics of Households in Ottoman Egypt: The Rise of the Qazdağlis, Jane Hathaway
Hierarchy and Egalitarianism in Islamic Thought, Louise Marlow
Commodity and Exchange in the Mongol Empire: A Cultural History of Islamic Textiles, Thomas T. Allsen
State and Provincial Society in the Ottoman Empire: Mosul, 1540–1834, Dina Rizk Khoury
The Mamluks in Egyptian Politics and Society, Thomas Philipp and Ulrich Haarmann (eds.)
The Delhi Sultanate: A Political and Military History, Peter Jackson
European and Islamic Trade in the Early Ottoman State: The Merchants of Genoa and Turkey, Kate Fleet

The Ottoman City between East and West: Aleppo, Izmir, and Istanbul, Edhem Eldem, Daniel Goffman, and Bruce Masters
The Politics of Trade in Safavid Iran: Silk for Silver, 1600–1730, Rudolph P. Matthee
The Idea of Idolatry and the Emergence of Islam: From Polemic to History, G. R. Hawting
A Monetary History of the Ottoman Empire, Şevket Pamuk
Classical Arabic Biography: The Heirs of the Prophets in the Age of Al-Ma'mun, Michael Cooperson
Empire and Elites after the Muslim Conquest: The Transformation of Northern Mesopotamia, Chase F. Robinson
Poverty and Charity in Medieval Islam: Mamluk Egypt, 1250–1517, Adam Sabra
Culture and Conquest in Mongol Eurasia, Thomas T. Allsen
Christians and Jews in the Ottoman Arab World: The Roots of Sectarianism, Bruce Masters
Arabic Administration in Norman Sicily: The Royal Diwan, Jeremy Johns
Law, Society and Culture in the Maghrib, 1300–1500, David S. Powers
Revival and Reform in Islam: The Legacy of Muhammad al-Shawkani, Bernard Haykel
Tolerance and Coercion in Islam: Interfaith Relations in the Muslim Tradition, Yohanan Friedmann
Guns for the Sultan: Military Power and the Weapons Industry in the Ottoman Empire, Gábor Ágoston
Marriage, Money and Divorce in Medieval Islamic Society, Yossef Rapoport
The Empire of the Qara Khitai in Eurasian History: Between China and the Islamic World, Michal Biran
Domesticity and Power in the Early Mughal World, Ruby Lal
Power, Politics and Religion in Timurid Iran, Beatrice Forbes Manz
Postal Systems in the Pre-Modern Islamic World, Adam J. Silverstein
Kingship and Ideology in the Islamic and Mongol Worlds, Anne F. Broadbridge
Justice, Punishment and the Medieval Muslim Imagination, Christian Lange
The Shiites of Lebanon under Ottoman Rule, 1516–1788, Stefan Winter
Women and Slavery in the Late Ottoman Empire, Madeline Zilfi
The Second Ottoman Empire: Political and Social Transformation in the Early Modern World, Baki Tezcan
The Legendary Biographies of Tamerlane: Islam and Heroic Apocrypha in Central Asia, Ron Sela
Non-Muslims in the Early Islamic Empire: From Surrender to Coexistence, Milka Levy-Rubin
The Origins of the Shi'a: Identity, Ritual, and Sacred Space in Eighth-Century Kufa, Najam Haider
Politics, Law, and Community in Islamic Thought: The Taymiyyan Moment, Ovamir Anjum
The Power of Oratory in the Medieval Muslim World, Linda G. Jones
Animals in the Qur'an, Sarra Tlili
The Logic of Law Making in Islam: Women and Prayer in the Legal Tradition, Behnam Sadeghi

Empire and Power in the Reign of Süleyman: Narrating the Sixteenth-Century Ottoman World, Kaya Şahin
Law and Piety in Medieval Islam, Megan H. Reid
Women and the Transmission of Religious Knowledge in Islam, Asma Sayeed
The New Muslims of Post-Conquest Iran: Tradition, Memory, and Conversion, Sarah Bowen Savant
The Mamluk City in the Middle East: History, Culture, and the Urban Landscape, Nimrod Luz
Disability in the Ottoman Arab World, 1500–1800, Sara Scalenghe
The Holy City of Medina: Sacred Space in Early Islamic Arabia, Harry Munt
Muslim Midwives: The Craft of Birthing in the Premodern Middle East, Avner Giladi
Doubt in Islamic Law: A History of Legal Maxims, Interpretation, and Islamic Criminal Law, Intisar A. Rabb
The Second Formation of Islamic Law: The Hanafi School in the Early Modern Ottoman Empire, Guy Burak
Sexual Violation in Islamic Law: Substance, Evidence, and Procedure, Hina Azam
Gender Hierarchy in the Qur'an: Medieval Interpretations, Modern Responses, Karen Bauer
Intellectual Networks in Timurid Iran: Sharaf al-Din 'Ali Yazdi and the Islamicate Republic of Letters, Ilker Evrim Binbaş
Authority and Identity in Medieval Islamic Historiography: Persian Histories from the Peripheries, Mimi Hanaoka
The Economics of Ottoman Justice: Settlement and Trial in the Sharia Courts, Metin Coşgel and Boğaç Ergene
The Mystics of al-Andalus: Ibn Barrajan and Islamic Thought in the Twelfth Century, Yousef Casewit
Muhammad's Heirs: The Rise of Muslim Scholarly Communities, 622–950, Jonathan E. Brockopp
The First of the Modern Ottomans: The Intellectual History of Ahmed Vasif, Ethan Menchinger
Non-Muslim Provinces under Early Islam: Islamic Rule and Iranian Legitimacy in Armenia and Caucasian Albania, Alison Vacca
Women and the Making of the Mongol Empire, Anne F. Broadbridge
Slavery and Empire in Central Asia, Jeff Eden
Christianity in Fifteenth-Century Iraq, Thomas A. Carlson